The War
Against Excellence

The War against Excellence

The Rising Tide of Mediocrity in America's Middle Schools

Cheri Pierson Yecke

Foreword by William J. Bennett,
Former U.S. Secretary of Education

ROWMAN & LITTLEFIELD EDUCATION
Lanham, Maryland • Toronto • Oxford
2005

Published in the United States of America
by Rowman & Littlefield Education
A Division of Rowman & Littlefield Publishers, Inc.
A wholly owned subsidiary of The Rowman & Littlefield Publishing Group, Inc.
4501 Forbes Boulevard, Suite 200, Lanham, Maryland 20706
www.rowmaneducation.com

PO Box 317
Oxford
OX2 9RU, UK

British Library Cataloguing in Publication Information Available

Library of Congress Cataloging-in-Publication Data

Yecke, Cheri Pierson, 1955–
    The war against excellence : the rising tide of mediocrity in America's
schools / Cheri Pierson Yecke.
        p.   cm.
    Includes bibliographical references and index.
    ISBN 0-57886-227-2 (alk. paper)
    1. Gifted children—Education (Middle school)—United States.   2. Middle
schools—United States—History.   I. Title.
LC3993.9.Y43   2003
371.9473—dc21   2003048807

♾ The paper used in this publication meets the minimum requirements of
American National Standard for Information Sciences—Permanence of
Paper for Printed Library Materials, ANSI/NISO Z39.48-1992.
Manufactured in the United States of America.

Copyright Acknowledgments

To my parents, Leo and Marcy Pierson,
who raised me to believe in my abilities.

To my daughters, Anastasia and Tiffany,
whose educational experiences led to this book.

To my husband, Dennis,
for his patience and understanding
over the many years of this project,
and for his unwavering support and belief in my efforts.

Contents

Foreword

Had we been spectators watching the class of 2003 run its 12-year academic course, we would have seen it start strong, lose steam, and then finish decidedly behind its peers from abroad. To see such promise squandered is to wonder what goes wrong, mid-course, in American education. Cheri Pierson Yecke helps us to understand one major source of the problem: a trend toward mediocrity resulting from the middle school movement.

The middle school agenda has been about much more than buildings and busing for middle-grade students. Like so many other twentieth-century education movements, it has artificially pitted equality against excellence. The quest to make all students equal has left all children equally disadvantaged academically. The effort to use the middle school to accomplish social goals, as Dr. Yecke documents, has left true educational goals further out of reach.

As I wrote in *The Educated Child*, "All children deserve access to a rich curriculum, a common core of worthwhile knowledge, important skills, and sound ideals. Good schools may vary the pace and pedagogy as appropriate, but they take pains to retain the content for all."

A number of reports on education, including the pivotal *A Nation at Risk* (1983), have observed that an enemy power could develop no better strategy for subduing the United States than to cripple its education system. Yet our educational breakdown has been self-inflicted.

It is too late to talk about how a social experiment as aggressive as the middle school movement described here was propagated through a monopoly government education system, but it is not too late to do something about it. Dr. Yecke's book is a rallying cry to that end.

William J. Bennett, Former U.S. Secretary of Education

December 2002

POSTSCRIPT

After this book was submitted for publication in 2002, Dr. Yecke became the Commissioner of Education for the State of Minnesota. She brought impeccable credentials as an award-winning teacher, having previously served as the Secretary of Education in Virginia and as a senior official at the U.S. Department of Education.

In only 16 months her leadership initiated and cemented profound changes in Minnesota's educational system, including the defeat of Minnesota's controversial and discredited "feel good" standards, widely known as the worst in the nation. She led the development of new, rigorous, grade-level specific academic standards that are content-rich, have higher expectations, and were developed by a coalition of parents, taxpayers, and educators. She developed the first-ever statewide accountability system for Minnesota's public schools and new school performance report cards that empower parents with a wealth of meaningful information.

By any measure, she produced more changes in Minnesota's education system than most Commissioners do in four years.

And the thanks she received for this effort?

The Democrats in the Minnesota State Senate rejected her confirmation on a straight party line vote.

According to Governor Tim Pawlenty:

In the dark of night, the Democrats in the Minnesota Senate have done a great disservice to our state. By rejecting Commissioner Yecke on a party line vote, they have rejected innovation and accountability for our education system. My disappointment in their action and the loss to our state is deep and profound.

Why would a highly regarded education reformer receive such appallingly shabby treatment? Why would someone with Dr. Yecke's qualifications and credentials be summarily dismissed? *Because she was successful.* The status quo had been put on notice that their nonacademic activities in the public schools would no longer be tolerated. The very people she exposes in this book—those who support using our schools for non-academic goals—were stung by the swiftness and completeness of the changes wrought by Dr. Yecke. These entrenched members of the education establishment, and the politicians they support, were so recoiled by the message in Dr. Yecke's book that they acted just as she predicted. Amidst vicious personal attacks, intense character assassination, and vilification of the message of this book, she was pilloried during her extensive confirmation hearings. Shunning the desires of parents and taxpayers and employing the politics of personal destruction, the education establishment orchestrated her dismissal.

According to Checker Finn, who served under me as an Assistant Secretary of Education:

Her sin was being an educator of strong principle who would not bend to expediency and whose concern for the state's children overrode the temptation to pander to adult interests. By which I mean not just the teacher unions but also the sizable band of frenzied ideologues that populates the education system of the Land of 10,000 Lakes.

She stoutly supported high standards, rigorous and substantive content (especially bona fide history), school choice, and results-based accountability. Educators balked. And by targeting her, Minnesota's faltering Democrat party was able to score a rare victory over GOP governor Tim Pawlenty.

Having dispatched Yecke, the legislature adjourned for the year. Dr. Yecke will live to fight another day, perhaps in another place. She's one of the all-too-rare human treasures of American education.

The lesson for education reformers is clear: Success at reform will be punished by members of the status quo as they grasp at any perceived means to keep the schools tightly under their control.

Minnesota was fortunate to have Dr. Yecke as a stalwart defender of higher academic expectations. She is a true champion of holding schools accountable to taxpayers for academic results. And like other education reformers who have blazed the path before her, she will not be silenced by political machinations that serve only special interests and not the interests of children.

William J. Bennett, Former U.S. Secretary of Education
October 2004

Preface

My dual passions for advocating for academic excellence and examining the motivations behind the contemporary middle school concept drove me to write this book. As the mother of two daughters who were academically gifted and as a middle school teacher, I experienced firsthand the frustrations of trying to meet the intellectual needs of high ability and highly motivated children within the prescriptive confines of the radical middle school plan.

My husband referred to my advocacy for our children as an example of the "she-bear" instinct—"if you mess with my cubs, you had better look out." While both of our daughters generally had very positive experiences in their schools, during their middle school years I had to fight one battle after another as I sought to ensure that their educational needs were met.

As a middle school teacher, I became increasingly frustrated with administrative policies that were implemented by fiat with the solemn declaration that "this is good for kids because everyone is doing it." Trendy new policies, such as the widespread elimination of ability grouping, the dumbing-down of the curriculum, and a wholesale embrace of cooperative learning and peer tutoring, were *not* good for all kids—and I didn't care who else was "doing it."

As a mom and as a teacher, I knew intuitively that these practices did not serve the best interests of all children, and I wondered where they were coming from.

As our district's Teacher of the Year and as a concerned parent, I had a voice to express my views, but it did not carry the weight of those who were looked to as experts. I found that concerned parents and dedicated educators were often made to feel ignorant and insignificant when they attempted to argue against the latest trends and fads. Self-proclaimed experts, cloaking themselves in pseudo-wisdom, often looked with disdain upon anyone who dared to question either their beliefs or the translation of their beliefs into practice.

I left the classroom and went back to earn my doctorate so that I could become more knowledgeable and perhaps obtain the same level of mainstream credibility as these so-called "experts." During those years, I became alarmed as I read article after article in which middle school activists expressed their arrogant assumption that America's public schools were their personal vehicles for social engineering. I came to see how radical middle school activists were driving many of the policies and practices that have been so damaging to the public education system in America at *all* grade levels, and how such policies and practices were responsible for damaging the trust between many parents and the public schools.

The battle to determine the focus of the middle school—either as a vehicle for social engineering or one that supports rigorous levels of academic achievement—crystallized in a war of words between advocates for the middle school concept and advocates for gifted learners.

This book chronicles the history of the middle school concept from its genesis to its current state. It shows how the middle school concept evolved from an academic orientation (as in junior high schools) into an activist movement designed to force radical social changes, regardless of the values or desires held by parents, students, or members of the community at large. It also details responses from advocates for gifted learners and those who envision the role of the public school as one that supports academic achievement.

Criticizing the beliefs and policies of self-proclaimed educational "experts" is not without its dangers. Consider the words of Arthur Bestor, who dared to criticize the education establishment in the 1950s:

The extreme unwillingness of professional educationists to submit their proposals to free public discussion and honest criticism frequently assumes the even uglier form of showering critics, no matter how upright and well-informed, with vituperation and personal abuse. A scientist or scholar who publishes a criticism of educational trends, even in a scientific journal, is liable to be denounced by professional educationists in responsible positions who do not think it beneath their dignity to hurl at him [assorted cruel and ugly] epithets. . . . The lesser lights of the educationist world [have] an arrogance such as one meets in no other profession, and which occasionally erupts in an attempt even to suppress freedom of discussion on public educational questions.[1]

Clearly, I anticipate that extreme charges and outlandish criticisms will be hurled at this book, along with an onslaught of personal attacks from both activists and the national organizations that support their causes. But, to put it simply, this is a story that has to be told.

This book is written to advocate for all children who have been impacted by the faddish policies supported by social engineers who try to disguise themselves as legitimate educators. It is written for all parents who need ammunition to fight battles on behalf of their children's education. And it is written for the many dedicated educators who have been coerced into silence for too long about the destructive practices and activist-driven policies they have been forced to implement, and which they know are not in the best interests of children.

NOTE

1. A. Bestor, *Educational Wastelands: The Retreat from Learning in Our Public Schools*, 2nd ed. (Urbana: University of Illinois Press, 1985), pp. 110–111 (orig. pub. in 1953).

Prologue

What I want to fix your attention on is the vast, overall movement toward the discrediting, and finally the elimination, of
every kind of human excellence—moral, cultural, social or intellectual.

C.S. Lewis, 1959[1]

Two decades ago, *A Nation at Risk* declared: "If an unfriendly
foreign power had attempted to impose on America the mediocre
educational performance that exists today, we might well have
viewed it as an act of war." How did American educators respond? In some instances there was an enthusiastic interest in
raising academic standards. However, radical middle school reformers had other ideas.

Rather than strengthen their commitment to higher academic
standards, activist reformers at the middle school level soon made
it clear that the middle school was not just a new educational
organization, but a means to an end—that end being the implementation of massive changes meant to promote social egalitarianism. The middle school was to become the vehicle for
implementing "social justice" by "making everyone equal." The
goal of creating mass equality is being pursued through policies
and practices implemented in many middle schools across the
country. Ability grouping is discouraged as elitist and in many

places has been replaced with "cooperative learning," where a few students do all the work and everyone shares the grade. High ability students are often not allowed to work at their own pace, but instead are held to the pace of the rest of the class in a twisted interpretation of "no child being left behind," and are required to tutor others, resulting in a loss in their own intellectual growth. Based on fraudulent interpretations of scientific "theories," the entire middle school curriculum has been dumbed-down because pre-adolescent brains can't possibly be expected to handle the strain of thinking too hard.

All of these policies and practices have been working together in a systemic fashion, encouraging at many middle schools a culture of disdain and contempt for high academic achievement. This is nothing less than a declaration of war against academic excellence.

Was this some sort of secret conspiracy? Not at all—in documents such as professional education journals, middle school activists were quite clear about their non-academic goals. This book documents these goals with numerous quotes from primary sources, as this is a story that can be told in the activists' own words.

Media reports often point to examples of political correctness in school curricula, such as "rainforest algebra" or revisionist interpretations of history. While such examples can be cited to demonstrate that some schools are guilty of indoctrinating rather than teaching, this book will not focus on the content of the curriculum. Rather, it will focus on changes in instructional practice that have negatively impacted the educational experiences of far too many American children.

The issue we face is how to meet the challenge of making a conscious national commitment to rigorous academic quality when the systemic dumbing-down of education, most notably at the middle school level, has had a negative impact on all of our children—especially those who are gifted, talented, or possessing above-average abilities. Achievement of students in other nations now regularly surpasses that of American students, and it will be impossible to reverse this trend within the confines of the radical middle school concept.

It is time for the American public to reject the policies and practices of the radical middle school movement. This book explains how the radical takeover of middle schools came about, and proposes solutions to this rising tide of mediocrity.

NOTE

1. C.S. Lewis, "Screwtape proposes a toast," in *The Screwtape Letters* (1942, 1959; reprint, San Francisco: HarperCollins, 2001), p. 201.

The War
Against Excellence

CHAPTER 1

Introduction

We report to the American people that while we can take justifiable pride in what our schools and colleges have historically accomplished and contributed to the United States and the well-being of its people, the educational foundations of our society are presently being eroded by a rising tide of mediocrity that threatens our very future as a nation and a people. What was unimaginable a generation ago has begun to occur—others are matching and surpassing our educational attainments.

A Nation at Risk, 1983[1]

Educational reforms of the last several decades suggest the presence of a strong underlying belief system that supports practices that work against children who are gifted, talented, or who possess high academic ability. Although evidence of this belief system can be seen in all grades, kindergarten through college, it is most obvious at the middle school level. In their quest to establish a more egalitarian society, activist middle school advocates and social reformers made it clear early on that the middle school was not just a new educational organization, but a means to an end—that end being the implementation of fundamental changes meant to promote social egalitarianism by coercing students who are gifted/high ability to be like everyone else. This is nothing less than a declaration of war against academic excellence—and against those children who possess high academic abilities.

It is well understood that not all middle school educators are anti-gifted activists, nor are all middle schools hostile environments for gifted or high ability children. But documentary evidence indicates that a small and influential cadre of like-minded people came to view the middle schools as vehicles for social engineering and made it clear that high ability children, and the programs that address their needs, stood in the way of their goals.

LOVE–HATE ATTITUDES TOWARD GIFTED LEARNERS

As gifted advocate James J. Gallagher points out, Americans demonstrate a strange love–hate relationship toward the quality known as giftedness. While we respect the outstanding accomplishments of athletes and entertainers, there is sometimes an underlying resentment toward children with high intellectual abilities. Like inherited wealth, intellectual ability is a trait that is often envied and seen as something that may be unfair—after all, those possessing it didn't earn it.[2]

It appears that these vacillating attitudes may be, in part, a reaction to the impact of both social and historical events. In a comprehensive history of gifted education in the United States from the 1950s through the 1970s, Abraham Tannenbaum noted:

The cyclical nature of interest in the gifted is probably unique in American education. No other special group of children has been alternately embraced and repelled with so much vigor by educators and laymen alike.

He pointed out that the 1950s saw "a commitment of the schools to deal with mediocrity rather than superiority." Serious attention to educational needs of gifted students in this country only came about in reaction to the Russian launch of Sputnik, which resulted in passage of the National Defense Education Act in 1958:

Despite the work of specialists on the gifted and the portents and premonitions concerning Russia's strides in building its talent reservoir, there was no serious action in America's schools until Sputnik was launched in 1957. . . . It was essential to build up our supply of high-level human resources quickly or else risk seeing a national emergency deteriorate into a national catastrophe. In time, school officials began to acknowledge that something was wrong with public education and that there was much overhauling to be done. . . . Professional journals were deluged with research reports and with exhortations to do something special for the gifted. So rapid was the buildup of literature in the field that one writer claimed there were more articles published in the three-year period from 1956–1959 than in the previous thirty years.[3]

The appearance of external threats to a nation's security thus appears to stimulate the desire to develop the talents of that nation's children. According to James J. Gallagher, "If the country feels threatened by outside forces or hostile neighbors, it tends to want to maximize all its resources."[4] In another analysis, he concludes:

Countries who perceive themselves under threat seem even more inclined to swing to the excellence side of the argument [supportive of services for the gifted]. . . . In other countries where a socialist philosophy dominates the political scene, the country leans toward the "equity" side of the argument.[5]

What does this cyclical precedent portend for the United States today? Our entrance into the twenty-first century was punctuated with a devastating wake-up call on September 11, 2001. The terrorist acts that killed thousands of innocent people and wreaked havoc on the American economy is evidence of an external threat unlike any we have seen before.

How can America respond? A report by the bipartisan U.S. Commission on National Security/21st Century, titled *Road Map for National Security: Imperative for Change*, was published in February 2001—seven months before the attack. It concluded that "without significant reforms, American power and influence cannot be sustained. . . . Despite the end of the Cold War threat, America faces distinctly new dangers."[6] Second only to securing the safety of American citizens on American soil came the recommendation that American education must be overhauled and strengthened:

The inadequacies of our systems of research and education pose a greater threat to U.S. national security over the next quarter century than any potential conventional war that we might imagine. American national leadership must understand these deficiencies as threats to national security. . . . In the next quarter century, we will likely see ourselves surpassed, and in relative decline, unless we make a conscious national commitment to maintain our edge.[7]

This is not the only recent report to raise serious concerns regarding American education. In March 2000, the Paris-based Organization for Economic Cooperation and Development released a report which showed that the United States has lost considerable ground on a number of important educational measures: "Thirty years ago, the United States was the 'undisputed leader' in educating its population. . . . But other countries are quickly catching up to or exceeding the United States."[8]

Both the Cold War and the September 11 terrorist atrocities were preceded by calls for more adequate educational opportunities for high ability students in the United States. The launch of Sputnik was followed by a concerted effort to provide such opportunities, but only time will tell if a renewed commitment to develop the talents of high ability students will occur in U.S. schools this time.

A NATION AT RISK

The report *Road Map for National Security: Imperative for Change* is not the first time our nation was warned about the consequences of neglecting the education of our children. In 1983, the publication of *A Nation at Risk* alerted the American public to the sharp decline in the academic performance of U.S. students, stating that society had "lost sight of the basic purposes of schooling, and of the high expectations and disciplined effort needed to attain them." It continued: "If an unfriendly foreign power had attempted to impose on America the mediocre educational performance that exists today, we might well have viewed it as an act of war."[9] The sentiments of *Road Map for National Security: Imperative for Change* are eerily similar:

Second only to a weapon of mass destruction detonating in an American city, we can think of nothing more dangerous than a failure to manage properly science, technology, and education for the common good over the next quarter century.[10]

A flurry of reform activity followed the publication *A Nation at Risk*. During the 1980s, many well-intentioned educators, hungry for improvement and with good intentions, bought into reform programs that looked exciting and promising. Many of the reforms, however, were nothing more than trendy fads with no track record of improving academic achievement—but what is worse is that some of the "reforms" were actually serious attempts at social engineering, where changes in instructional practices and policies were implemented in an attempt to reshape U.S. society into a sort of egalitarian utopia. Standing in the way of those who would restructure U.S. society were gifted/high ability students, their parents and advocates, and the programs that address their needs. As shall be documented, it became clear that middle school activists were intent on eliminating these "elitist" programs, and that, in the name of social equity, high ability children were to be forced to be like everyone else.

In many ways, the goals of middle school activists are only another example of twentieth-century attempts to "make everyone equal" through the redistribution of resources. While many of us are familiar with this when it is done with financial resources through excessive and confiscatory taxation, it is also happening to gifted/high ability children and their *intellectual* resources, which are viewed by some activists as "society's benefits" that need to be redistributed.[11]

There are several issues that need to be considered concurrently: the growth of anti-gifted attitudes and implementation of reforms that work against gifted/high ability students, and the middle school as the testing ground for the implementation of such changes—changes whose purpose is the fundamental restructuring of American society.

THE GROWTH OF ANTI-GIFTED ATTITUDES AND RELATED CONSEQUENCES

Initial stirrings of recent anti-gifted attitudes can be seen in the writings of social scientists in the 1980s. As noted by Matthew B. Miles, former Professor of Psychology and Education at Teachers' College, Columbia University, activists external to a given field are often the dominant initiators of massive change.[12] One example of such an activist influence is social scientist Mara Sapon-Shevin, who questioned whether it was moral to group students according to their abilities, noting that gifted students "might legitimately take some responsibility for enriching the lives of their non-gifted peers," an action that would serve as the beginning of the development of a "social conscience" among gifted students.[13] Another example is Jeanne Oakes, a social scientist with the Rand Corporation, who stated:

Until a major social reorganization occurs that results in cultural, political, and economic equity for all groups or until a major reconstruction of schooling takes place in which the educational process encourages individuals to refuse to tolerate an unequal social system, more limited reforms should be attempted to help equalize the effects of schooling.[14]

Slowly, quietly, and behind the scenes, beliefs such as these fueled anti-gifted practices that were promoted in American schools, especially at the middle school level.

By the late 1980s, a national survey conducted with educators of the gifted revealed that the most commonly shared concern was over negative attitudes toward gifted education:

Specifically, [the negative] attitudes held by classroom teachers, school administrators, and society at large toward gifted education are the concerns of many respondents. These problems of attitude appear often enough that one could surmise they go beyond the particular school or school district in which the respondent worked.[15]

By the early 1990s, expressions of concern were being voiced by leading educators of the gifted who saw that certain instructional practices promoted at the middle level were having a negative impact upon programs and services for the gifted.[16] These included the dilution of the middle school curriculum, the demise of ability grouping, and the unquestioning embrace of cooperative learning and peer tutoring. Even mainstream publications such as *Newsweek* ran articles on the issue, including one titled "Failing the most gifted kids: A generation goes to waste."[17] In the words of one advocate for the gifted:

There is an anti-intellectual stream meandering through our culture that sometimes overflows to drown those who exhibit too much of an academic streak. It is almost as if gifted children are viewed as deviants from the accepted norms of society.[18]

Concurrently, the alarm was sounded when a series of warnings appeared from influential leaders in the field of gifted education:

John Feldhusen, 1991: The question we now face is how to call a halt to a national reform agenda in which some school reformers have arrogated unto themselves a political-social agenda that is based on misinterpretation of current research evidence.[19]

James J. Gallagher, 1991: The potential for gifted students being further delayed in their academic development by participating in these middle school programs seems very real.[20]

Joseph Renzulli and Sally Reis, 1991: We believe that the field of education for the gifted and talented is currently facing a quiet crisis and that in many ways this crisis is directly related to the education reform movement in America.[21]

John Feldhusen and Sidney Moon, 1992: It seems clear that Oakes (1985) is calling for a cultural revolution in America starting with the schools but eventually permeating all aspects of American society. Homogenization of educational experiences is advocated primarily as a means to social change. The rush to heterogeneous grouping and cooperative learning is probably heavily influenced by social and political value systems.[22]

Joyce VanTassel-Baska, 1992: Only a small percentage of schools . . . [or] teachers across the United States currently employ instructional plans for *any* learner based on a diagnosed assessment of individual learning needs. How can we believe that less grouping and more heterogeneous [mixed ability] classrooms will enhance the learning process for *any* student with special needs?[23]

James Gallagher, 1993: The modest educational strategy of ability grouping has become hostage to major social forces in the society struggling for power and influence.[24]

Although these warnings were made in the early 1990s, they were largely ignored until the dismal performance of American middle school students on international achievement tests became front-page news. In 1995, the Third International Mathematics and Science Study (TIMSS) compared the academic achievement of students from 41 countries. American fourth graders scored above the international average, but by eighth grade, the performance of U.S. students started to lag. Eighth grade students from 16 other countries registered performance that was higher than the United States in science, and for 9 countries this difference was statistically significant. In math, the performance of students in 27 other countries was higher than that of U.S. students—a statistically significant difference in the case of 20 of these countries. Worse yet, by twelfth grade students from the United States were among the lowest performing students in both subjects, with only Cyprus and South Africa scoring lower. And it should be noted, contrary to the claims of some, that this is not a case of average U.S. students being compared to only the top students in other nations.[25]

The results came as a shock to many. A policy brief on the results issued by the U.S. Department of Education declared: "U.S. students don't start out behind; they fall behind."[26] According to Dr. William Schmidt of Michigan State University, the U.S. research coordinator for the study: "These essentially are just devastating results. There's no other way to cast them."[27] He continues: "I believe that one of the single most important policy implications of the TIMSS study is this precipitous decline in our international ranking from fourth to eighth grade." In other words, the decline takes place during the middle school years.

As related to our highest achieving students, Schmidt has somber words:

The results are quite startling: We are at the bottom of the international distribution. In the past, when international results have been reported, many people have suggested, "It's really not a problem because our best students are doing okay. This is really about those 'other' kids in the cities who are pulling our averages down. Everything is really okay at our best schools." That's simply not true: Even our best students are not world class. The problems we must address affect not only our average kids, but even our best kids.[28]

The realization that U.S. children appear to lose their achievement advantage once they leave elementary school and enter middle school was one reason officials decided to repeat the study in 1999 as the TIMSS-R (TIMSS-Repeat), with 38 countries participating and only eighth grade students being tested. It was speculated that curriculum changes from the early 1990s had produced positive results in 1995 for fourth graders only, and that achievement for this group of students would be sustained and increase by the time they were eighth graders. Unfortunately, the results indicate otherwise.[29]

Some comparisons can be made between the 1995 and 1999 data

that provide a picture of where U.S. student performance has gone over time. Although the 1995 math scores of U.S. fourth graders were right at the international average, by 1999 their scores as eighth graders were *22 points below* the international average, suggesting a sharp decline in performance.[30] The results in science are even more dramatic. In 1995, U.S. fourth graders scored 28 points above the international average, but in 1999, their scores as eighth graders had dropped to 9 points below the international average—*a full 37-point decline.*[31] In response to these results, one educator stated:

It would be interesting to know how much of our "averageness" and the "drop" between fourth and eighth grade are attributable to our failure to help our high achieving students make gains during those years.[32]

For parents of and advocates for gifted children, this alarming evidence indicated that U.S. schools are failing our top students. But the news gets worse.

Further evidence from international comparisons shows that high ability U.S. students are underachieving when compared to the top students in other nations. If the TIMSS-R was a competition held to select the top 10 percent of all science students internationally, 15 percent of our students would be selected—but 11 other countries would have *larger* percentages of their students selected. Singapore had 32 percent of its students score in the top 10 percent internationally, followed by Taipei with 31 percent. In math, only 9 percent of U.S. eighth graders scored in the top 10 percent of all students internationally, with the top students in 16 other countries being ranked ahead of us. Once again, Singapore (46 percent) and Taipei (41 percent) top the list. It needs to be re-emphasized that this is not a case of other countries spiking their averages by testing only their top students, and it should further be noted that these findings are consistent with the comments by immigrant students that U.S. schools are far less demanding than the schools in their home countries.[33] In addition, an extensive survey of foreign exchange students studying here in the United States found that these students express the belief that American education is far less rigorous than that of their home countries:

Overwhelmingly, the foreign exchange students found U.S. classes easier than classes in their home countries. More than half, 56 percent, described the U.S. classes they attended as much easier and 29 percent as a little easier. In contrast, only 5 percent found U.S. classes much harder and 6 percent a little harder. Even considering that exchange students are excellent students . . . while in the U.S. they usually attend above average schools and take the toughest classes that American high schools have to offer. Compared to the classes they are familiar with back home, which probably serve high achieving students, the American classes do not seem very rigorous.[34]

Regarding the TIMSS-R study, project manager Patrick Gonzales states: "What I think we can hypothesize from these results is that the pace of learning in some of the other nations is faster between fourth and eighth grades than it is in the United States."[35] However, there is more at play here than just the pacing of the curriculum. Exacerbating the decline in rigor of the middle school curriculum is a growing misconception that bright students do not need to be challenged. As will be seen, the belief of the following middle school teacher reflects the attitudes of many in the field:

We represent all children, and it is morally wrong to give different instruction to these gifted students. I, for one, do not believe the so-called research that indicates that these children have educational needs other children do not. If they are so smart they can find something useful to do with their time. . . . They need to learn discipline and to fit in.[36]

Serious questions must be raised. What is causing the general decline in academic achievement once U.S. students leave the elementary school? And what is causing fewer of our top students to perform competitively with their international peers? I believe the answers can be found in the growth of the middle school movement.

THE MIDDLE SCHOOL AS A VEHICLE FOR CHANGE

The founders of the middle school movement believed that there would be less resistance to significant instructional changes if such changes appeared to naturally accompany a new organizational structure for schools, thus allowing middle schools to serve as a testing ground for such changes. As this book will show, these changes reflected attitudes and behaviors that were directed against gifted/high ability children in the name of social

equity. Those driving the changes viewed public schools as vehicles for covertly implementing a type of social engineering. Consider this 1968 statement by early leaders of the middle school
movement:

The justification of a middle school organization as a means of accelerating the change process in education . . . is a very real factor in many
school districts. The belief that it is easier to innovate in a new than in
an old organization is widespread.[37]

This belief was expressed again, 25 years later, in a discussion of
the history of the middle school movement:

[The middle school could serve] as an ideal setting for implementation
of needed innovations. It was thought that perhaps it would be easier to
make significant changes needed if the school was a new one in the
school organizational plan.[38]

But just what sorts of "significant changes" were these activists
seeking? And why do they express the need to "accelerate the
change process?" Evidence consistently points to the middle
school as the vehicle for achieving the goal of societal changes, as
stated by prominent middle school activist Paul George. In 1988,
he declared that American middle schools had become "the focus
of societal experimentation, the vehicle for movement toward increased justice and equality in the society as a whole."[39]

The role of the middle school as a place for academic learning
that is focused on the acquisition of foundational knowledge has
been disparaged for nearly 30 years. A 1975 publication of the
influential Association for Supervision and Curriculum Development (ASCD) criticized the existence of "departmentalized
subject-matter curriculum" at junior high schools, and lamented
that middle schools "have continued these same sins."[40] As recently as 1999, the *Middle School Journal* published an article which
warns that the "democratic values promoted by some middle
school educators" are "at risk," and then laments that, in their
absence, "the middle schools are left as an institution devoted to
content coverage and bereft of any larger social meaning."[41] Current conference sessions hosted by the National Middle School
Association (NMSA) continue to describe middle level education
reforms as "massive systemic social reform."[42]

The fervor of belief among many middle school activists is intense. One of the founders of the middle school movement, John Lounsbury, called for activism based upon religious and patriotic principles to support the radical middle school movement, stating: "It has to succeed. It has God and the U.S. Constitution on its side."[43] And over a decade ago, when murmurs of dissent began to be heard regarding the implications of the middle school concept, activist Paul George declared that "we are in a race between the middle school concept and all the threats that imperil its existence."[44]

The radicalization of the middle school movement away from its original educational mission has had a profound effect on American education and American society. As evidenced in the following chapters, vocal middle school proponents are striving to homogenize or level academic achievement, and in doing so are adamant in their attitudes against gifted/high ability students. Such attitudes are manifested in behaviors such as reducing the rigor of the middle school curriculum, supporting the elimination of ability grouping, and increasing the use of cooperative learning and peer tutoring—in spite of research evidence that such practices are academically and emotionally harmful to many children, most notably gifted/high ability learners.

CONCLUSION

In 1986, Miriam Goldberg asserted that the relationship between attitudes toward education for the gifted and changes in the sociopolitical climate had not been identified:

There is, as yet, no systematic analysis of the relationship between the variations in the American stance toward the education of the gifted and changes in the socio-political climate of the country.[45]

I would posit that this is no longer true. This book traces the history of the middle school movement along with the anti-gifted educational practices that accompanied it. Through their own words, middle school activists reveal that their utopian goal of social equity has driven them to view the American middle school as the vehicle to reach this goal.

To meet their egalitarian social goals, middle school activists have promoted a number of classroom practices designed to homogenize or level academic achievement. A series of beliefs driving the implementation of these anti-gifted practices can be inferred from documentary evidence. These include: (1) a belief in equality of outcomes and the leveling of achievement; (2) a belief in the questioning of individualism; (3) a belief in the supremacy of the group; (4) a belief that advanced students have a duty to help others at the expense of their own needs; and (5) a belief in what is perceived as the destructive effects of competition, and the need to eliminate it. Each belief appears to be held with varying degrees of intensity, and echoes beliefs currently driving policies in the larger societal context. In turn, these beliefs support three fundamental convictions that I identify as *radical equity*, *group rights*, and *coercive egalitarianism*.

The middle school movement has been characterized by some as the current American anti-intellectual movement.[46] According to Arthur Bestor, former professor at the University of Illinois: "the good sense of the American people can be trusted to repudiate it [anti-intellectualism], once they grasp what it is about."[47] He advocated a pro-active approach toward eradicating anti-intellectualism:

In the long run, anti-intellectualism is bound to be self-defeating. But if powerful interests promote and sustain it, the run can be long and dangerous indeed. To destroy anti-intellectualism we need to do more than combat its arguments. We need to identify and expose the groups that are promoting it, so that we may check their disastrous influence upon policy making.[48]

That is the purpose of this book—to identify and expose educational practices, and the beliefs that undergird them, that are driving anti-intellectualism and anti-gifted practices in American schools. By analyzing documents from multiple sources, such as journal articles, surveys, books, monographs, and NMSA annual conference programs, we see that anti-gifted activists clearly reveal their underlying beliefs and driving convictions, as well as the strategies being used to implement their radical agenda.[49] Taken together, this documentary evidence will make the case that radical middle school activists view the public schools as their personal vehicles for engineering an egalitarian society, in complete disregard of American values and in spite of what the American public desires.

NOTES

1. *A Nation at Risk: The Imperative for Educational Reform*, National Commission on Excellence in Education (April 1983), available online at http://www.ed.gov/pubs/NatAtRisk/.

2. J. J. Gallagher, "Educational reform, values, and gifted students," *Gifted Child Quarterly*, vol. 35, no. 1 (Winter 1991), p. 13.

3. A. Tannenbaum, "Pre-Sputnik to Post-Watergate concern about the gifted," in *The Gifted and the Talented: Their Education and Development* (Ed. A.H. Passow), *The 78th Yearbook of the National Society for the Study of Education* (Chicago: University of Chicago Press, 1979), pp. 5, 8, 9, 10, 12.

4. J.J. Gallagher, "Our love/hate affair with gifted children," *Gifted Child Quarterly* (January/February 1988), p. 55.

5. J.J. Gallagher, "Equity vs. excellence: An educational drama," *Roeper Review*, vol. 8, no. 4 (May 1986), p. 234.

6. *Road Map for National Security: Imperative for Change*, The Phase III Report of the U.S. Commission on National Security/21st Century (Washington, D.C., February 15, 2001), p. iv.

7. Ibid., p. ix.

8. J. Gehring, "U.S. seen losing edge on education measures," *Education Week* (April 4, 2000), p. 3.

9. *A Nation at Risk.*

10. *Road Map for National Security*, p. 30.

11. See C.B. Howley, A. Howley, and E.D. Pendarvis, *Out of Our Minds: Anti-Intellectualism and Talented Development in American Schooling* (New York: Teachers College Press, 1995), p. 212. Note that, in spite of its title, this is clearly an anti-gifted book.

12. See M.B. Miles, *Innovation in Education* (New York: Teachers College Press, 1964), pp. 409–424.

13. M. Sapon-Shevin, "Mainstreaming the handicapped, segregating the gifted: Theoretical and pragmatic concerns," paper presented at the annual meeting of the American Educational Research Association (1982), ERIC document number ED-218-835, p. 27.

14. J. Oakes, *Keeping Track: How Schools Structure Inequality* (New Haven, Conn.: Yale University Press, 1985), p. 211.

15. J.R. Delisle & S.P. Govender, "Educators of gifted and talented students: Common bonds, unique perspectives," *Roeper Review*, vol. 11, no. 2 (1988), p. 74.

16. See Susan Allan, "Ability grouping research reviews: What do they say about grouping and the gifted?" *Educational Leadership*, vol. 48, no. 7 (April 1991), pp. 60–65; J.F. Feldhusen, S.M. Moon, and P.J. Rifner, "Educating the gifted and talented: Strengths, weaknesses, prospects," *Educational Perspectives*, vol. 26, nos. 1 & 2 (1989), pp. 48–55; J.J. Gallagher, "Education reform, values, and gifted students," *Gifted Child Quarterly*,

vol. 35, no. 1 (1991), pp. 12–19; C.J. Mills & W.G. Durden, "Cooperative learning and ability grouping: An issue of choice," *Gifted Child Quarterly*, vol. 36, no. 1 (1992), pp. 11–16; J.S. Renzulli & S. Reis, "The reform movement and the quiet crisis in gifted education," *Gifted Child Quarterly*, vol. 35, no. 1 (1991), pp. 26–35; A. Robinson, "Cooperation or exploitation? The argument against cooperative learning for talented students," *Journal of the Education of the Gifted*, vol. 14, no. 1 (1990), pp. 9–27; K. Rogers, *The Relationship of Grouping Practices to the Education of the Gifted and Talented Learner*, The National Research Center on the Gifted and Talented Research-Based Decision Making Series, No. 1 (Storrs: University of Connecticut, 1991); P.K. Sicola, "Where do gifted students fit? An examination of middle school philosophy as it relates to ability grouping and the gifted learner," *Journal for the Education of the Gifted*, vol. 14, no. 1 (1990), pp. 37–49; C.A. Tomlinson, "Gifted education and the middle school movement: Two voices on teaching the academically talented," *Journal for the Education of the Gifted*, vol. 15, no. 3 (1992), pp. 206–238; J. VanTassel-Baska, *Planning Effective Curriculum for Gifted Learners* (Denver, Colo.: Love Publishing, 1992); S. Willis, "Cooperative learning fallout? Some see 'exploitation' of gifted students in mixed-ability groups," *Association for Supervision and Curriculum Development Update* (October 1990), pp. 6–8.

17. B. Kantrowitz & P. Wingert, "Failing the most gifted kids: A generation goes to waste," *Newsweek* (November 15, 1993), p. 67.

18. P.O. Rogne, "Reflections on 'the research,'" *Gifted Child Today*, vol. 16, no. 1 (January/February 1993), p. 14.

19. J.F. Feldhusen, "Susan Allan sets the record straight: Response to Allan," *Educational Leadership*, vol. 48, no. 6 (March 1991), p. 66. Copyrighted material used with permission from the Association for Supervision and Curriculum Development (ASCD).

20. Gallagher (1991), p. 16.

21. Renzulli & Reis (1991), p. 26.

22. J.F. Feldhusen & S. Moon, "Grouping gifted students: Issues and concerns," *Gifted Child Quarterly*, vol. 35, no. 2 (Spring 1992), p. 64. Copyrighted material used with permission from the National Association for Gifted Children (NAGC).

23. VanTassel-Baska (1992), p. 13.

24. J.J. Gallagher, "Ability grouping: A tool for educational excellence," *College Board Review*, no. 168 (Summer 1993), p. 26.

25. *Mathematics and Science Education in the Eighth Grade: Findings from the Third International Mathematics and Science Study*, National Center for Educational Statistics, statistical analysis report (July 2000). See also *Highlights from TIMSS: Overview and Key Findings across Grade Levels*, Office of Educational Research and Improvement (Washington, D.C.: U.S. Department of Education, 1999), NCES document 1999–081.

26. *Policy Brief: What the Third International Mathematics and Science Study (TIMSS) Means for Systemic School Improvement*, Office of Educational Research and Improvement (Washington, D.C.: U.S. Department of Education, November 1998), p. vii.

27. Debra Viadero, "U.S. seniors near bottom in world test," *Education Week*, vol. 17, no. 25 (March 4, 1998).

28. W. Schmidt, "The implications of TIMSS for teacher quality," in *Shaping the Profession that Shapes the Future: Speeches from the AFT/NEA Conference on Teacher Quality* (Washington, D.C.: AFT/NEA, 1998), pp. 48, 49.

29. See David J. Hoff, "U.S. students' scores drop by 8th grade," *Education Week* (December 13, 2000).

30. *Pursuing Excellence: Comparisons of International Eighth Grade Mathematics and Science Achievement from a U.S. Perspective, 1995 and 1999, Initial Findings from the Third International Mathematics and Science Study—Repeat*, Office of Educational Research and Improvement (Washington, D.C.: U.S. Department of Education, December 2000), p. 41. See also *Highlights from the Third International Mathematics and Science Study—Repeat (TIMSS-R)*, Office of Educational Research and Improvement (Washington, D.C.: U.S. Department of Education), NCES document 2001-027.

31. Ibid., p. 42. See also Hoff (2000).

32. Dave Shearon, quoted in C. Colgan, "U.S. students show no progress in latest TIMSS results," *School Board News* (December 19, 2000).

33. M.A. Zahr, "Immigrant students find U.S. schools less demanding," *Education Week* (January 17, 2001), p. 8.

34. T. Loveless, *The 2001 Brown Center Report on American Education: How Well Are American Students Learning?* vol. 1, no. 2 (September 2001), p. 21.

35. Colgan (2000).

36. B. Clark, "Social ideologies and gifted education in today's schools," *Peabody Journal of Education*, vol. 72, nos. 3–4 (1997), p. 83.

37. W.M. Alexander, E.L. Williams, M. Compton, V.A. Hines, & D. Prescott, *The Emergent Middle School* (New York: Holt, Rinehart & Winston, 1968), p. 17.

38. C.K. McEwin, "William M. Alexander: Father of the American middle school," *Middle School Journal*, vol. 23, no. 5 (May 1992), p. 35.

39. P.S. George, "Education 2000: Which way the middle school?" *The Clearing House*, vol. 62, no. 1 (1988), p. 14.

40. T.E. Gatewood & C.A. Dilig, *The Middle School We Need* (Washington, D.C.: Association for Supervision and Curriculum Development, 1975), p. 4.

41. J.A. Beane, "Middle schools under siege: Points of attack," *Middle School Journal*, vol. 30, no. 4 (March 1999), p. 6.

42. National Middle School Association annual conference session (1998), p. 84.

43. H. Johnston, "Interview with John Lounsbury," *Middle School Journal*, vol. 24, no. 2 (November 1992), p. 50.

44. George (1988), p. 17.

45. M.L. Goldberg, "Issues in the education of gifted and talented children," *Roeper Review*, vol. 8, no. 4 (1986), p. 227.

46. For a thorough discussion of anti-intellectualism, see R. Hofstadter, *Anti-Intellectualism in American Life* (New York: Random House, 1963). For discussions of anti-intellectualism in a more current context, see Feldhusen (1991), p. 66; Feldhusen & Moon (1992), pp. 63–67; Gallagher (1991), pp. 12–19; J.J. Gallagher, "Academic effectiveness or social reform: A response to Robert Slavin and Jomills H. Braddock, III," *The College Board Review*, no. 168 (1993), pp. 18–34; J.J. Gallagher, "Least restrictive environment and gifted students," *Peabody Journal of Education*, vol. 72, nos. 3–4, (1997), pp. 153–165; Rogne (1993), pp. 8–14.

47. A. Bestor, *Educational Wastelands: The Retreat from Learning in Our Public Schools*, 2nd ed. (Urbana: University of Illinois Press, 1985), p. 101.

48. Ibid., p. 101.

49. Document analysis is a research method that involves the study and analysis of written documents containing information pertinent to the issue being studied. See K.D. Bailey, *Methods of Social Research* (New York: The Free Press, 1982). A significant strength of document analysis is the utilization of a variety of sources written for many different purposes (see Bailey, 1982; O.R. Holsti, "Content analysis," in G. Lindzey & E. Aronson (Eds.), *The Handbook of Social Psychology*, Reading, Mass.: Addison-Wesley, 1968, pp. 596–692; and K. Krippendorff, *Content Analysis: An Introduction to Its Methodology*, Beverly Hills, Calif.: Sage Publications, 1980). Document analysis also provides a stable source of information and a rich repository of detailed information. See Y.S. Lincoln & E.G. Guba, *Naturalistic Inquiry* (Newbury Park, Calif: Sage Publications, 1985), p. 277. When approaching a subject from the perspective of assessing changes over time, this approach is recommended, and will be the primary method used in this analysis.

CHAPTER 2

The Growth of the Middle School Movement

When we come to the realization that not every child has to read, figure, write and spell . . . then we shall be on the road to improving the junior high curriculum. Between this day and that a lot of selling must take place. But it's coming . . . the next step is to cut down on the amount of time and attention devoted to these areas in general junior-high courses.

National Association of Secondary School Principals, 1951[1]

A HISTORY OF CONTROVERSY

The middle school movement appears to have been poised for controversy from the start. The National Middle School Association (NMSA) was founded in 1973, held its first conference in 1974, and by 1979, three conference sessions had already addressed the issue of controversy. These included "Controversial Issues Confronting Middle School Educators: Are You Ready?" and "The Mission that Unites Us—Issues that Divide Us."[2] More than two decades later it is apparent that the controversy is continuing, with sessions such as "Hot Topics and Their Solution" appearing in NMSA conference programs.[3]

The controversy surrounding the middle school movement has not eased with the passage of time. In fact, it has grown more intense. According to middle school activists Paul George and Walter Grebing:

Our experience with the strife surrounding the issue of grouping, the gifted, and the middle school concept leads us to conclude that middle school educators in many parts of the country are in a struggle for what might legitimately be called the "soul" of the middle school.[4]

This statement begs a question—just what is the "soul" of the middle school movement? And who should define it?

To understand the impact of the middle school movement and how it has been influenced by a specific set of beliefs, it is imperative to look at its chronological development and to consider its historical treatment of student diversity, especially academic diversity.

CHRONOLOGICAL HISTORY OF THE MIDDLE SCHOOL MOVEMENT

Genesis of the Junior High School

During the latter part of the nineteenth century, the most common and nearly universal grade configuration for American schools had the elementary school containing the first eight grades and high school containing the last four (8/4). Education leaders expressed concerns about upper-level elementary students spending too much time in a repetitious curriculum, so in 1894 the Committee of Ten on Secondary Studies issued a report recommending a 6/6 grade-level split, thus removing students in grades 7 and 8 from the elementary school and including them in the high school with grades 9–12, with the intent of exposing them to a more rigorous curriculum in the latter part of what had previously been their elementary school years.[5]

Other committees soon followed with a series of proposals between 1908 and 1911, which included a modified proposal to split the upper half of the 6/6 organization into junior and senior levels.[6] This suggested grade-level modification reflected an interest in presenting an option which would have the potential for allowing students to receive more than six years of schooling before many of them dropped out.[7] Consequently, the first junior high schools on record appeared around 1909.[8]

The rise in elementary school enrollment shortly after World War I provided a pragmatic reason to accelerate the growth of the junior high movement. As a result of increased elementary enrollment, it made good economic sense to shift several grades out of the elementary schools, thus preserving the neighborhood school for the youngest students while constructing fewer, more centralized buildings for older students. Therefore, what had commonly been an 8/4 or 6/6 grade arrangement in the early part of this century became a 6/3/3 arrangement, or some variation thereof, over the following decades.[9]

Another element that helped to propel the junior high movement was the desire to jump on the proverbial bandwagon—a motivation that still influences the field of education today. As stated by one educator in 1927, the movement toward establishing junior high schools was:

not unlike the force of a fad. It often operates without any clear understanding of the purposes of reorganization and it not uncommonly results in change which, rather than being fundamental, restricts itself to such a superficiality as the mere regrouping of grades.[10]

The new junior high schools, which generally included grades 7, 8, and 9, were true to their name in that they were similar to high schools in both organization and curriculum. The presence of the ninth grade contributed to maintaining ties between the junior and senior high schools, a fact that troubled some educators. The high school orientation was strong enough to drive both the organizational structure and curriculum of junior high schools, and thus, they differed little from senior high schools.

A growing number of educators at that time came to believe that one of the greatest problems in education was "the failure of schools to recognize and provide for individual differences."[11] By the 1920s, an idea was promoted to address individual differences by providing "differentiation of work through partially variable curricula, groups moving at differing rates, promotion by subject, permitting brighter pupils to carry more courses, and supervised study."[12] In terms of academic diversity, it was noted that "there was abundant evidence of the fact of learning variation in the school and of the need to recognize it in the instruction and administration of the nation's schools."[13]

Had such a proposal been faithfully implemented, junior high schools may have been in the forefront of providing appropriate educational opportunities for all students. However, other events intervened.

Emergence of the Middle School

During the 1940s and 1950s, an educational proposal known as the "Life-Adjustment Movement" began to gain a strong following among American educators. As described by Pulitzer prize-winning historian Richard Hofstadter, this movement justified a less rigorous curriculum in the name of pragmatism and equity, and discounted the needs of gifted/high ability learners:

Formerly, it had been held that a liberal academic education was good for all pupils. Now it was argued that all pupils should in large measure get the kind of training originally conceived for the slow learner. . . . In the name of utility, democracy, and science, many educators had come to embrace the supposedly uneducable or less educable child as the center of the secondary-school universe, relegating the talented child to the sidelines.[14]

The fervor of this belief was strong among many, such as Dr. Charles A. Prosser, who praised individuals attending the 1947 national life-adjustment conference and their revolutionary ideas with unabashed intensity: "Never in the history of education has there been such a meeting as this. . . . What you have planned is worth fighting for—it is worth dying for . . . God bless you all."[15] A similar level of fervor can be seen in the remarks of another supporter of the life-adjustment movement, a principal who addressed the National Association of Secondary School Principals (NASSP) in 1951 with a presentation called "How can the junior high curriculum be improved?":

When we come to the realization that not every child has to read, figure, write and spell . . . that many of them either cannot or will not master these chores, then we shall be on the road to improving the junior high curriculum. Between this day and that a lot of selling must take place. But it's coming. . . . If and when we are able to convince a few folks that mastery of reading, writing, and arithmetic is not the one road leading to happy, successful living, the next step is to cut down on the amount of time and attention devoted to these areas in general junior-high courses.[16]

Consequently, dissatisfaction with "the tendency for the burgeoning junior high to mimic the high school program"[17] resulted in the formal call for junior high reform with the 1961 publication of *The Junior High School We Need*.[18] Subsequently, the Cornell Junior High School conference in 1963 amplified the call for the reorganization of the junior high.[19]

Whether junior high schools gradually evolved into middle schools or were directly supplanted by them is a matter of perspective; but regardless, by the late 1950s and early 1960s the first schools known as middle schools began to emerge.[20] This change involved moving ninth grade up to the high school and sixth grade (occasionally fifth as well) out of the elementary school and into the middle school. What emerged was a new 5/3/4 grade arrangement, and the removal of a direct high school influence at the middle level. The belief was that "without the ninth grade, these new schools would be less controlled by the high school and freer to adapt to the real life needs of older children and younger adolescents."[21]

Changes in demographics also affected the growth of middle schools. The movement toward racial integration helped accelerate the growth of middle schools, since children who attended segregated neighborhood elementary schools were often sent to integrated middle schools to comply with federal mandates, and such plans were approved by federal courts. School enrollment was increasing only at the elementary level, and this increase in the number of younger students encouraged administrators to make building-level changes resulting in the continued growth of the 5/3/4 model.[22]

A Movement in Search of a Mission

However, these physical reorganizations were not enough of a change for some middle school advocates, who had a specific vision of what a middle school should be. An apparent disconnect between their vision of the middle school concept and the reality of middle school practice began to be noted in the early 1970s, as educators and organizations began to raise their voices to echo supporters of the life-adjustment movement. In advocating programming unique to the middle school, many advocates saw the opportunity to use middle schools as the means to attain noneducational ends.

Early writings by middle school proponents in the 1970s shed light on this issue. A speech titled "The Middle School: An Opportunity for Humanized Education" hearkens back to the life-adjustment movement and appears to be the first in a series of efforts to create and control a new vision for the middle school:

This long-standing emphasis upon intellectual performance to the virtual exclusion of human development remained more than adequate as long as the basic family grouping . . . provided that cohesion and sense of belonging necessary for a viable society. But society has changed and the old solutions no longer work. . . . The middle school would seem to offer the opportunity to humanize the learning experiences of young people at a stage in their physical and social development where feelings and beliefs and understandings and relationships are critical. . . . The program in the middle school would most probably include limited instruction in what could be termed the learning skills—the abilities to read, write [and] perform arithmetic computation. . . . Students should be as free as possible to come and go, to study or not study, to take this course or that course. . . . The curriculum would likely emphasize the development of healthy relationships between people, encouraging the social development of the individual while helping each human being better understand his own needs. . . . Learner achievement would most probably be evaluated in ways which avoided comparing one student to another . . . [and] the curriculum would likely discourage any emphasis upon working independently.[23]

This middle school proponent was prescient in his description of the radical notion of the ideal middle school, as the evolving middle school concept ultimately included many of his recommendations. However, that these goals had not yet been achieved by the mid-1970s can be seen in the fact that many of these sentiments were echoed in a 1975 publication of the Association for Supervision and Curriculum Development (ASCD):

The available research indicates a significant gap between the main tenets of the theoretical middle school concept proposed by leading middle school authorities and actual education practices in most middle schools. It appears that many middle schools have adopted the educational programs and practices of junior highs, thus not successfully achieving the middle school concept. The junior high school, although its philosophy from the time of its inception in the early 1900s was almost identical to the present espoused philosophy of the middle school, has long been criticized for being too much a "true" junior to the senior high school. Many alleged characteristics of the senior high have "contaminated" the junior high—a departmentalized subject-matter curriculum, interscholastic athletics. . . . And now it appears that many middle schools have continued these same sins. . . . Thus, it should come as no surprise that the only real difference between many middle schools and junior highs have been in name and grade organization.[24]

It was around this time that the National Middle School Association (NMSA) was organized. Its first annual convention was held in 1974, but other than making it clear that the middle school should be very different from the junior high school, the movement was struggling with establishing an identity. For a span of approximately 15 years (1975–1990), no fewer than nine major reports on middle-level education and early adolescence emerged from different sources, including the Association for Supervision and Curriculum Development (ASCD, 1975), the Ford Foundation (1979), the National Society for the Study of Education (NSSE, 1980), the National Middle School Association (NMSA, 1982, 1988), the National Association of Secondary School Principals (NAASP, 1985, 1989), the Carnegie Council on Adolescent Development (1989), and The John Hopkins University Center for Research on Elementary and Middle Schools (1990).[25] While all of these reports focused on the extensive diversity among middle school students in terms of physical maturity, intellectual ability, social skills, and emotional development, one report in particular came to have a major influence on the direction of the middle school movement.

The Middle School Movement Finds Its Soul

The period from 1988 to 1989 was a pivotal time in the evolution of the contemporary middle school concept. In 1988, middle school activist Paul George published an article subtitled "Which Way the Middle School?" This title indicates the search for a distinctive middle school identity, and claims that adherence to such an identity, or the failure to do so, will make or break the middle school movement. The author called the middle school concept "the nation's most promising educational innovation," but one has to ask—innovation for what? George made it clear that genuine middle schools must have goals beyond educational ones. He declared that middle schools are "the focus of social experimentation, the vehicle for movement toward increased justice and equality in the society as a whole."[26] The article is a call to action for middle school advocates, with the author warning that "if the middle school concept is not firmly in place . . . [middle schools] may disappear and the concept with them. . . . We are in a race between the middle school concept and all the threats that imperil its existence."[27]

The questions raised by George and the sense of urgency he expressed were addressed the following year with the 1989 publication titled *Turning Points: Preparing Youth for the 21st Century*, a product of the Carnegie Council on Adolescent Development. This report agreed with earlier ones that a high level of developmental diversity is common among middle school students. However, the report went much further than that.

Turning Points sought to manufacture a crisis that did not exist by making the assumption that nearly all early adolescents are dysfunctional. This is a page out of the playbook of social radicals from the 1960s and 1970s, known as the "Hegelian Principle": (1) create a crisis, (2) publicize the problem, and (3) present the solution. In other words, if you want to make changes in society, simply create a crisis by inflating facts and figures, make your "findings" widely known, and then volunteer the solution that you wanted to implement in the first place. In this way, the public implores you to step in and provide the very solution that you wanted to implement before the "crisis" was invented.

If it could be established that all early adolescents are dysfunctional, then there surely is a crisis. Consider the descriptions in *Turning Points* regarding middle school–aged children. Phrases such as "grave situation" and "serious jeopardy"[28] are used to describe their situation, and both traditional education and an apathetic public are blamed:

The crisis our country faces with respect to the preparation of youth for the twenty-first century is largely unrecognized by the general public.

As currently organized, these middle grades constitute an arena of casualties—damaging to both student and teachers.

By age 15, millions of American youth are at risk. . . . These young people often suffer from underdeveloped intellectual abilities, indifference to good health, and cynicism about the values that American society embodies.

Many young people feel a desperate sense of isolation. Surrounded by their equally confused peers, too many make poor decisions with harmful or lethal consequences.

As the number of youth left behind grows . . . we must face the specter of a divided society. . . . We face an America at odds with itself.[29]

Thus, in one move, the publication of *Turning Points* both created a crisis and publicized it as well. Once the existence of the "crisis" was established, *Turning Points* presented the solution:

A fundamental transformation in the education of young adolescents is urgently required.

Middle grade schools—junior high, intermediate, and middle schools—are potentially society's most powerful force to recapture millions of youth adrift.

All sectors of society must be mobilized to build a national consensus to make transformation of middle grade schools a reality.

The middle grade school proposed here is profoundly different from many schools today.

This report . . . sets out recommendations for a fundamental transformation in middle grade schools.[30]

There were many recommendations in *Turning Points*, including organizing students into pseudo-families called "houses" and into teams within each "house," assigning an adult advisor to each individual student who would become "the primary contact between the school and the parents," providing health services in schools, a change declared to be something that "middle grade schools *must* accept [as] a significant responsibility" (emphasis added), and teaching students to be active citizens so they can learn a "desire for social justice."[31]

In terms of academics, a topic not given much prominence, the report recommends integrating subject matter across disciplines. However, far more space is devoted to the "elimination of tracking by achievement level and promotion of cooperative learning." A related recommendation for the use of peer tutoring echoes the statements of social activist Mara Sapon-Shevin, as the reader is told that "high achievers develop a sense of responsibility for those less advanced."[32]

This report marks a momentous shift in the history of the middle school movement. Those who ascribed to the life-adjustment and anti-intellectual philosophies were now given a vehicle with which to implement their vision. After all, an external organization possessing a high degree of credibility (via the Carnegie name) had staged the crisis and set the agenda, and leaders of the middle school movement saw this opportunity and flocked to it.

The impact of *Turning Points* cannot be underemphasized, as references to it appear again and again in middle school literature, and all but one of its recommendations were taken to heart and implemented with vigor by middle school activists.[33] NMSA conference programs reveal that the topic of *Turning Points* was quite popular at its annual conferences, especially in the mid-1990s. (See Appendix A.) When middle school proponents claim that "there were major conceptual differences in the development of the contemporary middle school movement from the earlier establishment of junior high schools,"[34] they are referring to the changes that came about after *Turning Points*. For example, in 1991, two years after the publication of *Turning Points*, one of the founders of the middle school movement echoed the crisis-creating strategy that was used in *Turning Points* as the underpinnings of the call for radical change. John Lounsbury declared: "Are not all young adolescents at risk as they negotiate this major developmental level?" He continued:

We can no longer achieve success by simply making further adjustments or refinements in the prevailing program. . . . We need to go back, then, and build up anew from the foundations of democratic values, social realities, and our knowledge of human growth and development. We have to be free to think outside of and beyond the big four subjects. . . . We need a common curriculum for our common clients in our common school. . . . In such a common curriculum, diversity is dealt with by varied activities and responsibilities rather than by separate programs. . . . Our [current] educational practices have . . . over-emphasiz[ed] the knowledge acquisition objective of education and virtually ignor[ed] in any official way the more important behavioral objectives. . . . Schooling, it is widely assumed, is a matter of acquiring knowledge, and that, further, knowledge is power. Human behavior, however, is much more driven by attitudes than knowledge, by feelings rather than facts. . . . Public education now, whether we like it or not, has new responsibilities—life building, character forming, personal growth responsibilities— that cannot be effectively carried out in a system and by a curriculum that was designed for transmitting prescribed knowledge. . . . The misguided and timid reform efforts of the past decades have obviously not gotten to the heart of the matter. . . . "Dare the school build a new social order?" George Counts asked in 1932. It was a proper question then and it is a proper one now. I, for one, believe the school does have a social and political responsibility to work toward change for the better in our larger society. [And I recognize] the key role that only the middle school can play in building better human beings.[35]

The middle school concept that began to emerge in the 1970s and evolved through the 1980s had finally found its voice. In the early 1990s, life-adjustment, non-academic, and anti-intellectual philosophies came to gain ascendancy over all other viewpoints, driving the agenda for the middle school movement for years to come. Although earlier rhetoric asserted the importance of honoring all types of diversity, along the way that "balance" came to be tipped in favor of every imaginable sort of diversity—except academic diversity.

The Middle School Moves Away from Academics

The astonishing impact of *Turning Points* can be seen in a close analysis of NMSA conference programs over time. This documentary evidence supports the existence of a dramatic move away from addressing the academic diversity of students in favor of other forms of diversity. Fifteen types of student diversity were identified and tracked over the course of nearly 30 years of NMSA annual conference programs. These specific areas of student diversity were then categorized into three groups: cultural diversity (including multicultural, ethnic, socio-economic, language, urban, and rural diversity), gender diversity (including gender equity and gender identity issues), and academic diversity (including but not limited to special education, gifted/talented, and at-risk of academic failure). The annual frequencies of sessions in each category were identified (Appendix B), and then the specific percentage of diversity-related sessions addressed annually by each category was determined (Appendix C).

Until 1990, the number of NMSA annual conference sessions addressing academic diversity surpassed the number addressing cultural diversity. Beginning in 1991, however, a new trend can be seen in the shift away from academic diversity in favor of cultural diversity. The shift accelerates in 1992, with over half of the sessions on diversity from 1992 to 1994 being centered on cultural diversity (Appendix C), reaching a peak of 82 sessions (66 percent of the total sessions on diversity) in 1993 (Appendix B). In this same year, the percentage of sessions addressing academic diversity reached an all-time low of 28 percent.

A gradual decline in the percentage of sessions on cultural diversity can be seen from 1995 to 2000. The reason for this decline is unknown, but it may reflect that the public seems to be indicating the desire for a more inclusive and less divisive atmosphere in the schools. For example, the findings of a recent survey of over 800 parents suggest that an overwhelming majority of parents want their schools to emphasize to children that they are Americans, not members of various ethnic and cultural groups. The survey, conducted by a non-partisan organization, found that a large majority of parents agreed that "the best place for kids to learn to take pride in their ethnic or racial identity is at home—school is where they should be learning what it means to be an American."[36] And nearly all parents agreed with this statement: "There's too much attention paid these days to what separates racial and ethnic groups and not enough to what they have in common."[37] Another survey of over 1,000 public school teachers found very few teachers overall, and a similar percentage of black teachers, believe that schools should adapt to the backgrounds of students, "such as using street language to teach inner-city kids."[38]

Interestingly, as large percentages of the public express their disagreement with the obsession of some activist educators with cultural and ethnic differences, recent research suggests that training opportunities for teachers in "special topics workshops" that address issues such as "gender, linguistic, class and racial inequalities in math classrooms" do nothing to help student academic performance for any group of students. The authors of this study call this "a very important result."[39]

Another recent study finds that education policymakers appear to be in agreement with the findings from national surveys that indicate the desire of the public for a color-blind approach to educating children:

It appears that policymakers, like practitioners and members of the public, choose to identify students by learning characteristics more so than by race or ethnicity.... It appears that both policymakers and practitioners see their students primarily as learners with specific academic strengths and weaknesses, and only secondarily as members of a specific ethnic group.[40]

Such an attitude is profoundly different from that which was expressed by early middle school advocates, who made declarations such as: "Ethnic and cultural identities should be emphasized."[41]

Diminished Focus on the Needs of Gifted Learners

Within the category of academic diversity, the number of annual sessions on special education students, students at risk for academic failure, and gifted/talented learners was compiled and charted (Appendix D), and the percentage for each of these three areas within the category of academic diversity was calculated (Appendix E). With the exception of only two years, the combined number of sessions dealing with special education students and students at risk of failure surpassed those dealing with gifted learners. Only in 1982 and 1983 did the number of sessions on gifted learners predominate. Furthermore, in the 1990s, only four years saw the percentage of sessions for gifted learners exceed 20 percent (Appendix E).

Another indicator is the percentage of total conference sessions dedicated to gifted and talented learners (Appendix F). A declining emphasis on gifted learners can be seen over time. From 1978 to 1983, with the exception of only one year, more than 2 percent of the total number of sessions addressed gifted learners, peaking in 1982 at 4.24 percent. However, in the 1990s, only three of ten years saw the number of sessions on gifted learners exceed 1 percent, with an all-time low of .26 percent in 1995. The 1990s were clearly the dark ages for sessions on gifted learners at NMSA conferences.

It should come as no surprise then to note that the Council of State Directors of Programs for the Gifted announced in 1994: "There is broad consensus that services for gifted students are in serious jeopardy throughout the country."[42]

RESPONSE FROM ADVOCATES FOR THE GIFTED

Initial Acceptance

Early on, the middle school movement was not an issue of importance to advocates for gifted/high ability learners. In the late 1980s, many members of the gifted community were focused instead on the positive changes occurring within their field. The 1988 passage of the Jacob K. Javits Gifted and Talented Children and Youth Education Act reestablished the Office of Gifted and Talented at the U.S. Department of Education and provided funding for teacher training and programs for gifted and talented students.[43] It was in this same year that Abraham Tannenbaum published *The Gifted Movement: Forward or on a Treadmill*, which included "A Much Needed Bill of Rights for the Gifted." One highlight from this "Bill of Rights" was "a right to differentiated education that is especially appropriate for [gifted learners]," which sounded amazingly like early middle-level educators' prescription for individualized instruction:

Tannenbaum, 1988: If we truly believe in individualized education, then we have to vary our educational objectives and programs to accommodate individual differences.[44]

Turning Points, 1989: Young adolescents show great variability among themselves and within themselves, yet we put them in classrooms where we ignore their variability and need for flexibility.[45]

Around this time, John Feldhusen of Purdue University and several associates expressed a profound sense of optimism for the field of gifted education:

The future of gifted education is easy to predict.... Gifted education is thriving.... The decade of the 1990s promises to move our nation much closer to the goal of an appropriate education for every gifted student in the United States.... Middle school and high school programs will turn increasingly to honors classes, seminars, advanced placement and concurrent college enrollment to meet the needs of academically gifted students.... We expect that good sense will prevail among many school personnel who will see a continuing need to group gifted youth for all or a part of the school day in order to meet their need for higher-level, fast-paced, and conceptually differentiated instruction.[46]

As noted earlier, major organizations issued statements that spoke glowingly of the need to address student diversity. But while advocates for gifted learners understood this to include academic diversity, middle school activists set their sights on promoting other types of diversity. In spite of statements on the part of middle school proponents that the middle school concept addressed the needs "of a most diverse and varied population," some types of diversity clearly took precedence over others.

From Optimism to Suspicion

By the early 1990s, the tone among members of the gifted community shifted. Advocates for gifted/high ability learners began to vocalize serious concerns about what was seen, at best, as a growing movement against ability grouping at the middle school level, and at worst, as an attempt to do away with all services for the gifted. Pamela Sicola noted that middle schools were "being encouraged by recognized experts and associations" to abandon ability grouping, in spite of the fact that "for the gifted student the effects of strict heterogeneous (mixed-ability) grouping are tremendous, yet generally disregarded in the middle school literature." She contended that the middle school focus was on affective needs, rather than on a balance between affective and academic needs, and sounded a warning and a call for action:

It is time to step back and assesses the goals and programs involved in middle school education. More specifically, it is essential that experts in the field of gifted education become familiar with the middle school philosophy and its impact on gifted learners and take an active role in researching and determining where exactly the gifted student's place is in the middle school.[47]

As noted in Chapter 1, a series of warnings appeared from a number of influential sources in the gifted education community in the early 1990s:

James J. Gallagher, 1991: The potential for gifted students being further delayed in their academic development by participating in these middle school programs seems very real and should be a major concern to those who formed the "excellence" movement only six years ago.[48]

John Feldhusen, 1991: [There is] an emerging national agenda among nearly all the school reform constituencies [that] ability grouping is bad, it is racist, it must be eliminated. Research is cited and twisted to support that agenda. . . . The question we now face is how to call a halt to a national reform agenda in which some school reformers have arrogated unto themselves a political-social agenda that is based on misinterpretation of current research evidence.[49]

Joseph Renzulli and Sally Reis, 1991: We believe that the field of education for the gifted and talented is currently facing a quiet crisis and that in many ways this crisis is directly related to the education reform movement in America.[50]

Over the course of a few short years, the mood in the field of gifted education swung from unbridled optimism to the declaration of a crisis. It is particularly telling that this change of mood occurred in spite of the establishment in 1990 of the federally funded National Research Center on the Gifted and Talented.

NMSA ATTEMPTS TO ADDRESS THE ISSUE OF GIFTED EDUCATION

In 1992, a NMSA policy paper was published on the topic of gifted education that purported to present "a balanced and well-documented tour that synthesizes and reviews the significant literature on these two topics." Unfortunately, the author appears more interested in justifying the middle school concept than in addressing the needs of gifted learners, turning the policy paper into an advocacy piece supporting the radical middle school concept and attacking gifted learners and the programs that address their needs. The author implies that gifted programs are elitist when he describes "labeling students who thereafter qualify for special services to the exclusion of others," and states that identification of students for gifted programs should not be the same as "membership applications for a private club."

Grouping gifted/high ability learners together for instruction is described pejoratively as an elitist instructional practice. Instruction for gifted children outside of the middle school–approved heterogeneous (mixed-ability) classroom is not presented as an option, although the author does concede that there are problems in the implementation of this favored middle school practice when it comes to gifted learners:

More and more parents are pointing out that indeed their children's academic needs are not being met in regular classrooms. If it were not, so they say, for that afternoon a week that my child spends in the gifted classroom, she or he would not be challenged at all in school. This is a serious indictment that suggests middle level educators are not yet delivering on the potential of middle school organization.[51]

But the author views differentiation of instruction in a mixed-ability classroom simplistically, obviously not understanding the difficulty it presents. He states: "Individual differences among students can *easily* be accommodated within a common curricular framework without having to rely on rigid ability grouping" (emphasis added).[52] This contrasts with the acknowledgment by many others that curriculum differentiation is a challenge for teachers that requires training, guidance, and experience.[53]

The portrayal of gifted/high ability children as elitists who keep other children away from educational opportunities can also be seen in a 1991 NMSA conference session description: "[This] entire school is focusing all of its energies on doing for all children what is presently reserved for the gifted and talented."[54] The titles of two sessions at the 1995 conference are equally informative: "Skill exploration: A gifted program for all students," and "The accelerated schools process incorporates powerful learning and teaches all students as if they were gifted."[55]

Attempts at Dialogue

In the early 1990s, gifted advocate Carol Tomlinson made it clear that any sort of compatibility between middle schools and gifted education, noted only a few short years before, appeared to be superficial, indicating a disconnect in middle school rhetoric between belief and behavior, philosophy and action, theory and practice. According to Tomlinson, "many middle school practices designed to benefit typical adolescents can create significant problems for the academically advanced student."[56] Statements that professed the importance of honoring all forms of student diversity apparently did not translate into practice, as *academic* diversity came to be ignored—and even disdained.

An attempt between the two groups to enter into a dialogue appears to have started in the early 1990s. Mary Ruth Coleman's presentation at the 1992 NMSA conference addressed "blending the goals for middle school and gifted education." Likewise, Tomlinson's presentation in 1993 suggested "ways of linking goals of the two fields so that teachers and administrators can help highly able middle school students receive the most appropriate education possible."[57]

This outreach was the beginning of an attempt at a dialogue that resulted in a series of articles in professional journals, a joint meeting between leaders of both groups, and the issuance of policy statements. The following policy statements were published in the January 1995 edition of the *Middle School Journal*:

The National Association for Gifted Children (NAGC) applauds and supports the fundamental principles of the middle school movement. We endorse, in particular:

- The emphasis on individual student needs;
- The teaching of thinking strategies and decision making;
- The teacher as facilitator, rather than knowledge giver;
- The use of interdisciplinary curricula;
- The encouragement of each student working at his/her own pace;
- The students belonging to a ["teamed"] group;
- The extension of learning beyond the textbooks.

In addition, the NAGC believes that the flexible use of grouping for student instruction and accelerated programs in content fields to match students' advanced abilities and knowledge can meet the needs of gifted students while maintaining the important social goals of the middle school movement.[58]

The National Middle School Association:

- Whereas, the development of gifted students is accelerated in one or more areas in comparison to their peers; and,
- Whereas, research identifies that these students want to be with their age peers and not feel alone in the learning process; and,
- Whereas, self-concept and self-esteem are directly related to all areas of school success;

Therefore, be it resolved that NMSA provide information about these issues and offer professional development experiences to help middle level educators respond more effectively to the needs of these students.[59]

Although the NAGC statement was accommodating and deferred to the middle school movement by expressing support for key tenets, documentary evidence indicates that the statement from the NMSA was mere lip service, as a decidedly negative tone continues in other official NMSA publications. For example, a 1993 NMSA conference session states that "instruction for gifted learners" should not be "like membership in a private club,"[60] echoing the "private club" language in the NMSA policy paper mentioned earlier. For the statements to be so similar one has to speculate that the tone of the policy paper appears to have influenced at least some practitioners in the field.

A series of articles addressing the needs of gifted middle school learners was published in the *Middle School Journal* in 1994 and 1995.[61] The editor's note accompanying the first article states that this series is "part of the continuing effort to open up communication" between middle school proponents "and those who argue for curricular and instructional reform aimed at developing the talents of those thought to be especially 'gifted.' "[62] The tone of the editor's note and the content of the articles by advocates of the middle school concept make it clear that, in spite of the *appearance* of searching for common ground, negative attitudes toward gifted learners still had a firm hold. Note, for example, that the editor places the word *gifted* into quotation marks, denoting the use in an ironic sense and indicating his disagreement with the term.

In the first of these articles, the author implies that addressing the needs of gifted students is an inconvenience with which one is forced to deal. After listing social, athletic, and extracurricular activities in which many middle school students are involved, the author states:

As we begin to believe that middle school students do not have room on their educational plates for another morsel, another entrée is brought to the table. The entrée that may be introduced is the fact that . . . [high ability students are] in need of even greater academic challenges. This additional entrée is one that could cause the heads of the school's principals and teachers to spin. As students choose to become involved in a multitude of school and community activities, providing these additional academic challenges to identified gifted students has always been demanding at the middle level especially if there are few study halls included in the school's master schedule.[63]

Note the assumption that the academic needs of gifted learners should be addressed only as an add-on and not as a part of the regular daily curriculum. Challenging the gifted is treated as an extra, an "entrée"—as though it is one of many extracurricular activities from which students can pick and choose. The idea of integrating an appropriate level of challenge for gifted/high ability learners within the regular school day is not even considered—the only allowable option is during "study halls."

Another article in this series continues the sort of confrontational language that was common from the mid-1980s through the early 1990s. The two groups in question are presented as diametrically opposed—proponents for elitism versus proponents for the democratic ideal:

Many parents whose children have been labeled gifted argue that, for their children to be properly educated and successful in high school and college, they must be continually challenged academically, and permitted to move as fast and as far as their abilities permit. Other, slower students should not be permitted to slow down their gifted student. Ability grouped classes and special opportunities for the gifted are the result. Middle school proponents, on the other hand, feel the pressure from parents and other advocates for the gifted as a direct challenge to their commitment to provide success for all children. . . . Many middle school educators believe that gifted students can be effectively educated within heterogeneous interdisciplinary teams without tracking and elitism.[64]

According to the authors, addressing the needs of gifted learners means "special opportunities" and "elitism." Anti-gifted attitudes are also seen in the authors' subsequent denial that the needs of gifted learners are not being met. Rather than acknowledge that this is a shortcoming of the operationalized middle school concept, as do some,[65] it is attributed to unreasonable parental demands: "Attempts to meet the needs of all gifted and talented students sometimes fall short of parental expectations."[66] Parents of gifted learners are viewed as obstacles to be overcome, as they "must be helped to welcome opportunities for their students to explain concepts and skills to other students."[67] It should be noted that many middle school activists view the concerns expressed by parents of gifted learners as selfish and unreasonable.[68]

The only article in this series that was written by advocates for gifted learners takes a more practical and accommodating approach. Mary Ruth Coleman and James Gallagher present a positive response and define the argument logically and with little acrimony:

There seems to be strong congruence between the goals of the middle school movement and accepted goals for the education of gifted students. . . . But in spite of this clear overlap of goals, little collaboration has existed between the two fields.[69]

The authors conducted a survey that compared attitudes toward gifted learners among middle school proponents and gifted advocates. Some of their findings indicate several points upon which both groups agree, including: "the regular curriculum does not challenge gifted students," "most middle school teachers need more preparation on meeting the needs of gifted learners," and "little collaboration currently takes place between the two areas [regular middle school teachers and gifted education teachers]." The only items "truly polarizing" the two groups were the issues of ability grouping and the effects of the label *gifted*.[70]

The second part of their article delineated the results of a study of five exemplary middle schools and their dealings with gifted learners:

Teachers at each site used a variety of curriculum differentiation strategies to meet the needs of gifted students, with enrichment and grouping by ability/performance in use at all five schools. . . . In every case . . . the education of gifted students was not addressed merely as an afterthought. Rather, when school personnel planned for the education of all their students, they intentionally differentiated the school program for their most capable learners.[71]

This article does not focus on divisiveness or theoretical solutions to the controversy, but presents the reality of solutions currently being implemented. As such, proponents of education for the gifted appear to be more willing to work toward a solution than proponents of the middle school concept.

The Summit

This was further evidenced during January 1995 when a summit was held to provide an opportunity for discussion between both groups. The purpose of the summit, which was hosted by the Council for Exceptional Children, was to provide the opportunity for a dialogue between leaders in the area of gifted education and leaders of the middle school movement.

Although the summit was billed as a positive sign that a dialogue had begun, the text from the presentations at this event indicate that middle school advocates remained adamantly close-minded toward issues dealing with gifted learners. Their language continued to be harsh and confrontational.

Representing advocates for the middle school concept, Thomas Erb continued strident calls for a continued restructuring of schools according to the middle school model:

Our energies will then be focused on developing human potential as opposed to dissipating our energy trying to figure out who is talented and who is not so we can sort children into rigid categories that all too often have the unfortunate consequences of limiting their potential.

Furthermore, he implied that gifted learners are hurt academically by gifted pull-out programs, as opposed to programs based upon the middle school model:

Since all students are exposed to the same core curriculum, no gaps can creep into the backgrounds of students who have in the past been pulled out of core classes to engage in "gifted" activities.[72]

Activist Paul George, often looked to as a spokesperson for the middle school movement, was clearly angry in his remarks:

I think I hear an understanding emerging that schools are systems and that when you change one part of a system, there's a cost. And what I hope we're becoming aware of is that gifted programs involve costs that I'm not sure other children should be asked to pay. . . .

Schools are about the redistribution of future wealth. That's what they're about. They're not about talent development. They're not about taking each child as far as he or she can go. They're about redistributing the wealth of the future.[73]

In contrast, presentations by advocates for gifted learners indicated their efforts to seek common ground and presented pragmatic solutions to the problems being addressed. Mary Ruth Coleman and James Gallagher, whose presentation was based on the results of their survey and five case studies, presented real-life implementation options, not just theory and opinion. They concluded:

The results of the two studies indicate that it was more than just "possible" for educators from middle schools and gifted education to work together profitably—in some schools it is a current reality.[74]

Carol Tomlinson gave a balanced overview of the issue along with presentations on differentiated instruction, as well as instructional and management strategies for mixed-ability classrooms. In her overview, Tomlinson asserted optimistically that "there are enough areas of shared belief to bridge the practice between gifted education and middle school education."[75] She lists problems and proposes potential solutions for an array of issues, including the emphasis on heterogeneity, equity, cooperative learning, affective needs, and appropriate curriculum.

The few years following the summit saw attempts to continue the dialogue. At the 1996 NMSA conference, a joint presentation that included advocates for both the middle school concept and gifted education was titled "Meeting the needs of the gifted in middle level programs." The tone was more conciliatory, even if it did not reflect the current reality:

Past misunderstandings have given way to an emerging vision, some established successful programs, and growing recognition of some promising opportunities to better accommodate students of widely diverging gifts, abilities, and interests.[76]

This was followed by an assembly at the 1997 NMSA conference titled "Gifted and Talented Discussion," which was billed "as an attempt to find common ground upon which educators can proceed in educating all students, including high achievers."[77]

Growing Discontent

As promising as this looked, the words of middle school advocates have rarely been followed by matching action. A growing discontent with the middle school concept continues to be expressed. In early 1998, *Education Week* carried a special section titled "Muddle in the Middle" that stated:

Thirty years after districts began shifting away from junior versions of high school, the middle school model has come under attack for supplanting academic rigor with a focus on students' social, emotional, and physical needs.[78]

In November 1998, *School Board News* ran an article titled "School Leaders, Researchers, Re-examining Middle School Reform," that noted similar concerns:

Has the middle-school concept gone too far in catering to the social and emotional developmental needs of young adolescents at the expense of academic performance? That's exactly what some education experts and school leaders are charging.[79]

Even *Teacher Magazine* addressed the issue in 1998:

After more than 30 years, the middle school reform movement has done little to improve the education young teenagers get.[80]

A 1998 NMSA conference session also addressed this growing discontent:

While the middle level movement has grown in terms of professional advocacy and school implementation, there is a growing criticism of middle schools and philosophy. In this session the presenters will provide a description and analysis of the source of criticism, from right and left, and ideas for how middle school advocates might respond.[81]

A growing concern among middle school proponents is that many parents of gifted/high ability students, tired of the battles for securing instructional practices that meet their children's needs, are giving up on the public schools and seeking educational opportunities elsewhere. It has been noted that "parents can make or break school change,"[82] and a 1998 NMSA conference session even addressed the issue of how a middle school could prevent "losing its best and brightest students."[83] Middle school activist Paul George, strangely unaware that the very practices he has zealously promoted have been among the primary reasons parents of gifted/high ability students are removing their children from the egalitarian embrace of the "ideal" middle school, laments:

Nor can public education survive as anything other than pauper schooling if parents of gifted and talented students, frustrated in their attempts to secure the best the school has to offer, withdraw their children from the public schools and create a whole new system of private education based on the ability to pay.[84]

Likewise, other authors claim that educators are "forced to choose between equity-based reforms and the flight of elite parents from the public school system."[85] However, some see the problem differently, as though there is a conspiracy of sorts, warning that middle school proponents "very clearly run the risk of losing the public education system to those whose political agenda is to dismantle the public schools."[86]

Writing in *Phi Delta Kappan*, a concerned parent notes that supporters of those reforms embraced by middle school activists are "the worst enemy of public schools," because under their philosophical control:

The exodus of the best and the brightest from the nation's public schools will only accelerate, and the widespread public perception that public schools are places of mediocrity rather than excellence will only deepen and, indeed, be confirmed. The public schools must stand for excellence, or they are finished, and American democracy will truly be the casualty.[87]

CONCLUSION

So it was, during the late 1980s and early 1990s, that the smoldering fire of suspicions regarding the effect of middle school practices on gifted learners erupted into a contentious debate between middle school advocates and advocates for the gifted. Fueling the fire were social scientists who claimed that practices such as ability grouping were immoral.

Behind the scenes and in conflict with earlier rhetoric, in the early 1990s the middle school movement lurched into a new identity, and in many cases middle schools became laboratories for anti-gifted practices. Although a dialogue between advocates for the middle school concept and advocates for the gifted was initiated in the mid-1990s, these attempts at conciliation did not bear fruit. It should be noted that middle school advocates participate in such dialogues only when the needs of gifted learners are addressed strictly within the context of heterogeneous grouping, which remains a key component of the middle school concept.

It is clear now that an attempt was being made to change the commonly accepted definition of "school." According to the title of an article in the *Middle School Journal*: " 'School' no longer means what you thought."[88]

From this point forward, the rigor of the curriculum in many middle schools was weakened, the use of ability grouping declined, and the practice of cooperative learning and peer tutoring grew with vigor. All of these practices had as their focus the homogenization of academic performance. Details of how these practices evolved, and the related implications, will be discussed in detail in the next several chapters.

NOTES

1. A.H. Lauchner, "How can the junior high curriculum be improved?" *Bulletin of the National Association of Secondary School Principals*, vol. 35, no. 177 (March 1951), pp. 299–300; as cited in A. Bestor, *Educational Wastelands: The Retreat from Learning in Our Public Schools*, 2nd ed. (Urbana: University of Illinois Press, 1985), pp. 55–56.

2. National Middle School Association annual conference program (1979), pp. 6, 8, 11.

3. National Middle School Association annual conference program (1988), p. 164.

4. P.S. George & W. Grebing, "Talent development and grouping in the middle grades: Challenging the brightest without sacrificing the rest," *Middle School Journal*, vol. 26, no. 4 (March 1995), p. 17. Copyrighted material used with permission from the National Middle School Association (NMSA).

5. *Report of the Committee of Ten on Secondary School Studies*, National Education Association (New York: American Book Company, 1894), as cited in S.N. Clark & D.C. Clark, *Restructuring the Middle Level School: Implications for School Leaders* (Albany: State University of New York Press, 1994), p. 8.

6. C.F. Toepfer, "Middle level school curriculum: Defining the elusive," in J.L. Irvin (Ed.), *Transforming Middle Level Education: Perspectives and Possibilities* (Needham Heights, Mass.: Allyn and Bacon, 1992), pp. 205–243.

7. Ibid.

8. Clark & Clark (1994).

9. W. Gruhn & H. Douglass, *The Modern Junior High School* (New York: Ronald Press, 1971); and W.M. Alexander & P.S. George, *The Exemplary Middle School* (New York: Holt, Rinehart & Winston, 1981).

10. L.V. Koos, *The Junior High School* (Boston: Ginn and Company, 1927), as cited in Clark & Clark (1994), p. 23.

11. Clark & Clark (1994), p. 110.

12. Koos (1927), p. 50, as cited in Clark & Clark (1994), p. 12.

13. Clark & Clark (1994), p. 11.

14. R. Hofstadter, *Anti-Intellectualism in American Life* (New York: Random House, 1963).

15. Ibid., p. 352.

16. Lauchner (1951), pp. 299–300; as cited in Bestor (1985), pp. 55–56.

17. W.M. Alexander, "Schools in the middle: Rhetoric and reality," *Social Education*, vol. 52, no. 2 (1988), p. 107.

18. J. Grantes, C. Noyce, F. Patterson, & J. Robertson, *The Junior High School We Need* (Washington, D.C.: Association for Supervision and Curriculum Development, 1961).

19. Alexander & George (1981).

20. Alexander (1988); Alexander & George (1981); P.S. George, C. Stevenson, J. Thomason, & J. Beane, *The Middle School—And Beyond* (Alexandria, Va.: Association for Supervision and Curriculum Development, 1992), p. 6.

21. George et al. (1992).

22. Alexander & George (1981); George et al. (1992).

23. C.L. Midjaas, "The middle school: An opportunity for humanized education," speech delivered at Northern Michigan University Planning Symposium (May 8, 1970), ERIC document number ED 046 110, pp. 2, 4, 5.

24. T.E. Gatewood & C.A. Dilig, *The Middle School We Need* (Washington, D.C.: Association for Supervision and Curriculum Development, 1975), pp. 3, 4. Copyrighted material used with permission from the Association for Supervision and Curriculum Development (ASCD).

25. See *Report of the Working Group on the Emergent Adolescent* (Alexandria, Va.: Association for Supervision and Curriculum Development, 1975); J. Lipsitz (Ed.), *Barriers: A New Look at the Needs of Young Adolescents* (New York: The Ford Foundation, 1979); *Seventy-ninth Yearbook of the National Society for the Study of Education* (Chicago: University of Chicago Press, 1980); *This We Believe* (National Middle School Association, 1982); *This We Believe* (National Middle School Association, 1988); *An Agenda for Excellence at the Middle Level* (Reston, Va.: National Association of Secondary School Principals, 1985); *Middle Levels Education's Responsibility for Intellectual Development* (Reston, Va.: National Association of Secondary School Principals, 1989); *Turning Points: Preparing American Youth for the 21st Century* (Washington, D.C.: Carnegie Council on Adolescent Development, 1989); "Education in the middle grades: A National survey of practices and trends," Johns Hopkins University Center of Research on Elementary and Middle Schools, *Phi Delta Kappan*, vol. 71, no. 6 (February 1990), pp. 436–469.

26. P.S. George, "Education 2000: Which way the middle school?" *The Clearing House*, vol. 62, no. 1 (1988), p. 14.

27. Ibid., pp. 15, 17.

28. *Turning Points*, p. 25.

29. Ibid., pp. 85, 13, 21, 22, 9.

30. Ibid., pp. 36, 8, 10, 36, 33.

31. Ibid., pp. 40, 61, 45.

32. Ibid., pp. 9, 52.

33. The only recommendation in *Turning Points* to be ignored by middle school activists was the caution against subscribing to the theory of brain periodization. Although *Turning Points* warned that "The ability of young adolescents to cope is often further jeopardized by a middle grade curriculum that assumes a need for an intellectual moratorium during early adolescence" (p. 32), middle school activists ignored this warning. See Chapter 3 for a more detailed discussion.

34. Toepfer (1992), p. 209.

35. J.H. Lounsbury, "A fresh start for the middle school curriculum," *Middle School Journal*, vol. 23, no. 2 (November 1991), pp. 4, 3–7. Copyrighted material used with permission from the National Middle School Association (NMSA).

36. S. Farkas & J. Johnson, *A Lot to Be Thankful For: What Parents Want Children to Learn about America* (New York: Public Agenda, 1998), p. 39.

37. Ibid., p. 35.

38. S. Farkas & J. Johnson, *Given the Circumstances; Teacher Talk about Public Education Today* (New York: Public Agenda, 1996), p. 41.

39. D.K. Cohen & H.C. Hill. "Instructional policy and classroom performance: The mathematics reforms in California," *Teachers College Record*, vol. 102, no. 2 (February 2000), pp. 305, 326.

40. C. Yecke, *Policymakers' Views on Issues at the Middle School Level*, doctoral dissertation (2001), p. 182.

41. Lipsitz (1979), p. 49.

42. *1994 State of the States Gifted and Talented Report*, Council of State Directors of Programs for the Gifted (Jefferson City, Mo., 1994), p. 2.

43. J. Harrington, C. Harrington, & E. Karnes, "The Marland Report: Twenty years later," *Journal for the Education of the Gifted*, vol. 15, no. 1 (1991), pp. 31–43.

44. A.J. Tannenbaum, "The gifted movement: Forward or on a treadmill" (West Lafayette, Ind.: Gifted Education Resource Institute, 1988), ERIC document no. ED 315 949, pp. 47–50.

45. *Turning Points* (1989), p. 36.

46. J.F. Feldhusen, S.M. Moon, & P.J. Rifner, "Educating the gifted and talented: Strengths, weaknesses, prospects," *Educational Perspectives*, vol. 26, nos. 1 & 2 (1989), pp. 48, 50, 53.

47. P.K. Sicola, "Where do gifted students fit? An examination of mid-

dle school philosophy as it relates to ability grouping and the gifted learner," *Journal for the Education of the Gifted*, vol. 14, no. 1 (1990), pp. 38, 47–48. Copyrighted material used with the permission of Prufrock Press.

48. J.J. Gallagher, "Education reform, values, and gifted students," *Gifted Child Quarterly*, vol. 35, no. 1 (1991), p. 16.

49. J.F. Feldhusen, "Susan Allan sets the record straight: Response to Allan," *Educational Leadership*, vol. 48, no. 6 (March 1991), p. 66. Copyrighted material used with permission from the Association for Supervision and Curriculum Development (ASCD).

50. J.S. Renzulli & S. Reis, "The reform movement and the quiet crisis in gifted education," *Gifted Child Quarterly*, vol. 35, no. 1 (1991), p. 26.

51. T.O. Erb, "Encouraging gifted performance in middle schools," *Midpoints*, vol. 3, no. 1 (1992), pp. 1, 21, 12, 20. Copyrighted material used with permission from the National Middle School Association (NMSA).

52. Ibid., p. 5.

53. For example, see C.A. Tomlinson, "Leadership for differentiated classrooms," *The School Administrator*, vol. 56, no. 8 (October 1999), pp. 6–11; C.A. Tomlinson, "Deciding to differentiate instruction in middle school: One school's journey," *Gifted Child Quarterly*, vol. 39, no. 2 (Spring 1995), pp. 77–87; C.A. Tomlinson, "Teach me, teach my brain: A call for differentiated classrooms," *Educational Leadership*, vol. 56, no. 3 (November 1998), pp. 52–55.

54. National Middle School Association annual conference program (1991), p. 36.

55. Ibid. (1995), pp. 191 and 136.

56. C.A. Tomlinson, "Making middle school work for gifted kids," *Principal*, vol. 74, no. 1 (1994), p. 52.

57. National Middle School Association annual conference program (1992), p. 91; and (1993), p. 141.

58. National Association for the Gifted (NAGC) Position Paper on Middle Schools (1994).

59. National Middle School Association (NMSA) Resolution 93.5 (1993).

60. National Middle School Association annual conference program (1993), p. 95.

61. M.R. Coleman & J.J. Gallagher, "Middle schools and their impact on talent development," *Middle School Journal*, vol. 26, no. 3 (January 1995), pp. 47–56; George & Grebing (1995), pp. 12–17; and R. Ruder, "A three-pronged approach to talent development," *Middle School Journal*, vol. 26, no. 2 (November 1994), pp. 61–63. Copyrighted material used with permission from the National Middle School Association (NMSA).

62. "Editor's Note," *Middle School Journal*, vol. 26, no. 2 (November 1994), p. 61.

63. Ruder (1994), p. 61.

64. George & Grebing (1995), p. 13.

65. For example, see Erb (1992).

66. George & Grebing (1995), p. 15.

67. Ibid., p. 16.

68. For other examples, see J.A. Beane, *Curriculum Integration: Designing the Core of Democratic Education* (New York: Teachers College Press, 1997), p. 79; P.S. George, "Tracking and ability grouping," *Middle School Journal*, vol. 20, no. 1 (September 1988), pp. 21–28; A. Kohn, "Only for *my* kid: How privileged parents are undermining school reform," *Phi Delta Kappan*, vol. 79, no. 8 (April 1998), pp. 569–577; J. Oakes & A.S. Wells, "Detracking for high student achievement," *Educational Leadership*, vol. 55, no. 6 (March 1998), pp. 38–41; A.S. Wells & J. Oakes, "Potential pitfalls of systemic reform: Early lessons from research on detracking," *Sociology of Education*, vol. 69 (1996), p. 138; and A. Wheelock, "Winning over gifted parents," *School Administrator* (April 1995), p. 17.

69. Coleman & Gallagher (1995), p. 47.

70. Ibid., pp. 48, 50.

71. Ibid., p. 55.

72. T.O. Erb, "The middle school: Mimicking the success routes of the information age," in *Gifted Education and Middle Schools* (Reston, Va.: Council for Exceptional Children, 1995), p. 12.

73. P.S. George, "In balance: Gifted education and middle schools," in *Gifted Education and Middle Schools* (Reston, Va.: Council for Exceptional Children, 1995), p. 48.

74. M.R. Coleman & J.J. Gallagher, "Middle schools and their impact on talent development," in *Gifted Education and Middle Schools* (Reston, Va.: Council for Exceptional Children, 1995), p. 25.

75. C.A. Tomlinson, "Gifted learners and the middle school: Problem or promise?" in *Gifted Education and Middle Schools* (Reston, Va.: Council for Exceptional Children, 1995), p. 31.

76. National Middle School Association (NMSA) annual conference program (1996), p. 70.

77. National Middle School Association (NMSA) annual conference program (1997), p. 171.

78. A. Bradley, "Muddle in the Middle," *Education Week* (April 15, 1998) p. 38.

79. D. Brockett, "School leaders, researchers re-examining middle reform," *School Board News* (November 10, 1998), p. 5.

80. D. Ruenzel, "Coming of age," *Teacher Magazine*, vol. 9, no. 5 (February 1998), p. 32.

81. National Middle School Association (NMSA) annual conference program (1998), p. 123.

82. A. Wheelock, "The case for untracking," *Educational Leadership*, vol. 50, no. 2 (October 1992), p. 9.

83. National Middle School Association (NMSA) annual conference program (1998), p. 161.

84. George & Grebing (1995), p. 17.

85. A.S. Wells & I. Serna, "The politics of culture: Understanding local political resistance to detracking in racially-mixed schools," *Harvard Educational Review*, vol. 66, no. 1 (1996), p. 116.

86. Erb (1995), p. 2.

87. J.M. Rochester, "What's it all about, Alfie? A parent/educator's response to Alfie Kohn," *Phi Delta Kappan*, vol. 80, no. 2 (October 1998), p. 168. This was written in response to Kohn (1998), pp. 569–577.

88. T. Erb, "School no longer means what you thought," *Middle School Journal*, vol. 27, no. 4 (March 1996), p. 2.

CHAPTER 3

Middle School Curriculum

Phillip, my 12-year-old son, is an excellent student who wants to learn. Unfortunately, he is being de-motivated by a school system that publicly proclaims its academic standards but privately has put a higher priority on social concerns. . . . Academic accomplishment is no longer paramount. Instead, the curriculum has softened and playtime activity frequently passes for teaching. . . . The unintended results of this absence of academic rigor are diminished student achievement and motivation.

Parent in Montana, 1996[1]

THE ISSUE DEFINED

Discussions regarding middle school curricula can focus on two different aspects of what is taught: content and rigor. The political correctness and lack of solid content in the offerings at some middle schools could fill volumes. Examples of "rainforest algebra" and "fuzzy math" abound, and self-proclaimed "ethnomathematicians" even claim that math is an artifact of Western culture, used by white males to oppress all other cultures and genders. Examples of PC science have been noted by many, and as one parent described her daughter's middle school experience: "social science was a course in political correctness with little history content."[2] The reach of political correctness often goes beyond the "academic" part of the school day and permeates the school culture. In places like Ann Arbor, Michigan, and Woodbury, Minnesota, students have had to go to court to uphold their right to express opinions that run counter to the politically correct views espoused by their school systems.

This discussion will focus only on the level of rigor of the middle school curriculum and not on its content. However, abuses of rigor and content often go hand-in-hand. Middle school reading classes that emphasize environmentalism have consisted of a teacher reading *The Acorn People* to her seventh grade class, followed by the students making necklaces by gluing acorns onto yarn. In math classes, some students have spent 12 days designing cereal boxes as a way to learn important math skills, such as scaling.[3] And for the first anniversary of 9/11, it was reported that the nation's largest teachers' union, the National Education Association (NEA), established a web site that recommended materials such as those that emphasized "historical instances of American intolerance" and purported that the 9/11 tragedy must be viewed "through a multicultural lens."[4]

Political correctness aside, why have the expectations for middle school students been so dumbed down? A common belief held by middle school educators about how middle school students learn is based upon a questionable theory that misinterprets scientific data. For many years, adherence to the theory of brain periodization drove a dumbing-down of the academic curriculum at the middle school level—and survey research indicates that its influence was present well into the 1990s.[5] Brain periodization is a theory which claims that brain growth reaches a plateau around the ages of 12–14, at which time "the brain virtually ceases to grow."[6] As a result, researchers recommended (and many educators embraced) altering the middle school curriculum to avoid the introduction of new and challenging material—a decision with debilitating consequences for all students, but especially for gifted/high ability students.

Emerging from the data presented below is evidence that a belief in the equality of outcomes through the leveling of achievement may be driving the enduring embrace of the theory of brain periodization, more so than any current credible scientific evidence. Although the theory has been scientifically discredited for over a decade, many educators remain committed to it—a commitment that appears to be based in ideology as opposed to scientific fact.

EVOLUTION OF THE CONTROVERSY

Dissatisfaction with the curriculum for pre-adolescents was voiced early in the middle school movement by leaders who viewed individualization of curriculum and instruction as one of the justifications to support the middle school movement.[7] One would assume that this would mean providing varying levels of academic challenge for students, but before many educators could even contemplate a shift in this direction, the theory of brain periodization appeared on the educational scene, giving radical middle school advocates a "scientific" reason to dilute the quality and rigor of the middle school curriculum. Proponents of the life-adjustment and anti-intellectual movements thus had a "scientific" reason to demand changes to the middle school curriculum—changes that would support their non-academic goals.

1970s–Middle 1980s: Support for Brain Periodization

The theory of brain periodization was first articulated to educators in a 1978 edition of *Educational Leadership*, a publication of the Association for Supervision and Curriculum Development (ASCD). It introduced the notion that around the ages of 12–14, "the brain virtually ceases to grow," and teaching complex material during this time would have damaging effects on children. According to the authors, Herman Epstein (a professor of biophysics) and Conrad Toepfer (an education professor):

With virtually no increase of brain size and mass in the large majority of 12- to 14-year-olds, there is no growth in the capacity of the brain to handle more complex thinking processes usually introduced in grades seven and eight. This continued demand for the youngster's brain to handle increasingly complex input, which he or she cannot comprehend during this period, may result in the rejection of these inputs and the possible development of negative neural networks to dissipate the energy of the inputs. Thus, it is possible that even when the subsequent growth of the brain between the ages of 14 and 16 could support the development of more complex cognitive skills, the untold numbers of individuals who have developed such negative networks have been so "turned off" that they literally can no longer develop novel cognitive skills.

The authors presented a forceful argument, even to skeptics, when they followed their claims with the solemn pronouncement that "These biological data provide a validated neuroscience framework in which educators can have confidence."[8]

Formally introduced to the middle school community at the 1979 National Middle School Association (NMSA) conference, this theory was "largely unquestioned and viewed as a possible new dogma by advocates,"[9] and it quickly began to drive the development of less challenging middle school curricula. After all, the "fact" of brain periodization necessitated the avoidance of new and higher level cognitive skills.[10] Toepfer and another co-author reinforced this trend by stating that the move toward challenging curriculum was a "dangerous and naively irresponsible effort . . . being enacted in complete ignorance of the truth that transescents cannot think at the level possible for high school adolescents."[11] In addition, both the NMSA and the influential National Association of Secondary School Principals (NASSP) used this theory as the basis for officially recommending that educators use caution in exposing middle school students to challenging content and higher-level cognitive skills.[12]

In 1981, the NMSA hosted four different presentations on this topic at its annual conference (see Appendix G), and in the following year it formally endorsed the theory of brain periodization in the policy handbook, *This We Believe*. The NMSA stated that addressing the intellectual characteristics of the middle-level learner must include "consideration of the brain growth periodization data identified by Epstein:"

Transescents are pressured, often excessively, to succeed academically. . . . 12 to 14 year olds may experience problems if expectations for continued development of higher thinking skills are held when a plateau in brain growth exists.[13]

Although challenged in subsequent conference sessions and journal articles,[14] the theory nonetheless became a pervasive belief among many middle school educators. With the exception of only two years, from 1979 through 1985 brain periodization was the dominant annual NMSA conference topic addressing how students learn (see Appendix H).

Late 1980s–Middle 1990s: Reconsideration—and Entrenchment

Turning Points, the publication that provided the primary impetus for the contemporary middle school movement, stated in 1989 that a "thorough review of recent studies on adolescent cognitive development found no persuasive evidence that young adolescents cannot engage in critical and higher order thinking."[15] However, in a 1990 article titled "Implementing *Turning Points*: Major Issues to be Faced," Conrad Toepfer, prominent middle school activist and co-author of the seminal article on the theory of brain periodization, continued the broad caution against "overchallenging students in the middle grades."[16] This article appeared in the official NMSA publication, the *Middle School Journal*, indicating that while middle school leaders were happy to implement many of the recommendations in *Turning Points*, they were selective about which ones. It appears that the *Turning Points* recommendation against the theory of brain periodization was simply ignored by many middle school proponents.

However, other voices made their concerns known. One such researcher stated that "most evidence on the development of adolescent thinking suggests that such delays [as advocated by the theory of brain periodization] may actually be harmful."[17] Finally, in 1993—a full four years after *Turning Points* cautioned against it—an article appeared in the NMSA publication *Midpoints* criticizing the theory of brain periodization by stating "there is no supporting evidence" for the theory, and that "it is simply blasphemous for teachers to believe that young adolescents are intellectually inert."[18]

Nonetheless, the NMSA continued to host presenters at its annual conferences who disparaged challenging curriculum, with any focus on academic rigor being viewed negatively. Criticism was presented toward "parents who want their child challenged" and those who questioned "the quality of what we should be teaching to early adolescents." Interestingly, some conference sessions appear to be a response to the growing backlash against the move away from academic rigor. One stated that "middle school curricula are being attacked as the weakest link in current middle school programs," while another, by posing a question, implied that the issue was not hypothetical but was currently being asked: "How do we respond to community fears that academics will suffer, that our product will be somehow inferior?"[19]

In 1995, gifted advocate Carol Tomlinson recommended that educators "disavow theories that present middle school students as incapable of high level thought and complex learning."[20] The evidence against brain periodization was mounting. A full *16 years* after both introducing and embracing the theory of brain periodization, the *Middle School Journal* finally published an article criticizing the concept—but by then, the damage was done.[21]

Current Beliefs

The tragedy is that although the theory of brain periodization was discredited in the mid-1990s, it still maintains a firm hold on the belief system of many educators. A survey of middle school practitioners found that *nearly half* of all middle school teachers surveyed agreed with the statement that their students are in a "plateau learning period." The authors of this startling finding concluded:

Perhaps the most troubling set of responses in the study relates to principal and teacher beliefs about the nature of early adolescents. If educators teach with an audience in mind, one would assume that teacher beliefs about the nature of that audience would profoundly shape both what is taught and how it is taught. If that is the case, then beliefs reported by both principal and teacher respondents in this study appear to be the harbinger of curriculum and instruction which would vastly underchallenge advanced middle school learners—and likely underchallenge most other middle schoolers as well. . . . It is certainly cause for concern that nearly half of principals and teachers still believe that middle school learners are in a plateau learning period.[22]

Related to this, and indicative of the fact that many other teachers are alarmed by this belief, are the results of a survey conducted in 1996 by researchers Farkas and Johnson who found that over half of the teachers surveyed believed that low academic standards and low academic expectations were "very serious" or "somewhat serious" problems. An even greater percentage of the general public agrees with this view.[23] A more current survey

(2000) indicates that fewer than 10 percent of parents nationwide believe that teachers are putting too much academic pressure on their children,[24] and students themselves appear to agree with this finding. In 1997, well over half of the students surveyed admitted that they could perform better in school if they tried, suggesting that they are currently not being adequately challenged.[25]

A survey of policymakers indicates that their beliefs are closer to those of the public than to those held by many educators. Overwhelming majorities of all groups of education policymakers disagree with the theory of brain periodization, ranging from a low of 88 percent among local school board members to a high of 100 percent among state legislators.[26]

Although seven years had passed with no NMSA conference sessions addressing brain periodization, the topic reappeared in 1996, greatly softened and with different focus—but presented by the same 1970s proponents: "The brain growth data clearly show that the daycare ages and the middle school years are the most difficult periods for intellectual and psycho-social development."[27] Clearly, there are some advocates that do not want to let go of this notion.

This can be seen in the current resurgence of interest in a number of brain-related theories and their implications for education. The ASCD, which published the first article extolling the virtues of the theory of brain periodization in 1978, has recently sponsored workshops on brain-based learning theories, and the National School Boards Association (NSBA) recently ran a front-page story on the topic.[28] And after several years of minimal interest, the number of annual NMSA conference sessions on the general topic of how the brain influences learning has shown a sharp increase. (See Appendices G and H.)

However, in the April 2001 edition of *Basic Education*, education policy expert Kathleen Madigan issued the following caution:

Once again, educators have taken a leap of faith rather than use good science. . . . Some educators are extrapolating piecemeal from certain findings and creating curriculum specifications without actual research to back up their claims. . . . Using the term "brain-based" has become fashionable, but unfortunately, it is only that—a fashionable fad that may actually undermine serious research in a very complex field.[29]

Her advice echoes that of Kurt W. Fischer, director of the Mind, Brain, and Education program at Harvard's Graduate School of

Education, who stated: "You can't go from neuroscience to the classroom because we don't know enough about neuroscience." Another expert, John T. Bruer, president of an organization that supports neuro-scientific research, cautions that a wholesale embrace of such theories is premature, meaning that some educators "are making a very big mistake by wasting their time on 'brain-based' curricula."[30]

Concurrent with the embrace of the theory of brain periodization was the belief that the middle school would be failing in its mission if it focused exclusively on academics. Thus, the void left by the dilution of academics was quickly filled by middle school activists with an assortment of other, non-academic offerings:

[Middle] school now offers the best possibilities of assisting increasing numbers of students to deal with developing identity needs. . . . Identity development must become a major middle level education curriculum goal. . . . [In addition], middle level curricula should . . . be organized around local social needs and [community] problems requiring study and action.[31]

Turning Points had helped to set the stage for this shift away from academics by emphasizing that middle schools should address "the emotional, physical, and social development of their students," including expectations of community service and immersion in opportunities to solve current social problems—so as to produce "fundamental social change." In summary, *Turning Points* declared that "Preparing all youth for the demands of the twenty-first century requires a *redefinition* of middle grade education"[32] (emphasis added).

RESPONSE FROM ADVOCATES FOR GIFTED LEARNERS

Early on, advocates for gifted learners appeared to be on a parallel track with advocates of the middle school movement in the areas of individualization of instruction and differentiation of curriculum.[33] According to gifted advocate Carol Tomlinson:

An initial reading of the literature of both fields suggests that the compatibility is great. . . . There appears on the surface little conflict between what these middle school educators seek for middle school students and what educators of the gifted have espoused for gifted students.[34]

Nonetheless, as it became clear that changes in middle school curriculum included concessions to those who advocated the theory of brain periodization, advocates for the gifted became increasingly alarmed.

Implications of the theory of brain periodization were serious for all students, but especially for gifted/high ability learners. Those middle school gifted programs that were "based on an acceleration model rather than upon enrichment" were criticized,[35] as was the "contemporary infatuation with improving performance in academic achievement."[36] Attempts to introduce more challenging academic opportunities at the middle grades were attacked as "dangerous and naively irresponsible efforts . . . being enacted in complete ignorance of the truth that transescents cannot think at the levels possible for high school adolescents."[37]

Such beliefs ignored the needs of gifted/high ability students. As noted by Tomlinson in 1992:

In spite of the repeated cautions against overchallenging middle school students . . . there is no balance of caution in the middle school literature against *underchallenging* students whose thinking may be far more mature than the level which is stressed throughout middle school literature. . . . We may be affronting middle school age students (and certainly gifted middle schoolers) by assuming that they haven't the will or ability to respond to an academic program with a serious intellectual focus.[38]

Another advocate for the gifted, Joyce VanTassel-Baska, recommended a dialogue between middle school advocates and advocates for gifted learners:

If middle school educators and gifted educators could map out a plan to ensure balance and flexibility . . . the hard lines of perceived disagreement between the two special interest groups might be overcome.

She also expressed the concern that, without cooperation among teachers in the planning of curriculum, gifted learners may be "left to stagnate in an unresponsive environment primarily geared to the needs of other groups of learners."

This need for extensive differentiation of instruction was seen as critical due to several realities of the early 1990s: the embrace of the theory of brain periodization, the shift in middle schools to non-academic goals, the growing movement away from the use of ability grouping, and the lack of teacher training in differentiating instruction. All of these threatened to reduce the academic curricula to an insipid set of minimal standards expected for all students. VanTassel-Baska stated:

Equality of opportunity and equality of treatment in education, however, are not the same—nor should they be. In any profession, the client's needs dictate the nature of the prescription. High-quality services should be available to all, but the nature and organization of those services should vary based on diagnosed need. Education can ill-afford to level its services lest the pill of mediocrity be absorbed into the blood stream of all our students.[39]

Very early in the middle school movement, advocates for the middle school concept had stated their support for "optimum individualization of curriculum and instruction for a population characterized by great variability."[40] However, as articulated 25 years later in a 1993 U.S. Department of Education report titled *National Excellence: A Case for Developing America's Talent*, it was apparent that this concept had not been implemented at the middle school—or anywhere else:

The vast majority of talented students spend most of the school day in a regular classroom where little is done to adapt curriculum to their special learning needs . . . the gap between the level of curriculum and the abilities of talented students is the largest of all student groups. . . . Classroom teachers do little to accommodate the different learning needs of gifted children. . . . Most teachers said they give the same assignments to both gifted and average students almost all the time. . . . Most students with outstanding talent spend most of their time in the regular curriculum with few differentiated opportunities.[41]

It was not only advocates for the gifted who were expressing concerns—parents had become painfully aware of the move away from academics in the middle school. According to one father:

Phillip, my 12-year-old son, is an excellent student who wants to learn. Unfortunately, he is being de-motivated by a school system that publicly proclaims its academic standards but privately has put a higher priority on social concerns. . . . Academic accomplishment is no longer paramount. Instead, the curriculum has softened and playtime activity frequently passes for teaching. The talk is all about sharing, celebrating and facilitating; not about working, studying, and teaching. . . . The unintended results of this absence of academic rigor are diminished student achievement and motivation.[42]

These are not the sentiments of a single individual. A study by two prominent middle school advocates found that many parents share the same concerns. Only 13 percent of parents surveyed believed that the program in their child's middle school was "rigorous and challenging." The remaining 83 percent either disagreed or were unsure. Parents reported that they have concerns about low levels of expectation:

I think my kid writes rather poorly, yet she brings home As in English and social studies. They must not be expecting her to write very much or they're accepting pretty low-quality work.

These parents reported being frustrated: "The middle school doesn't even want to talk about what they do for gifted kids. I just keep getting stonewalled."[43]

A less rigorous curriculum naturally means that more students will be earning higher grades. While some educators believe this is a way to help students gain self-esteem, recent research demonstrates that such a practice may actually be detrimental to academic achievement. Contrary to popular middle school beliefs, the students of teachers with high expectations who are tough graders tend to show markedly increased achievement as measured by non-classroom (i.e., standardized) assessments.[44]

CURRENT STATUS

Since the early 1990s, there appears to be a growing acceptance of the concept that curriculum can and should be differentiated for diverse learners, and that teachers should receive training in the most effective ways to accomplish this.[45] This may be driven by the realization that the widespread embrace of heterogeneous [mixed-ability] grouping is causing serious problems for teachers:

Many classroom teachers are pulling their hair out or leaving the profession due to the fact that they are being asked to teach in an inclusive [mixed-ability] setting without training, resource personnel/materials, or planning time. . . . Many educators say the gifted students in these situations are the ones suffering the most.[46]

The need for teacher training was highlighted in a 1994 study which found that 61 percent of public school teachers and 54 percent of private school teachers reported that they had never received any training on meeting the needs of gifted students. In a follow-up study, it was found that gifted students received no curricular differentiation in 84 percent of their instruction,[47] and in a 1995 survey of middle school educators it was reported that many middle level teachers expressed a high degree of discomfort with the idea of differentiating curriculum.[48]

However, some radical voices suggest that a move in this direction is an attempt to "retrack" schools. According to education reform critic Gerald Bracey: "The parents of the former high-track students thus put pressure on school administrators to resegregate instruction by offering differentiated curricula."[49] Similarly, in a 1995 study of eighth grade students, the authors viewed the results of differentiation as negative, noting that "differentiated instruction may lead to unequal results for students,"[50] a sentiment similar to that expressed by those who contend that differentiated curriculum is inequitable.[51] The fear of "unequal results" must be questioned, and indicates a desire to produce "equality" through the redistribution of intellectual capital. Some educators appear intent on pursuing equal *outcomes*—something far different than equal *opportunities*. This reveals the radical leanings of many middle school activists, as it highlights the shift away from academics and toward the social goal of egalitarianism.

Advocates for gifted learners have made the case that differentiation of curriculum is a moral imperative for these students,[52] and have provided practical advice, examples, and encouragement for educators of the gifted through numerous articles and publications.[53] However, the combination of having the theory of brain periodization still embraced by many middle school teachers, and with middle school activists continuing to downplay the academic role of middle schools, there are profound implications regarding the instructional decisions made by teachers for middle school students.[54]

The late 1990s saw a growing backlash against the dumbing-down of the middle school curriculum. A special section in *Education Week* reported that the "overemphasis on the social, emotional, and physical needs of the middle school student has led to neglect of academic competencies."[55] A 1998 survey of parents with children in middle school revealed that they saw the academic curriculum as "trivial" and "disjointed," and lamented the lack of rigor and low expectations. They further noted that their children were often bored.[56] Parents and many concerned teachers who had intuitively recognized the need for a stronger, faster-paced curriculum at the middle level saw their instincts validated when the results from the TIMSS-R were made public in December of 2000, as discussed in Chapter 1.

The need for a more rigorous curriculum requires teachers who can rise to the challenge. However, it has been found that only 44 percent of middle school teachers hold an undergraduate or graduate major in an academic field.[57] Anecdotally, this may be due to weaker teacher candidates seeking middle school endorsements. According to one teacher educator who is concerned over the lack of academic preparation among middle school teachers:

What we are finding is that the only students [at colleges of education] who select a middle school program (as opposed to mid/secondary 7–12) are those who are weak students and see that they will not make it through a major in an [academic] discipline.[58]

Another survey indicates that 28 percent of all middle school teachers currently hold a middle-level certificate, compared to 11 percent in both 1980 and 1992, indicating that the tenets of the middle school movement are being taught to growing numbers of teachers—while the percentage of middle-level teachers with subject-specific secondary certificates is rapidly declining, dropping from 80 percent in 1980, to 63 percent in 1992, to only 52 percent in 2000.[59] In fact, the National Center for Education Statistics reported that during the 1999-2000 school year, the percentages of middle school students who were taught by teachers who did not have a college major or certification in the areas they were teaching were staggering. This included nearly 6 out of every 10 middle grade students in English (58 percent), science (57 percent), and foreign language classes (61 percent). In some classes, the percentage of students being taught by teachers lacking such credentials was even higher: math (69 percent), history (71 percent), and physical science (93 percent). According to the report:

Compared to high school grades, higher percentages of students in the middle grades were in classes led by teachers who did not hold certification and a major in the subject taught. . . . Teachers who teach specific subjects in the middle grades are less likely to have the recognized credentials than their contemporaries teaching in the high school grades.[60]

Incredibly, many middle school principals are not as concerned over this drop in subject area expertise as they are over the number of teachers who have not been prepared to teach specifically at the middle level. Only 47 percent of middle school principals express concern over the growing lack of subject area expertise, while 77 percent express concerns regarding the lack of teachers trained specifically for the middle school.[61] This should be a major cause for concern, as there is strong evidence that strong subject area knowledge among teachers correlates with higher student achievement.[62]

Regardless, one leading middle school advocate declares that teachers without specific training in the middle school concept are guilty of "malpractice." He is one of many who believe that obtaining an educational license specific to the middle grades should be mandatory for anyone who teaches at the middle school level.[63]

However, the days of weak preparation and low expectations for many middle school teachers are numbered. The new federal *No Child Left Behind* legislation requires that new middle school teachers must, by 2006, demonstrate subject area expertise—either by passing a test, holding an academic major, or through some other means—for each content area taught.

CONCLUSION

Although leading proponents of the middle school concept embraced the theory of brain periodization in 1979 and the NMSA formally endorsed it in 1982, by the early 1990s the theory had little credibility among scientific experts. Nonetheless, after having spent over a decade being actively endorsed and advocated by both the NMSA and radical middle school activists, support for this theory appears to still remain entrenched. If it is not being driven by scientific fact, then what may account for its longevity?

The theory provided a convenient rationale to support the dumbing-down of the middle school curriculum, an act driven by the belief of many middle school activists that the academic role of schools should be downplayed in order for schools to address identity development, social issues, and myriad other non-academic endeavors.

The damage has been done, and the dire results of the policies driven by this belief can be seen in the dismal performance of U.S. middle school students on international measures of academic achievement, such as the TIMSS exams. With nearly half of all classroom teachers subscribing to the theory of brain periodization, and with many middle school activists sneering at the idea that middle schools should have an academic role, it is no wonder that members of the public, and even middle school students themselves, feel that there is a profound lack of challenge in their schools.

NOTES

1. A.H. Bloom, "What are you teaching my son?" *Educational Leadership*, vol. 53, no. 7 (April 1996), p. 83. Copyrighted material used with permission from the Association for Supervision and Curriculum Development (ASCD).

2. N. Granstrom, "A parent criticizes middle school theory," *Basic Education* (May 1999), Council for Basic Education, Washington, DC.

3. Ibid.

4. For more information, see D. Limbaugh, "NEA exploiting the attack," *The Washington Times* (August 22, 2002); E. Sorokin, "NEA plan for 9/11 not backed by teachers," *The Washington Times* (August 20, 2002); and G. Will, "The NEA's sensitivity tutors" (August 26, 2002), available online at www.townhall.com.

5. T. Moon, C.A. Tomlinson, & C.M. Callahan, *Academic Diversity in the Middle School: Results of a National Survey of Middle School Administrators and Teachers*, monograph no. 95124 (Charlottesville, VA: National Research Center on the Gifted and Talented, 1995).

6. H.T. Epstein & C.F. Toepfer, "A neuroscience basis for reorganizing middle grades education," *Educational Leadership*, vol. 35, no. 8 (May 1978), p. 657. Copyrighted material used with permission from the Association for Supervision and Curriculum Development (ASCD).

7. W.M. Alexander, E.L. Williams, M. Compton, V.A. Hines, & D. Prescott, *The Emergent Middle School* (New York: Holt, Rinehart & Winston, 1968), p. 19.

8. Epstein & Toepfer (1978), pp. 657, 657–658, 660.

9. B.A. Hutson, "Brain growth spurts: What's left by middle school?" *Middle School Journal*, vol. 16, no. 2 (February 1985), p. 8.

10. E.N. Brazee, "Brain periodization: Challenge, not justification," *Middle School Journal*, vol. 15, no. 1 (November 1983), pp. 8–10; Epstein & Toepfer (1978); J.P. Hester & P.J. Hester, "Brain research and the middle school curriculum," *Middle School Journal*, vol. 15, no. 1 (November 1983), pp. 4–30.

11. D.B. Strahan & C.F. Toepfer, "Transescent thinking: Renewed rationale for exploratory learning," *Middle School Journal*, vol. 15, no. 2 (February 1984), p. 8.

12. See *This We Believe* (Columbus, Ohio: National Middle School Association, 1982); and *Middle Level Education's Responsibility for Intellectual Development* (Reston, Va.: National Association of Secondary School Principals, 1989).

13. *This We Believe* (1982), pp. 7, 7–8.

14. Hutson (1985), pp. 8–11; National Middle School Association annual conference program (1981), p. 14; R. McQueen, "Spurts and plateaus on brain growth: A critique of the claims of Herman Epstein," *Educational Leadership*, vol. 41, no. 5 (February 1984), pp. 67–72.

15. *Turning Points: Preparing American Youth for the 21st Century* (Washington, D.C.: Carnegie Council on Adolescent Development, 1989), p. 42.

16. C.F. Toepfer, "Implementing *Turning Points*: Major Issues to Be Faced," *Middle School Journal*, vol. 21, no. 5 (May 1990), p. 19.

17. D.P. Keating, "Adolescent thinking," in S.S. Feldman & G.R. Elliott (Eds.), *At the Threshold: The Developing Adolescent* (Cambridge, Mass.: Harvard University Press, 1990), p. 63.

18. J.F. Arnold, "A curriculum to empower young adolescents," *Midpoints*, vol. 4, no. 1 (1993), pp. 4, 5.

19. National Middle School Association annual conference program (1991), pp. 127, 67, 91.

20. C.A. Tomlinson, "Gifted learners and the middle school: Problem or promise?" in *Gifted Education and Middle Schools* (Reston, Va.: Council for Exceptional Children, 1995), p. 33.

21. J.L. Irvin, "Cognitive growth during early adolescence: The regulation of developmental tasks," *Middle School Journal*, vol. 27, no. 1 (September 1995), pp. 54–55.

22. Moon, Tomlinson, & Callahan (1995), pp. 52, 70.

23. S. Farkas & J. Johnson, *Given the Circumstances: Teacher Talk about Public Education Today* (New York: Public Agenda, 1996).

24. "Survey finds little sign of backlash against academic standards or standardized tests" (New York: Public Agenda, 2000).

25. J. Johnson & S. Farkas, *Getting By: What American Teenagers Really Think about Their Schools* (New York: Public Agenda, 1997).

26. C. Yecke, *Policymakers' Views on Issues at the Middle School Level*, doctoral dissertation (2001).

27. National Middle School Association annual conference program (1996), p. 152.

28. D. Stover, "Educators taking an interest in the latest brain research," *School Board News* (February 6, 2001), pp. 1, 3.

29. K. Madigan, "Buyer beware: Too early to use brain-based strategies," *Basic Education*, vol. 45, no. 8 (April 2001), p. 9.

30. V. Strauss, "Brain research oversold, experts say," *Washington Post* (March 12, 2001), p. A09.

31. C.F. Toepfer, "Curriculum for identity: A middle level educational obligation," *Middle School Journal*, vol. 23, no. 3 (January 1992), p. 8.

32. *Turning Points* (1989), pp. 32, 66, 80.

33. J.J. Gallagher, *Teaching the Gifted Child* (Boston: Allyn & Bacon, 1975); S.N. Kaplan, *Providing Programs for the Gifted and Talented: A Handbook* (Ventura, Calif.: Office of the Ventura County Superintendent of Schools, 1974); J.S. Renzulli, *The Enrichment Triad: A Guide for Developing Defensible Programs for the Gifted and Talented* (Wethersfield, Conn.: Creative Learning Press, 1977); and V.S. Ward, *Educating the Gifted: An Axiomatic Approach* (Columbus, Ohio: Merrill, 1961).

34. C.A. Tomlinson, "Gifted education and the middle school movement: Two voices on teaching the academically gifted," *Journal for the Education of the Gifted*, vol. 15, no. 3 (1992), pp. 207, 209. Copyrighted material used with the permission of Prufrock Press.

35. Hester & Hester (1983), p. 7.

36. C.F. Toepfer, "What to know about young adolescents," *Social Education*, vol. 52, no. 2 (1988), p. 110.

37. Strahan & Toepfer (1984), p. 8.

38. Tomlinson (1992), pp. 214, 216.

39. J. VanTassel-Baska, *Planning Effective Curriculum for Gifted Learners* (Denver, Colo.: Love Publishing, 1992), pp. 15, 10–11, 11, 13.

40. Alexander et al. (1968), p. 19.

41. *National Excellence: A Case for Developing America's Talent* (U.S. Department of Education, 1993), pp. 19–20.

42. Bloom (1996), p. 83.

43. J.H. Johnston & R.D. Williamson, "Listening to four communities: Parent and public concerns about middle level schools," *NASSP Bulletin*, vol. 82, no. 597 (April 1998), pp. 48, 51.

44. D. Figlio & M. Lucas, *Do High Grading Standards Affect Student Performance?* (Cambridge, Mass.: National Bureau of Economic Research, working paper number 7985, 2001).

45. See J.J. Gallagher, "Accountability for gifted children," *Phi Delta Kappan*, vol. 79, no. 1 (September 1998), pp. 739–742; K. Goree, "Making the most out of inclusive setting," *Gifted Child Today*, vol. 19, no. 2 (March/April 1996), pp. 22–24; Goree (1996); L.R. Marcus & T. Johnson, "New possibilities for teaching diverse populations in tomorrow's high school," *High School Journal*, vol. 79, no. 2 (1996), pp. 134–138; NMSA,

1995; Reis et al. (1994), as cited in R.R. Culross, "Concepts of inclusion in gifted education," *Teaching Exceptional Children* (January/February 1997), pp. 24–26; S. Reis, J. Renzulli, & K. Westberg, "Effects of inclusion on high ability students: Concerns raised by current research," unpublished manuscript (Storrs: University of Connecticut, 1994), as cited in Culross (1997); C.M. Shields, "To group or not to group academically talented or gifted students?" *Educational Administration Quarterly*, vol. 32, no. 2 (1996), pp. 295–323; A. Smith, "Eliminating tracking in the middle schools: Derailing the pursuit of excellence?" *American Secondary Education*, vol. 23, no. 3 (1995), pp. 9–12; C.A. Tomlinson, "The easy lie and the role of gifted education in school excellence," *Roeper Review*, vol. 16, no. 4 (1994a), pp. 258–259; C.A. Tomlinson, "Making middle school work for gifted kids," *Principal*, vol. 74, no. 1 (1994b), pp. 52–53; C.A. Tomlinson, " 'All kids can learn': Masking diversity in middle school," *The Clearing House* (1995), pp. 163–165; C.A. Tomlinson, T.R. Moon, & C.M. Callahan, "How well are we addressing academic diversity in the middle school?" *Middle School Journal*, vol. 29, no. 1 (1998), pp. 3–11; VanTassel-Baska (1995); and J. VanTassel-Baska, L.D. Avery, C. Little, & C. Hughes, "An evaluation of the implementation of curriculum innovation: The impact of the William & Mary Units on schools," *Journal for the Education of the Gifted*, vol. 23, no. 2 (2000), pp. 244–272.

46. Goree (1996), p. 22.

47. Reis, Renzulli, & Westberg (1994), as cited in Culross (1997).

48. Moon, Tomlinson, & Callahan (1995).

49. G.W. Bracey, "The smarts of teachers," *Phi Delta Kappan*, vol. 78, no. 4 (1996), p. 331.

50. A. Gamoran, M. Nystrand, M. Berends, & P.C. LePore, "An organizational analysis of the effects of ability grouping," *American Educational Research Journal*, vol. 32 (1995), p. 687.

51. R.S. Weinstein, "High standards in a tracked system of schooling: For which students and with what educational support?" *Educational Researcher*, vol. 25, no. 8 (1996), pp. 16–19.

52. Gallagher (1998); Tomlinson (1994b); Van Tassel-Baska (1995).

53. Gallagher (1998); Tomlinson (1994a, 1994b, 1995); Tomlinson, Moon, & Callahan (1998); VanTassel-Baska (1995); VanTassel-Baska et al. (2000).

54. Moon, Tomlinson, & Callahan (1995).

55. A. Bradley, "Muddle in the middle," *Education Week* (April 15, 1998).

56. Johnston & Williamson (1998), pp. 48, 50.

57. *Teacher Quality: A Report on the Preparation and Qualifications of Public School Teachers*, U.S. Department of Education (Washington, D.C.: National Center for Education Statistics, 1999), p. 11.

58. I.L. Shannon, Professor and Director of Secondary Education, Vir-

ginia Wesleyan College, correspondence to the Virginia Department of Education regarding proposed changes to teacher licensure regulations (October 25, 1996).

59. D. Clark, V. Petzko, S. Lucas, & J. Valentine, "Research Findings from the 2000 National Study of Leadership in Middle Level Schools," paper presented at the National Middle School Association annual conference, Washington, D.C. (November 1, 2001). See pp. 5–6.

60. *Qualifications of the Public School Teacher Workforce: Prevalence of Out-of-Field Teaching 1987–88 to 1999–2000* (Washington, D.C.: National Center for Education Statistics, 2002).

61. Clark et al. (2001).

62. See G.R. Whitehurst, "Research on Teacher Preparation and Professional Development," a speech presented at the White House Conference on Preparing Tomorrow's Teachers (March 5, 2002), available online: www.ed.gov/inits/preparingteachersconference/whitehurst.html.

63. K. McEwin, "This We Believe, Now We Must Act," session # 2551, National Middle School Association annual conference (November 2, 2001).

CHAPTER 4

Ability Grouping

There exists a body of philosophic absolutes that should include this statement: The ability grouping of students for educational opportunities in a democratic society is ethically unacceptable. We need not justify this with research, for it is a statement of principle, not of science. It should become a moral imperative along with the beliefs that slavery is immoral and that all people are created equal under the law.

Elementary school principal in Texas, 1992[1]

THE ISSUE DEFINED

The issue of ability grouping can be intensely controversial, often because the term *ability grouping* is sometimes confused with "tracking."[2] When it was still practiced, tracking involved placing all students into rigidly separated groups on what was commonly a permanent basis. Very often, this meant relegating disadvantaged and minority students to the lowest track and affluent whites to the highest track. By contrast, ability grouping is a flexible option which allows students with specific needs in specific disciplines to be grouped together for more targeted and efficient instruction.[3]

The ability grouping debate has been called one of the most contentious and acrimonious in educational history.[4] Historically, this debate has been framed as the contrast between the Jacksonian ideal, with education as the great leveler, and the Jeffersonian ideal, providing, at public expense, specialized education for the most able.[5] Our nation has vacillated between one ideal or the other as both international and domestic situations have changed.[6] However, over the past several decades, activist social policies, politics, and anti-gifted attitudes often played a larger role than an assessment of individual educational needs in determining whether or not ability grouping should be practiced.[7]

Heterogeneous (mixed-ability) grouping is favored by those who see public education as the opportunity to address social issues by leveling the playing field—clearly a Jacksonian ideal. These anti–ability grouping advocates view ability grouping as elitist and/or racist in nature, and express support for what they call "educational equity," that is, educating children so they all have similar levels of achievement, as a means of producing a more equitable society.[8]

Homogeneous (like-ability) grouping is favored by those who look to the individual needs of students over group needs or the perceived needs of society. Proponents of ability grouping generally view the purpose of public education to be the fulfillment of individual potential, as opposed to the attainment of social goals, and express support for helping all children to be challenged to the extent of their abilities.[9] This view reflects the Jeffersonian tradition of acknowledging the responsibility of a constitutional republic in furthering excellence:

By . . . [selecting] the youths of genius from among the classes of the poor, we hope to avail the State of those talents which nature has sown as liberally among the poor as the rich, but which perish without use if not sought for and cultivated. (Thomas Jefferson, 1782)[10]

The larger question may not be the issue of supporting ability grouping, in spite of the pressures to be "politically correct," as much as, in the words of John Feldhusen, of "how to call a halt to a national reform agenda in which some school reformers have arrogated unto themselves a political-social agenda that is based on misinterpretation of current research evidence."[11]

Where did the current movement to eliminate ability grouping originate? Evidence indicates that it had its genesis as part of the contemporary middle school movement.

EVOLUTION OF THE CONTROVERSY

1970s–1980s: Early Trends

The position of the middle school movement on ability grouping reflects an evolutionary change. A national study conducted from 1977 to 1979 found that while *local* middle school administrators expressed support for ability grouping, *national* leaders of the middle school movement appeared equally divided between supporting and opposing it.[12] Unlike in later years, in the late 1970s only one reference could be found that claimed ability grouping was a practice contrary to the goals of the middle school movement.[13]

In fact, in the late 1970s and early 1980s, it appeared that any early hesitations regarding ability grouping were being reconsidered. In 1978, the National Association of Secondary School Principals (NASSP) published the results of a study of the highest-performing high schools in the country, and found that it did not matter if these schools were exclusive private academies or public schools located in middle-class neighborhoods—they all had three things in common: (1) the belief that academics was the first and primary responsibility of the school; (2) an emphasis on a traditional liberal arts curriculum; and (3) ability grouping. In fact, so few schools among those identified as high performing had moved toward any sort of heterogeneous (mixed-ability) grouping that a statistically significant difference was found for this factor between the high achieving schools and those that had experienced substantial declines in performance.[14]

A few short years later, two national leaders of the middle school movement published an exhaustive handbook titled *The Exemplary Middle School* (1981). It is notable that although the authors alluded to the presence of a growing anti–ability grouping sentiment, they suggested that the middle school movement might soon be moving *toward* ability grouping:

It is possible that ... the reader expected a considerably more lengthy discussion of topics such as ability grouping. ... Such topics are of tremendous concern and will continue to be for many years; they are of sufficient importance as to require detailed treatment beyond the scope of the present volume. New research on teacher effectiveness, suggesting the value of more direct large group instruction when teaching skills to problem learners, may cause a reevaluation of prevalent anti–ability grouping attitudes.[15]

The first edition of *This We Believe* (1982), a policy handbook for the National Middle School Association (NMSA), contains only one short paragraph on ability grouping, noting that "Homogeneous [like-ability] grouping may be a proper requisite for some instruction while heterogeneous [mixed-ability] grouping is best for most instruction."[16]

However, in the early 1980s, social scientist Mara Sapon-Shevin presented a paper at the annual conference of the American Educational Research Association (AERA) in which she stated: "the key question concerns whether or not educational services should be offered in homogeneous or heterogeneous groups." In noting the use of differentiated instruction for gifted learners, she questioned "educational decisions that attend to the exclusive needs of only a small segment of learners." She also asserted that gifted students have an obligation to develop a "social conscience" by attending to the needs of their non-gifted peers.[17] Although not overtly negative at this point in time, the author nonetheless raises the issue of radical equity in the context of educational outcomes.

An article that appeared the following year in the *Middle School Journal* appears to have initiated a decidedly negative tone to the discussion. Although entitled "What Research Says to the Practitioner about Ability Grouping," the authors, middle school activists J. Howard Johnston and Glenn Markle, discuss *tracking*, not ability grouping, and they do so in highly emotional terms, evoking images of classism and elitism:

Initial grouping is done very early in a child's school career. . . . Such groupings, which likely reflect the family's socioeconomic status more than the child's ability or potential to learn, result in higher socioeconomic status children receiving favored treatment. . . . Differences, initiated in kindergarten or first grade, are enhanced through second and third grade, where higher status children stay together as an elite group which tends to remain fixed and rigid, regardless of the children's performance.

The authors cite several studies that failed to show evidence of a positive correlation between ability grouping and academic performance. Rather than note that these studies analyzed only the effects of *grouping*, and not grouping in concert with different instructional practices tailored to each group, the authors conclude that "the practice of grouping students by ability for instructional purposes is not supported by research. . . . *The practice is especially antithetical to the goals and objectives of the middle school movement*"[18] (emphasis added).

As the 1980s progressed, those calling for the elimination of ability grouping became increasingly vocal and often cited the issue of social equity to justify their calls for change. By 1984, Sapon-Shevin had refined and sharpened her arguments and convictions, presenting the call to eliminate ability grouping as an "argument for social justice," concluding that ability grouping results in "segregated programs for gifted students" and "accompanying social consequences [that] are substantially disparate."[19]

In 1985, Jeanne Oakes, a social scientist with the Rand Corporation, published *Keeping Track: How Schools Structure Inequality*, expressing views congruent with those of Sapon-Shevin. The book received a substantial amount of attention, with no fewer than 18 reviews in a few short years: three in 1985,[20] ten in 1986,[21] and five more in 1987.[22] Oakes addressed the issue of social equity and claimed that the elimination of ability grouping in schools would address it:

Until a major social reorganization occurs that results in cultural, political, and economic equity for all groups or until a major reconstruction of schooling takes place in which the educational process encourages individuals to refuse to tolerate an unequal social system, more limited reforms should be attempted to help equalize the effects of schooling. A reorganization of secondary school grouping patterns appears to be one such necessary reform.[23]

Oakes viewed schools as the primary vehicle for social change, and the elimination of ability grouping was the primary means to accomplish this goal. In a 1988 article she further articulated her vision of the school as an essential component in reforming society as a whole, according to her set of values:

The concept of the school as the center of change must not be interpreted to mean that the school alone can do what is necessary. The school exists in a larger ecosystem that often hampers the school's efforts to become a renewing culture in which the very best educational and social values permeate daily life. It is difficult to disagree with those social reformers who believe that reform of the school without reform of the larger society is futile. However, we argue that the two must proceed simultaneously.[24]

What she failed to point out in her zeal, however, is the fact that her mission to eliminate ability grouping is based upon her study of only 13 senior high schools and 12 junior high schools—a mere fraction of the thousands of schools across the country. Oakes generalized to *all* schools what she perceived as the "evils" of ability grouping in these schools. Using this generalization as her justification, she set out on a mission to eradicate ability grouping from all American schools. And as the historical record shows, she was quite successful.

Late 1980s: Negative Attitudes Grow

The latter half of the 1980s saw opponents of ability grouping becoming increasingly vocal. Journal articles, reports by influential foundations, presentations, and speeches all echoed the theme that ability grouping had no place in public education, especially at the middle school level. In 1986, Johnston and Markle reprinted their 1983 critique on ability grouping in a book titled *What Research Says to the Middle Level Practitioner*. Their statement on ability grouping blames the practice for social inequities:

[Ability grouping] interferes with opportunities for students to learn from—and learn to accept—peers of different socio-economic backgrounds, and may perpetuate notions of superior and inferior classes of citizens. The practice is especially antithetical to the goals and objectives of the middle school.[25]

In the same year, *Phi Delta Kappan* published a two-part article based upon Oakes' 1985 book, which helped to more broadly distribute the idea that ability grouping results in "frightening patterns of curricular inequality."[26] This policy article was reprinted in *Equity and Excellence*, along with a study that echoed similar views, noting that within all the ability groups examined, "a narrow range of activities and instructional methodologies characterized the educational experiences of all students." Rather than criticize the lack of differentiated instruction in classrooms, the researchers illogically blamed ability grouping for the lack of tailored instruction by concluding that the "numbing similarity of practices and content . . . raise serious doubts about the continued use of ability grouping."[27]

In 1988, middle school activist Paul George published an article that continued the attack on ability grouping. Interspersed with research supporting his point of view are declarations of "facts" with no citations that insult the professionalism of many dedicated teachers: "Teachers behave differently toward low-track students. They tend to slow down the pace of learning. They prepare less vigorously. They may persist less strenuously." While he acknowledges that heterogeneous (mixed-ability) grouping "imposed serious lesson planning difficulties on teachers and presented obstacles to providing individual attention to all students," and that "teachers appear to experience considerable difficulty planning and teaching classroom groups of widely varying ability and achievement levels,"[28] he does little more than flippantly suggest that teachers receive more training to deal with these problems. In the same year, George further noted that middle schools had become "the focus of societal experimentation, the vehicle for movement toward increased justice and equality in the society as a whole."[29]

The first set of annual resolutions released by the NMSA in 1988 recommended a commitment to move away from "rigid" ability grouping, but the language was less strident than that of George. Although the resolution mentions flexible grouping, as will be seen, this was mere lip service to critics:

Whereas, young adolescence is a period of dramatic developmental diversity deserving responsive grouping practices; and whereas, common tracking and rigid ability grouping do not accommodate this diversity; and, whereas, research has demonstrated that such practices have either negative, or at best, no impact on either student achievement or self-concept: Therefore, be it resolved that NMSA urge school personnel to implement flexible grouping practices which place student needs above organizational and instructional convenience.[30]

The NMSA was not the only group to jump on the anti–ability grouping bandwagon. The NASSP moved from a position of supporting ability grouping (1978) to being noncommittal toward grouping issues (1985), to ultimately changing course completely (1989). In *Middle Level Education's Responsibility for Intellectual De-*

velopment, the NASSP ignored its own 1978 study which indicated a statistically significant relationship between ability grouping and higher academic achievement, and instead jumped on the anti–ability grouping bandwagon by citing the work of middle school activists Johnston and Markle to support a reversal of its stand on the issue:

Homogeneous grouping by ability clearly does not improve intellectual development or facilitate academic achievement. . . . Research evidence does not support the belief by some educators that academic and affective growth are enhanced by ability grouping.[31]

And as noted in Chapter 2, the influential 1989 Carnegie Council publication *Turning Points* amplified the call to abandon ability grouping. The report called for "fundamental social change," and equated ability grouping with tracking, referring to it as "one of the most divisive and damaging school practices in existence."[32] The publication of this report was followed by numerous articles supporting and commending its findings.[33]

Early 1990s: Negative Attitudes Continue

The popular press picked up the anti–ability grouping theme, resulting in a front-page commentary in the *Washington Post* Outlook titled: "Fast Track Trap: How Ability Grouping Hurts Our Schools, Kids, and Families."[34] This was followed a month later by a special section in the *ASCD Education Update*, questioning whether gifted students should be grouped by ability.[35]

Growing interest in the issue of grouping is further evidenced by the number of NMSA conference sessions on the topic, which made a massive leap from single digits in the 1970s and 1980s to double digits in the 1990s. The number of sessions peaked in 1992 at 49 sessions (see Appendix I).

The narratives describing NMSA conference sessions in 1990 and 1991 misstate research findings in an apparent attempt to support the elimination of ability grouping, stating that "research indicates that [all] middle school youngsters should be grouped heterogeneously"[36] and that the research "makes it clear that ability grouping, or tracking, has serious social and emotional side effects for [all] middle school students."[37]

Professional education associations also participated in the debate on ability grouping, and although these discussions were not always focused on the middle school, they indicate that the issue of ability grouping resonated at all educational levels. In 1990, the *ASCD Education Update* addressed the issue in a pro and con forum,[38] and a 1991 edition of *Educational Leadership*, another ASCD publication, carried a special section on "Grouping and the Gifted," featuring a lead story on ability grouping by Susan Allan. An advocate for gifted learners, Allan revealed how activists supporting heterogeneous (mixed-ability) grouping deliberately misstate research findings on grouping. Her article is followed by three responses: two supporting Allan and one disputing her assertions.[39]

One of the respondents framed the debate as a moral issue, stating that research was irrelevant when it comes to ability grouping:

There exists a body of philosophic absolutes that should include this statement: The ability grouping of students for educational opportunities in a democratic society is ethically unacceptable. We need not justify this with research, for it is a statement of principle, not of science. It should become a moral imperative along with the beliefs that slavery is immoral and that all people are created equal under the law.[40]

In 1992, the NMSA hosted a session at its annual conference titled: "Excellence and equity: Must middle schools choose between them? A symposium on ability grouping." The text of the session description noted the acrimonious nature of the debate:

Attacks on the practice of ability grouping challenge traditional programs for meeting the needs of the gifted student [while] advancing the need for equity. Proponents of education for the gifted and advocates of heterogeneous grouping appear poised for a series of confrontational clashes which may do little to advance the effectiveness of middle school education. This session will address the importance of excellence and need to attend to equity.[41]

The session did little to lay the issue to rest. In the years following the 1992 session, the rhetoric against ability grouping in session texts does not change. One session is titled "Integration and inclusion, NOT separation and seclusion." Another session promoted grouping all students together as a way to celebrate diversity: "Rather than sorting and excluding, special population students (i.e., ESL, learning disabled, gifted and talented, and at-risk) are included in regular classes."[42] The issue of equity also predominates in session titles such as "Equity and excellence for all: Untracking at the middle level," while another session urges participants to consider "philosophical, pedagogical, and legal reasons why heterogeneous grouping is necessary." Another session, titled "Just schools? The truth about tracking and ability grouping," is far more direct:

Living in a society that was built on the principles of equality, justice, and liberty for all, why do we persist with schooling practices that promote the contrary? What do we really do when we separate and sort students by ability? What are the alternatives and what can we do to reestablish real equity in America?[43]

Journal articles and formal NMSA publications during the early 1990s continued to indicate a strong negative attitude on the part of middle school advocates toward the issue of ability grouping. An NMSA position paper describes tracking and ability grouping as "artifacts from factory-model secondary schools,"[44] while an article in the *Middle School Journal* refers to ability grouping as "academic segregation" and a "serious manifestation of inequality in education."[45] Middle school activist Paul George published "Tracking and Ability Grouping in the Middle School: Ten Tentative Truths,"[46] which appears to be an update of his 1987 article "Ten Current Truths about Effective Schools" (which, interestingly, contained no mention of ability grouping). Even the *ERIC Digest*, compiled with federal funds, declared that "there has been a recent policy consensus that the negative effects of tracking on lower track students are so severe that schools should move towards detracking."[47] Slavin and others also continued the arguments for the elimination of tracking and ability grouping on social grounds, not on the basis of academics: "It undermines democratic values and contributes to a stratified society."[48]

As it had in 1991, *Educational Leadership* again dedicated nearly an entire issue to the controversy in 1992. Treatment of the issue was one-sided and included an interview with Jeanne Oakes and an article by Anne Wheelock, both of whom echo Paul George in their scathing attacks on ability grouping, blaming what they perceive as demands from excessively assertive, elitist parents as one reason for resistance to the elimination of this practice.[49]

It was also in 1992 that the ASCD published *The Middle School and Beyond*, which stated that the practice of grouping students "is to risk serious damage to self-concept in return for unproven and very limited benefits."[50] Another ASCD publication that year was *How to Untrack Your School*, a book by middle school activist Paul George. It contained many of the same anti–ability grouping arguments seen elsewhere: "Even if tracking produced higher academic achievement and higher self-esteem for most students—which it doesn't—it is an undesirable and unacceptable educational practice."[51]

Another professional organization, Phi Delta Kappa, also weighed in on the issue. The authors of a 1994 article in *Phi Delta Kappan* asserted that there was "growing agreement that tracking is unfair and injurious" and that "today the evidence clearly calls for its elimination."[52] Nearly the entire November 1995 issue of *Kappan* was dedicated to the subject of ability grouping, again presenting one-sided arguments. Three articles were included from those who supported the elimination of ability grouping with only one supporting its continued use.[53] A fifth well-balanced article presented policy options for consideration:

We merely wish to highlight the fact that the conventional wisdom on which detracking is based—that students in low-track classes (who are drawn disproportionally from poor families and from minority groups) are hurt by tracking while others are largely unaffected—is simply not supported by very strong evidence. . . . There is clearly a case for detracking on equity grounds; however, as a result, students currently in upper-track classes may suffer major losses in achievement test scores.[54]

In response, cooperative learning activist Robert Slavin disputed the authors' assertion:

It is fair to say that the jury is still out on how such untracking programs will work in practice, but *there is little basis for the fear that they will be detrimental to the performance of high achievers*.[55] (emphasis added)

The authors returned to *Kappan* with the following response:

It is worth stressing that we are neither opponents nor advocates of detracking. Our results point out that policymakers face a tradeoff between helping low-achieving students and hurting high-achieving ones.[56]

Ironically, the fact that achievement of high-ability students is harmed when educators blindly embrace heterogeneous grouping to the exclusion of all other options can be seen in Slavin's own research. He conducted a review of mastery learning, where students who did not reach mastery of the class subject matter are tutored by the teacher or other students who had already mastered the material. In Slavin's own words: "in several studies, positive effects were found for low-achievers only." He even used the term "the Robin Hood Effect" to describe this phenomenon, where the performance of low-achieving students rises as the achievement of high ability students falls. As stated by Slavin, who supports this practice: "whole-class instruction in effect holds back high achievers for the benefit of low achievers. Group-based mastery learning may thus be accentuating a 'Robin Hood' tendency."[57]

Calls for Social Equity

Some authors, looking beyond ability grouping to the larger issue of what they perceive as an expanded social role for public education, claim that "education is the only means by which society can prevent the passing of racism, sexism, and the privileges of class from generation to generation."[58] Thus, voices demanding social equity continued to be heard. In 1991, Elizabeth Cohen stated that heterogeneous (mixed-ability) grouping, in her perspective, was an imperative for achieving social justice:

What is at stake here is the attempt to undo the effects of inequality in society at large as it affects the day-to-day life of the classroom. Social scientists have documented the ways in which classrooms tend to reproduce the inequalities of the larger society. Undoing these effects is an ambitious undertaking. Nonetheless, the application of sociological theory and research to the problem of increasing equity in [the] heterogeneous classroom leaves room for hope that these goals are within our reach.[59]

This theme was continued by Sapon-Shevin in 1994, who stated that the goal of education was to "uncover and dismantle the structures that separate and damage children and reinvent schools that embody social and educational equity and justice."[60] Others continued the claim that there was a connection between social equity and the elimination of ability grouping: "Less grouping by ability and a less rigid departmental structure appear to promote social equality in achievement among students."[61]

Cooperative learning activist Robert Slavin articulated unsubstantiated criticisms of ability grouping and a continued misinterpretation of the research by noting:

Given the undemocratic, antiegalitarian nature of ability grouping, the burden of proof should be on those who would group rather than those who favor heterogeneous grouping, and in the absence of evidence that grouping is beneficial, it is hard to justify continuation of the practice.[62]

Although the number of sessions on grouping at NMSA conferences begins to decrease near the end of the 1990s, this does not mean that interest is not sustained (see Appendix I). Rather, it appears that the issue might have been seen by middle school activists as a battle that has already been won.

RESPONSE FROM ADVOCATES FOR GIFTED LEARNERS

The active dismantling of ability grouping by middle school advocates became a major area of concern for advocates of the gifted. Carol Tomlinson notes that many middle school activists characterize ability grouping as "not only ineffective for all students, but also somehow evil."[63] Opponents of ability grouping include leading activists who support both the middle school movement and the goal of social change. Proponents of ability grouping acknowledge its misuse in the past, but defend it as a viable option for meeting the diverse needs of students at both ends of the ability spectrum.

Gifted proponent Susan Allan defended ability grouping in a 1991 article in *Educational Leadership*, and pointed out that "the preponderance of evidence does not support the contention that children are academically harmed by [homogeneous] grouping." Furthermore, she challenges those who claim otherwise, stating that research results have been misinterpreted or accepted without question, a position that is "the most destructive aspect of the controversy."[64] Other educators have expressed similar sentiments, with one stating that "educators have uncritically accepted" the idea that homogeneous grouping is harmful and heterogeneous grouping is beneficial, "when little empirical proof has been presented," while another noted that the anti–ability grouping movement may have been fueled by resentment and envy toward those with gifted abilities.[65]

Also in 1991, a detailed report by gifted advocate Karen Rogers, titled *The Relationship of Grouping Practices to the Education of the Gifted and Talented Learner*, provided an analysis of over 700 studies on ability grouping. Results indicated that ability grouping, when coupled with differentiated curricula or enrichment, produces "substantial academic gains" for gifted students, and Rogers recommends that "students who are academically or intellectually gifted and talented should spend the majority of their school day with others of similar abilities and interests."[66] These results and recommendations echoed the findings of Kulik and Kulik,[67] which indicated that academic achievement increased significantly for those gifted learners who were grouped by ability and received a differentiated curriculum. Conversely, evidence indicates that the achievement of gifted learners suffers when ability grouping is eliminated.[68]

Further, advocates for the gifted point out that if high-achieving students are removed from the classroom, the achievement of neither average nor below average students suffers,[69] and gifted learners are allowed to "experience instruction with peers who accept them as they are, who will not ridicule or ostracize them."[70] Research by Dale Schunk indicated that students choose to model on those with similar abilities, which serves to neutralize the claim that gifted students are needed as role models.[71] Moreover, evidence indicates that grouping above average students together can actually *benefit* average and below average students by "providing some relief from the intellectual dominance" of those high-achieving students.[72]

In 1992, Feldhusen and Moon articulated what they believed to be the underlying source of the move to eliminate ability grouping:

It seems amazing, then, that at a time of mass underachievement among American youth, we have serious researchers such as Slavin and Oakes advocating heterogeneous grouping and opposing ability grouping. . . . It is important to recognize that value systems that have little to do with school learning and achievement may be at work in the proposals of some of these scholars. . . . Homogenization of educational experiences is advocated primarily as a means to social change. The rush to heterogeneous grouping and cooperative learning is probably heavily influenced by social and political value systems.[73]

The words of James Gallagher in 1993 regarding anti–ability grouping activist Robert Slavin echoes these thoughts:

Mr. Slavin promotes a social agenda for the schools rather than an academic one. He tries to convince the reader that his social agenda can be obtained at no cost to academic performance. That is a hard sell. Mr. Slavin points out that "Untracking must never be—or appear to be—taking from high achievers to give to low achievers." Yet that seems to be precisely what is happening out there in the countryside, with school systems abandoning honors courses and programs for gifted students—and citing Robert Slavin as their authority for doing so. This practice has not escaped the attention of those "active parents" of high-ability students to which Mr. Slavin refers—and they don't like it. Slavin would have us believe that high achievers will do just as well in heterogeneous [mixed-ability] settings; that the presence of low achievers does not cause teachers to slow down or "dumb down" their curriculum and that, besides, there is no evidence that ability grouping works anyway. Really!!! . . . Heterogeneous classes *do* slow down the bright students and . . . the curriculum *is* dumbed down.[74] (emphasis in the original).

The concerns of these leaders on the issue of ability grouping were not the isolated worries of a few individuals. The pessimism of advocates for gifted learners in the 1990s was reflected in other sources as well:

Only a small percentage of schools and teachers across the United States currently employ instructional plans for *any* learner based on a diagnosed assessment of individual learning needs. How can we believe that less grouping and more heterogeneous classrooms will enhance the learning process for *any* student with special needs?[75]

In our efforts to be democratic, we have forgotten Thomas Jefferson's statement: "nothing is so unequal as the equal treatment of unequal people." Although Oakes has acknowledged that ability grouping does benefit the highest ability students, she questions whether we can continue to meet their needs at the expense of all others. Can it be that our school systems are actually giving tacit approval to create underachievement in one ability group so that the needs of the other ability groups can be served? This, indeed, is egalitarianism at its worst.[76]

"Homogenization of educational experiences" and "creat[ing] underachievers" are clearly strategies employed in the quest to build an Orwellian sort of egalitarian society. By coercing egalitarianism, activists are attempting to "level the playing field" by reducing the achievement of high ability students.

SURVEY RESULTS ON ABILITY GROUPING

Changes over time in the behaviors of both middle school activists and practitioners can be analyzed by examining surveys of their practices.[77] While some of these surveys are methodologically sound, others are flawed. Both categories of surveys are discussed separately.

Valid Surveys: 1965, 1980, 1988, 1995, and 2001

In a 1965 survey, ability grouping by subject matter was ranked third by middle school principals in a list of 11 educational priorities. The authors stated:

The use of ability grouping as a means to reduce the wide range of individual differences that exist in a given classroom has become quite common. Almost 90 percent of the principals surveyed favored some type of ability grouping. The most frequently advocated system of grouping pupils was within all grade levels but only in selected subject areas.

In practice, 20 percent of principals reported that their school used tracking, 68 percent indicated the presence of ability grouping only in certain subject areas, and 9 percent reported no ability grouping at all (see Table 1). Practice and beliefs were consistent, with 19 percent of the principals reporting they believed in tracking, 69 percent in ability grouping only in certain subject areas, and 7 percent expressing the belief that there should be no ability grouping at all. Eighty-four percent of the principals surveyed indicated that their schools used at least two criteria for making decisions about group placement for individual students.[78]

Fifteen years later (1980), another survey asked middle school principals about the practice of ability grouping, and the responses fell into three general groups: 11 percent of the principals reported the use of tracking (classes grouped at all levels for all subjects), 74 percent indicated the use of ability grouping for some subject areas in all or some grade levels, and 11 percent indicated no ability grouping (see Table 1). In expressing their opinions about ability grouping, as in the 1965 survey, practices and beliefs were consistent, with 11 percent stating that they supported tracking, 76 percent supporting ability grouping in some subjects, and 8 percent expressing no support for ability grouping. However, the authors were dismayed at these results and stated: "It is apparent that research on the unfavorable effects of ability grouping has yet to influence the level of practice."[79]

In a 1988 survey, 18 percent of the participating middle school principals reported that they did not practice ability grouping, 26 percent grouped all classes by ability, and 56 percent used some ability grouping (see Table 1).

The authors presented a balanced analysis of their data:

The data show that most schools use homogeneous [like-ability] grouping in some but not all subject classes. Grouping by ability for some classes is not necessarily good or bad. The results and effects of grouping depend on appropriate placement, flexible membership, appropriate instructional materials, teaching practices that reward students for progress in learning, and other pedagogical and motivational factors. . . . For most middle grade schools, the Carnegie recommendation to eliminate homogeneous [like-ability] grouping is a long-term goal that depends on the availability of material and staff development approaches to enable all teachers to deal effectively with diversity in all subjects. . . . There is, presently, great variation in grouping practices. . . . It is clear from these data that educators have many options for organizing and assigning groups of students to their classes and need not rely on only one grouping strategy.[80]

In a 1995 survey, several questions were asked about different types of ability grouping and the frequency of their use. Of those middle school principals surveyed, 73 percent indicated that they had no ability grouping in their schools, 10 percent indicated some ability grouping, and 9 percent indicated that all classes are ability grouped (see Table 1).[81]

The most current survey was conducted in 2000 and results were reported at the NMSA national conference in November 2001. The middle school principals who responded to the survey indicated that ability grouping for specific classes has made an astonishing revival. While only 15 percent indicated that they

Table 1
Ability Grouping and Cooperative Learning at the Middle School
Level: Practices Reported by Principals* (Reported in Percentages)

	1965	1980	1988	1995	2001
Tracking at all or some grade levels	20	11	26	9	N/A
Ability grouping used for certain subjects	68	74	56	10	72**
No ability grouping or tracking	9	11	18	73	15

*Those surveys with noted interpretive problems as discussed in Chapter 4 are
    not included (Connors & Irvin, 1989; Valentine et al., 1993).
**This survey also reported that teachers grouped by ability within classrooms
    in 13 percent of schools responding.

have no ability grouping in their schools, 72 percent reported that
they group students by ability in specific classes, and 13 percent
reported within-class grouping (see Table 1). These reported practices are congruent with the principals' stated beliefs: 65 percent
report that their schools practice ability grouping and have no
plans to change.[82]

The middle school proponents who were the authors expressed
alarm at this change, which they characterize as "inching back to
1980." According to one of the authors:

There's a big disconnect between the research and the practice in this
particular area of middle level education . . . 65 percent of our principals
in 2000 say that they have ability grouping and don't intend to change
it. That's compared to 27 percent in 1992. . . . So again, we see some significant changes in attitude on ability grouping and we have to ask ourselves: Why? Why is this inching back? What's causing the disconnect
between the research and recommendations in the literature and the
practices that are happening in our schools? This is a very, very significant call for future research.[83]

Interestingly, one of the authors also makes a statement that
reveals the strange belief or illogical conclusion that ability grouping means "dumbing-down" the rigor of what is taught. In this
statement, she also implicitly acknowledges that high ability stu-

dents should not be allowed to work to their fullest potential because if they do, educational outcomes will not be the same:

In *Turning Points, In This We Believe*, and *Turning Points 2000*, there is a repeated denunciation of grouping students by ability. . . . However, you see that is not the current practice, and we have some significant concerns that in a worst case scenario, we may be looking at an increase in—excuse the pejorative expression—"dumbing down" the curriculum . . . or more specifically, the achievement gap widening.[84]

In response to a question from the audience, another author of the study stated: "By and large, ability grouping is still considered to have a negative impact upon the kids. That's how we read it."[85]

Problematic Surveys: 1989 and 1993

A close look at two other surveys of middle school instructional practices reveals that the authors reported the data in misleading ways, apparently with the hope of bolstering their activist anti–ability grouping agendas as opposed to accurately reporting the data that had been collected. The 1989 survey was published by the *Middle School Journal*, the official publication of the NMSA,[86] and the 1993 survey was published by the National Association of Secondary School Principals (NASSP).[87]

Respondents to the 1989 *Middle School Journal* survey were asked to answer *yes* or *no* to a number of statements, including: "Students remain in the same ability group for all academic subjects." However, in reporting their results, the authors took a flying leap of logic and reported the converse of this statement, "students are heterogeneously [mixed-ability] grouped," instead of the statement that was used to gather the data. The question on the survey, in essence, asked if schools *tracked* their students by keeping them in the same ability group for all subjects, but the authors reported the negative responses on tracking as evidence of almost a complete shift to heterogeneous [mixed-ability] grouping, disregarding the existence of per-subject ability grouping within heterogeneous classes. To collect research data that ask for one thing and then twist the way it is reported is either sloppy and unprofessional work or constitutes an unethical use of the data. One cannot assume that if a school does not track, it has thus eliminated any and all sorts of ability grouping—but that is the (flawed) logic that these authors took, perhaps because such data support the authors' activist stand and can thus be used to convince educators that "everyone is doing it." The authors stated:

A final and rather significant response was the high percentages of schools . . . that implemented heterogeneous [mixed-ability] grouping. . . . Perhaps more schools are moving away from ability grouping and beginning to realize the benefits of heterogeneous [mixed-ability] grouping and lack of research evidence to support homogeneous [like-ability] grouping in middle schools.

That they were apparently searching for data to support their position can be seen in their admission that their results "were contrary to recent reports." Finally, in their conclusion, the authors' advocacy becomes obvious as they address the growing opposition to the middle school movement itself:

Middle level educators, however, must continue to communicate to the public that what they are doing is effective and does make a difference for students. Furthermore, they must reinforce the concept that the middle school is unique and that the "50 percent humanistic, 50 percent academic" philosophy is successful in helping students achieve.[88]

The other problematic survey is the 1993 NASSP study in which the authors stated: "Ability grouping in this study is defined as the *assignment of students to classes based upon academic ability*" (emphasis in the original). The data chart on page 57 of the study, summarizing the results of question 38 of *Principal Survey: Form B,* clearly shows the total percentage of principals who reported grouping students into "specific classes by academic ability" as 69 percent, with those who reported grouping students *within a classroom* as 13 percent. Yet the authors proceeded to ignore their stated definition of ability grouping when they combined these numbers and declared that "eighty-two percent of the principals said their schools used some degree of ability grouping." In other words, they combined the responses for subject or per-class ability grouping (genuine ability grouping, according to their definition), and grouping that takes place within a single classroom (which, according to their own definition, is *not* ability grouping). This falsely inflated number is cited numerous times throughout the study, always as evidence that more work urgently needs to be done to eliminate ability grouping.[89] (See Table 2.)

It appears that the authors of the 1993 survey exaggerated the number of schools that *practiced* ability grouping in order to state a case for its elimination, while the authors of the 1989 survey exaggerated the number of schools that had *eliminated* ability grouping in an attempt to show that the trend was to move away from ability grouping.

The authors of the 1993 study reveal their anti–ability grouping bias when they refer to "the elimination of ability grouping" as "this important issue":

Grouping by ability, in spite of the research that shows its deleterious effect on early adolescents . . . still remains firmly entrenched in middle level schools. . . . As reported earlier, ability grouping was found in 82 percent of the schools in this study.

[Among the] most frustrating findings [is that] . . . [a]bility grouping is still widely supported and utilized in middle level schools (82 percent). Scholarly consensus opposes both tracking and most forms of ability grouping.

The authors also failed to point out the lack of internal consistency in their flawed interpretation of the principals' responses. The responses on instructional *practice* indicated that 18 percent of principals surveyed do not group students by ability, compared to 82 percent (by the authors' count) who do; while the responses to the question on *belief* indicate that 13 percent of principals do not believe in grouping by ability, compared to 64 percent who believe in it for specific classes and 23 percent who believe in it within classrooms.[90] The authors make no mention of this inconsistency in their text, but they consistently use the numbers more favorable for their argument (82 percent), when in actuality their figure of 69 percent for the practice of grouping classes by academic ability is more consistent with the 64 percent figure of those principals who hold this belief, since it is logical to assume that practice reflects belief (see Table 2).

As far as both of these studies are concerned, the questionable judgment inherent in each appears to be a thinly veiled attempt to misstate research findings to support the authors' ideological viewpoints and further their agendas. Unfortunately, but perhaps as part of the authors' covert goals, a ripple effect has occurred.

Table 2
1993 NASSP Study on Ability Grouping in the Middle School
(Reported in Percentages)

	Data: Percentage of principals who *practice* this	Authors' conclusions regarding current practice	Data: Percentage of principals who *believe* this
No form of grouping by academic ability	18	18	13
Students grouped into specific classes by academic ability	69	82 (69 + 13)	64
Students not grouped into specific classes by ability, but teacher groups within individual classes	13	0	23

Other authors and researchers who trusted that the conclusions were sound (without bothering to delve into the details) have cited and continue to cite these studies—and this is occurring, among other places, in NMSA publications.[91]

Survey Summaries

Key findings from these surveys are summarized in Table 1. The findings from the 1989 and 1993 surveys are not included in that table due to the interpretive problems noted earlier. One notable observation is that, according to the data, "tracking" was never practiced by more than 26 percent of American middle schools. This is interesting to highlight, since the rhetoric of many middle school activists leads one to believe that this "evil" practice was widespread and pervasive throughout the United States, necessitating an urgent drive for its eradication. But, as was noted previously, the outcry from social scientist Jeanne Oakes for the full elimination of ability grouping in the name of equity was based on the observations of a mere 25 schools.[92] She generalized her findings to all schools in the country, leading people to believe that a crisis existed because the "evil" practice of tracking was everywhere. The simple truth is that it was not. Once again, a "crisis" was created by those who were looking for an opportunity to foster massive social changes through their ready-made solution.

Wild claims of pervasive and unfair grouping practices cannot be substantiated when one examines the longitudinal survey data—in spite of the attempts of some middle school activists to do just that. What is evident, however, is that there was a massive shift away from ability grouping over time.

CURRENT STATUS OF THE DEBATE

Attempts at Dialogue

In 1995, *ASCD Education Update* presented the pros and cons of ability grouping in an article that reflected input from both sides of the issue,[93] and presentations by Carol Tomlinson at the summit hosted by the Council for Exceptional Children included strategies for addressing the needs of gifted learners within heterogeneously grouped classes.[94] However, this did not herald a new era of consensus or compromise as some had hoped, because a negative tone remained. Note activist Paul George's strident remarks from the summit:

Schools are about the redistribution of future wealth. That's what they're about. They're not about talent development. They're not about taking each child as far as he or she can go. They're about redistributing the wealth of the future. That's what they've always been about. Sorting, providing opportunities for some and denying them to others.[95]

Negative articles also appeared the following year in the *Harvard Educational Review* and *Educational Researcher*.[96]

The issue also received a fair amount of play in the popular press. In an article in *Education Week* titled "Massachusetts Leads Mounting Charge Against Ability Grouping,"[97] the author notes that the state was using fiscal leverage to encourage schools to move away from ability grouping by withholding grant money to schools that did not conform, and a 1994 *Washington Post* article called for the elimination of programs for gifted learners.[98]

Entrenched Attitudes: Contrary to Public Beliefs

Over the last several decades, heterogeneous (mixed-ability) grouping has come to be presented as the grouping plan of choice in many educational journals and by many education reformers, but the public has yet to be convinced that this practice makes sense. In 1994, members of the public were surveyed regarding their preferences for heterogeneous (mixed-ability) or homogeneous (same-ability) grouping. A mere one-third of the general public indicated support for heterogeneous (mixed-ability) grouping, leading the authors to conclude: "Heterogeneous (mixed-ability) grouping makes no intuitive sense to people and seems to fly in the face of their real-world experiences."[99]

Researchers also reported that over half of those teachers surveyed are either equivocal or do not see the practice of heterogeneous (mixed-ability) grouping as instrumental in improving academic achievement, and focus group discussions indicate that there is probably less support for heterogeneous (mixed-ability) grouping than survey percentages suggest:

Focus groups suggest that teachers and the public share similar concerns: They fear high achievers and average students will be held back while teachers attend to the needs of low achievers; or that students with difficulties will never get the attention they really need.[100]

The fears expressed by these focus group members have been addressed by researchers, many of whom agree that "the preponderance of evidence does not support the contention that children are academically harmed by (homogeneous) grouping."[101] Further, some studies suggest that if high-achieving students are removed from the classroom, the achievement of average or below average students does not suffer.[102] Other evidence indicates that grouping above average students separately can *benefit* average and below average students by "providing some relief from the intellectual dominance" of those high-achieving students.[103]

There will be those who claim that other research refutes these findings. However, there is ample evidence that such research has either been misinterpreted or accepted without question.[104] One researcher has asserted that "educators have uncritically accepted" the idea that homogeneous grouping is harmful and heterogeneous grouping is beneficial, "when little empirical proof has been presented."[105]

This "uncritical acceptance" of heterogeneous (mixed-ability) grouping as good and homogeneous (same ability) grouping as bad can be seen in a comprehensive survey of the attitudes of education school professors. A majority of all education professors surveyed would like to see *less* like-ability grouping, and half would like to see *more* mixed-ability grouping. A similar percentage believe that mixed-ability grouping will improve student academic achievement. Considering that only a small proportion of the public appears to support mixed-ability grouping, the attitudes of many education professors appear to be contrary to those held by members of the public.[106] As the authors of the study note:

Education professors speak with passionate idealism about their own sometimes lofty vision of public education and the mission of teacher education programs . . . [however, they hold] expectations that often differ dramatically from those of parents and teachers now in the classrooms.[107]

This is significant due to the powerful influence education professors have on those studying to become teachers:

Their convictions and beliefs, it seems, should have particular significance since they are the source of a chain reaction. Assuming that they are at least reasonably effective, what education professors teach about learning and schools shapes the goals, expectations, and priorities of the nation's teaching corps.[108]

Grouping as "Racist"

It has been noted that arguments regarding ability grouping have turned especially divisive when the topic of race is interjected:

An emerging national agenda among nearly all the school reform constituencies is claiming that "ability grouping is bad, it is racist, it must be eliminated." Research is cited and twisted to support that agenda. The linking of ability grouping to racism adds an emotional and inflammatory element to the agenda.[109]

One of the most vocal advocates for eliminating ability grouping, social activist Mara Sapon-Shevin, claims that "parental demand for and the increased interest in gifted programming can be traced directly to the increasing racial integration of many schools and communities."[110] She gives no context for this statement, so one can only assume she is referring to the increased interest in gifted programming which began in the late 1950s. She is implying that the increase in gifted programming at that time was the result of the 1954 Supreme Court ruling in *Brown v. Board of Education* which set the stage for school desegregation, suggesting that the move toward integration coincided with increases in gifted programming because parents were seeking segregation. However, one of the first lessons that any serious researcher should learn is that a correlation does not necessarily indicate causation. Documentary evidence suggests a very different reason for the increase in gifted programming during the late 1950s—specifically, the 1957 launching of Sputnik by the Russians in the middle of the Cold War, which "triggered unprecedented action on behalf of the gifted."[111]

The notion that homogeneous grouping is "a camouflage for racial prejudice" can also be deflated by observing what minority parents want for their own children. A recent Public Agenda survey found that "opposition to heterogeneous (mixed-ability) grouping is as strong among African-American parents as among white parents, and support for it is equally weak."[112]

This finding also disputes Sapon-Shevin's assertion that, when it comes to being vocal about the needs of high-performing children, "parents whose own educations have been constrained by racism or poverty often lack the confidence to speak out."[113] This is demeaning to the many minority parents who have overcome great odds themselves, and who want their children to have the opportunities that may have been denied to a different generation.

Other research also indicates that the "racist" myth surrounding ability grouping is simply not true. For example, in a 1995 study involving 1,100 American high schools, researchers found that schools practicing ability grouping used student *ability* as the placement criterion rather than socio-economic status or race. The authors state:

The greater the tendency of schools to assign students to tracks [ability groups] . . . the greater the schools' reliance on students' ability as the criterion of placement and the lesser their tendency to favor higher SES [socio-economic status] students.[114]

Likewise, in their 1997 study of over 600 students in schools with a college-prep "track," another group of scholars reported that they found "no empirical basis for the historical ambiguity concerning race and schooling."[115]

Court Opinions on Ability Grouping

In two landmark cases, the courts have ruled quite differently on the issue of student grouping.[116] In large measure, this is because in one case, *Hobson v. Hansen* (1967, 1969) the school district was practicing rigid tracking; while in the other case, *Marshall v. Georgia* (1984, 1985) the school district was practicing flexible ability grouping. Why did the courts rule *against* grouping in *Hobson* but *in favor* of it in *Marshall*? There are four fundamental differences between the two cases:

1. In the Hobson case, decisions on grouping depended on a single measure of general academic ability, while in the Marshall case, "a combination of academic indicators was taken into consideration with primary emphasis being placed on a child's actual performance."[117]
2. In the Hobson case, students were tracked—that is, they were assigned to the same group for all of their courses and this placement was essentially permanent. In the Marshall case, a student's assignment to a group depended on his or her ability in that specific subject. The school district also provided evidence that, over a two year period, 37 percent of the students in that district changed their instructional grouping assignments.
3. In the Hobson case, resources were not evenly distributed among the grouping levels, while in the Marshall case more services were available for students in the lower ability groups.
4. In the Hobson case, there was no evidence presented to demonstrate that lower ability students were benefiting academically from grouping, while in the Marshall case, data from standardized tests indicated academic improvement for the lowest-performing children.

The appeals court opinion on the Marshall case stated that ability grouping was not only acceptable, it was preferred to heterogeneous (mixed-ability) grouping because, in this situation, ability grouping was "designed to remedy the past results of past segregation through better educational opportunity for the present generation of black students."[118]

Beliefs of Teachers and Principals

Although evidence indicates that the majority of middle school teachers believe that ability grouping is the best way to address the needs of both high ability and remedial learners,[119] the majority of middle school principals appear to align their beliefs with middle school activists intent on discouraging the practice. In a 1995 survey, middle school principals ranked "advancement of student talent" as *last* in a list of priorities for the middle school, and likewise ranked differentiating the curriculum as 15/16 in a list of factors influencing their decisions on middle school instruction. Only 27 percent of the principals surveyed believed there to be considerable or a great deal of merit in providing some full-time classes for advanced students.[120] The tone of radical middle school leaders is sometimes reflected in the attitudes of practitioners. Consider again the words of one middle school teacher:

We represent all children and it is morally wrong to give different instruction to these gifted students. I, for one, do not believe the so-called research that indicates that these children have educational needs other children do not. If they are so smart they can find something useful to do with their time.[121]

As if in response, gifted advocate Carol Tomlinson noted that:

Unless differentiated instruction does evolve, chances are that heterogeneous grouping will fail and we may be forced to adopt alternative instructional arrangements to meet the varied learning needs of a diverse student population.[122]

Current evidence of the growing backlash against radical heterogeneous (mixed-ability) grouping practices, and against the middle school movement itself, suggests that her prediction may be coming true.

Current Research on Grouping

Current studies from other countries shed new light on the issue of ability grouping. The author of a 1995 study from England notes that the most significant student mobility in the schools he studied is the movement of South Asian students from lower into

higher ability groups, indicating that merit can overcome prejudice or perceived lack of ability in that system.[123] A 1998 study of
Israeli schools reports that ability and academic performance are
stronger predictors of group placement than socio-economic
standing, ethnicity, or gender.[124] And Singapore, a country whose
students have consistently scored above most others in international assessments such as the Third International Math and Science Study (TIMSS), credits ability grouping as one of the key
factors in its students' academic success.[125]

A 1997 study of middle school–aged students in Taiwan explains that school reputations there are based in large measure
upon how well students perform on three levels of difficult high
school entrance exams. According to the author, this sort of public
accountability

creates an incentive structure in which it is in the interest of school personnel to channel students with the greatest aptitude . . . into the high-
ability class-groups, with little or no regard for their social class
background.

As a result, there are higher academic aspirations among students
from *all* social classes, which places students from wealthy families on the same footing as all others—a fact that well reflects
Thomas Jefferson's desire to provide challenging educational opportunities for "the youths of genius from among the classes of
the poor." The author concludes:

Students from advantaged households cannot automatically reproduce
their parents' status, but must compete successfully on the high school
entrance examinations. Conversely, talented students from disadvantaged households face fewer educational barriers to educational achievement and advancement. . . . Ability grouping, as practiced within the
educational context and larger societal context of Taiwan, seems to contribute to greater equality of educational opportunity.[126]

Just as significant are the 1999 findings of Takehiko Kariya and
James E. Rosenbaum, who studied Japan's experience with eliminating ability grouping from its schools. They report that the
elimination of ability grouping led to "bright flight," with many
of the highest-achieving students leaving public schools in favor
of private ones:

The private schools do not seem to have superior resources; indeed, they have much worse student/teacher ratios. Nor do they use financial incentives to draw better teachers from public schools. Nor do private schools boast of better instructors, better instructional techniques, or better curricula. . . . Private schools boast that they can create homogenous [like-ability] classes of students who can proceed more quickly . . . which allows students to learn more over the course of their high school career. . . . In contrast, the wide heterogeneity in de-tracked public schools may slow the coverage of curriculum. This slower pace may explain the decision of faster students to leave the public schools. . . . We conclude that the best-intentioned detracking reforms may not fix tracking problems. . . . If detracking lowers the achievement or engagement of faster students, it may drive them out of the public schools. . . . We hope American reformers can learn from this experience and avoid these outcomes.[127]

In addition, the authors note that those prefectures (school divisions) that were among the first to eliminate ability grouping have mounted intense efforts to reverse this mistake in the hope of attracting top students back into the public schools. At the current time, such efforts have been unsuccessful.

It is evident that hard-core middle school activists are ignoring such warnings. The words of activist Robert Slavin, noted earlier, reflect this view: "The jury is still out on how such untracking programs will work in practice, but there is little basis for the fear that they will be detrimental to the performance of high achievers."[128] Thus, middle school activists continue to sneer at the concern that the quality of education is lowered when ability grouping is eliminated.

Furthermore, if one middle school goal is expanded opportunities for minority students, activists should think twice about the policies they are promoting—such as the elimination of ability grouping. We have seen how the results in Taiwan indicate that with ability grouping, talented children from disadvantaged backgrounds can access educational opportunities to match their abilities. However, in this country, research by Tom Loveless indicates that "black achievement may actually suffer from tracking's abolition."[129]

These findings match the conclusions of a comprehensive study that addressed the impact of current ability grouping practices by analyzing the relationship between ability grouping and achievement, as measured by the National Education Longitudinal Study

(NELS), a study that followed students over time from grade 8 to grade 12. The authors concluded:

We find no evidence that low ability students are harmed by being grouped together, and conclude that the trend away from tracking [ability grouping] has been misguided. . . . We find that tracking [ability grouping] programs are associated with test score *gains* for students in the bottom third of the initial test score distribution. We conclude that the move to end tracking may harm the very students that it is intended to help. . . . We can find no evidence that detracking America's schools, as is currently in vogue, will improve outcomes among disadvantaged students. This trend may instead hurt the very students that detracking is intended to help.[130] (emphasis in the original)

Occasionally, even the popular press is beginning to present a different perspective—a perspective critical of the movement to eliminate ability grouping: "The Miseducation of Our Gifted Children" appeared in *Education Week*[131] and "Sacrificing Kids on the Altar of Equality" appeared in the *Wall Street Journal*.[132] In November 1998, *School Board News* ran an article titled "School Leaders, Researchers, Re-examining Middle School Reform." The author raised the following question:

Has the middle-school concept gone too far in catering to the social and emotional developmental needs of young adolescents at the expense of academic performance? That's exactly what some education experts and school leaders are charging.[133]

Some politicians have even entered the debate. In 1996, British prime minister Tony Blair announced that government schools in Great Britain must abandon heterogeneous (mixed-ability) grouping and return to homogeneous (same-ability) grouping. An article titled "Blair turns on mixed-ability myth" declared that this move "amount[s] to a secondary school revolution." It goes on to say that:

Mixed-ability teaching, in which the most gifted and the slowest students are taught at the same speed in the same classrooms, has been identified by critics as a major contributor to sliding standards.

The article then quotes Blair's remarks:

True equality must give everyone the education that helps them achieve all they can. That implies special help for those who need it; a challenging education for the averagely gifted pupil; and the full extension of the capacity of the intellectually gifted.[134]

It appears that our friends across the Atlantic have already awakened to the devastation wrought by anti-gifted practices, and have taken bold and decisive steps to return to a more common-sense approach to meeting the educational needs of high ability students.

CONCLUSION

The attitudes of many middle school advocates remain unwavering in their strident opposition to ability grouping, in spite of reasonable requests for accommodations for gifted learners. It appears that middle school activists will consider options for gifted learners only if such options fit within the heterogeneous (mixed-ability) grouping organization of the middle school plan. A position statement on ability grouping issued by the NMSA in 2001 merely dances around the issue. In two and one-half pages of text, only one sentence directly addresses ability grouping: "When students are grouped and regrouped for purposes of instruction, the assignment is temporary and based on diagnosed needs, interests, and talents of students." Does the NMSA support this? Oppose it? The statement says little or nothing. It is notable that the majority of the text discusses how middle schools have a "non-negotiable commitment" not only to academic success, but more importantly to "healthy development," signaling that middle school activists still support a strong non-academic mission.

There is little doubt that the move away from ability grouping may be a motivating factor behind the growing movement in this country toward home schooling, vouchers, and other forms of school choice that favor options other than the public schools.[135] These options are well on their way to becoming the "alternative instructional arrangements" identified earlier by Tomlinson. Research indicates that, when public schools eliminate ability grouping, families with the means to do so often make other instructional choices, resulting in increasing proportions of students from low-income families remaining in the schools which others are fleeing.[136] So while the NMSA extols the perceived virtues of American middle schools with statements commending

support for a "commitment to social equity," and that "heterogeneous assignment of students is the norm," parents are becoming increasingly aware that when heterogeneous (mixed-ability)
grouping *is* the norm, students at both ends of the ability spectrum
stand to not have their needs met. One comprehensive study indicates that 71 percent of those schools which embrace heterogeneous grouping have also eliminated all programs for both gifted
and remedial students.[137]

Chapter 7 will provide an in-depth analysis of the beliefs that
undergird the movement to eliminate ability grouping, which include: (1) the belief in equality of outcomes through the leveling
of achievement, (2) the belief in questioning the value of the individual, (3) the belief in the supremacy of the group, (4) the belief
that gifted learners should address the needs of others at the expense of their own academic needs, and (5) the belief in the negative consequences of competition.

NOTES

1. C. Hastings, "Ending ability grouping is a moral imperative," *Educational Leadership*, vol. 50, no. 2 (October 1992), p. 14. Copyrighted material used with permission from the Association for Supervision and
Curriculum Development (ASCD).

2. For example, see B. Grossen, "How should we group to achieve
excellence with equity?" *Effective School Practices*, vol. 15, no. 2 (Spring
1996); E.D. Fiedler, R.E. Lange, & S. Winebrenner, "In search of reality:
Unraveling the myths about tracking, ability grouping, and the gifted,"
Roeper Review, vol. 16, no. 1 (1993), pp. 4–7; and J.F. Feldhusen & S. Moon,
"Grouping gifted students: Issues and concerns," *Gifted Child Quarterly*,
vol. 36, no. 2 (1992), pp. 63–67.

3. Fiedler, Lange, & Winebrenner (1993); Feldhusen & Moon (1992).

4. J.H. Johnston & G.C. Markle, "Gifted and talented education: Part
I: Definition, identification, rationale," *Middle School Journal*, vol. 23, no.
2 (November 1991), pp. 52–55.

5. M.L. Goldberg, "Issues in the education of gifted and talented
children," *Roeper Review*, vol. 8, no. 4 (1986), pp. 226–233.

6. J.J. Gallagher, "Equity vs. excellence: An educational drama," *Roeper Review*, vol. 8, no. 4 (May 1986), pp. 233–235; Goldberg (1986); T.R.
McDaniel, "Mainstreaming the gifted: Historical perspectives on excellence and equity," *Roeper Review*, vol. 11, no. 3 (1989), pp. 171–172.

7. See, for example: Feldhusen & Moon (1992); J.J. Gallagher, "Education reform, values, and gifted students," *Gifted Child Quarterly*, vol.
35, no. 1 (1991), pp. 12–19; J.S. Renzulli & S. Reis, "The reform movement

and the quiet crisis in gifted education," *Gifted Child Quarterly*, vol. 35, no. 1 (1991), pp. 26–35.

8. See J. Oakes, "Beyond tracking," *Educational Horizons*, vol. 65, no. 1 (1986a), pp. 32–35; J. Oakes, "Keeping track, part 1: The policy and practice of curriculum inequality," *Phi Delta Kappan*, vol. 68, no. 1 (September 1986b), pp. 12–17; J. Oakes, "Keeping track, part 2: Curriculum inequality and school reforms," *Phi Delta Kappan*, vol. 68, no. 2 (October 1986c), pp. 148–154; M. Sapon-Shevin, "The tug-of-war nobody wins: Allocation of educational resources for handicapped, gifted, and 'typical' students," *Curriculum Inquiry*, vol. 14, no. 1 (1984), pp. 57–81; and M. Sapon-Shevin, *Playing Favorites: Gifted Education and the Disruption of Community* (Albany: State University of New York Press, 1994a).

9. See, for example, Fiedler, Lange, & Winebrenner (1992); J.A. Kulik, *An Analysis of the Research on Ability Grouping: Historical and Contemporary Perspectives* (Storrs, Conn.: National Research Center on the Gifted and Talented, 1992), monograph no. 9204; A. Wallach, Review of the book *Keeping Track: How Schools Structure Inequality, Thrust*, vol. 17 (1987), pp. 36–39; K. Rogers, "Grouping the gifted and talented: Questions and answers," *Roeper Review*, vol. 16, no. 1 (1993), pp. 8–12.

10. Thomas Jefferson, *Notes on Virginia* Q.XIV (1782), Electronic Text Center, University of Virginia Library, ME 2:206.

11. J.F. Feldhusen, "Susan Allan sets the record straight: Response to Allan," *Educational Leadership*, vol. 48, no. 6 (March 1991), p. 66. Copyrighted material used with permission from the Association for Supervision and Curriculum Development (ASCD).

12. F.L. Splittgerber & R. Allen, *A Comparison of Principals' and National Leaders' Perceptions toward the Middle School* (Washington, D.C.: U.S. Department of Education Office of Educational Research and Improvement, 1981), ERIC document number ED 206 081.

13. W. Klingele, *Teaching in the Middle Schools* (Boston: Allyn & Bacon, 1979).

14. S.D. Thompson, *Guidelines for Improving SAT Scores* (Reston, Va.: National Association of Secondary School Principals, 1978). I would like to extend my thanks to Professor Daniel Singal of Hobart and William Smith Colleges for providing me with this difficult-to-find text. The first reference I saw to this study was in an excellent article by Dr. Singal: "The other crisis in American education," *The Atlantic Monthly* (November 1991), pp. 59–74.

15. W.M. Alexander & P.S. George, *The Exemplary Middle School* (New York: Holt, Rinehart & Winston, 1981), pp. 169, 170.

16. *This We Believe* (Columbus, Ohio: National Middle School Association, 1982), p. 11.

17. M. Sapon-Shevin, "Mainstreaming the handicapped, segregating the gifted: Theoretical and pragmatic concerns," paper presented at the

annual meeting of the Educational Research Association, 1982, ERIC document number ED 218 835, pp. 12, 27.

18. J.H. Johnston & G.C. Markle, "What research says to the practitioner about ability grouping," *Middle School Journal*, vol. 14, no. 4 (August 1983), pp. 28–30, 28, 30. Copyrighted material used with permission from the National Middle School Association (NMSA).

19. Sapon-Shevin (1984), pp. 74, 68, 65.

20. In 1985, the following authors published reviews of the book *Keeping Track: How Schools Structure Inequality*: C. Coffman, *NASSP Bulletin*, vol. 69 (November 1985), pp. 130–131; R. King, *The London Times Higher Education Supplement*, no. 667 (August 16, 1985), p. 15; M.D. Thomas, *The American School Board Journal*, vol. 172 (December 1985), pp. 22–23.

21. In 1986, the following authors published reviews of the book *Keeping Track: How Schools Structure Inequality*: N.L. Arnez, *The Journal of Negro Education*, vol. 55, pp. 244–246; L. Biemer, *Media and Methods*, vol. 23, pp. 52–54; Anonymous, *Delta-Kappa-Gamma Bulletin*, vol. 52, no. 4, p. 7; K. Dougherty, *The Review of Education*, vol. 12, pp. 34–38; A. Gamoran, *American Journal of Education*, vol. 94, no. 2, pp. 268–272; F.M. Hammack, *Phi Delta Kappan*, vol. 68, pp. 332–334; C. Jurkowitz, *Educational Leadership*, vol. 43, no. 3 (November), pp. 92–93; M. Oromaner, *Contemporary Sociology*, vol. 15, no. 1, pp. 93–94; Strike, *Teachers College Record*, vol. 87, no. 3, pp. 441–444; and M. Weinberg, *Educational Studies*, vol. 17, pp. 436–442.

22. In 1987, the following authors published reviews of the book *Keeping Track: How Schools Structure Inequality*: B. Heyns, *American Journal of Sociology*, vol. 93, no. 2, pp. 508–510; D. Karen, *Harvard Educational Review*, vol. 57, pp. 495–500; A.C. Kerckhoff, *Contemporary Sociology*, vol. 16, no. 4, pp. 573–574; G. Lewis, *Childhood Education*, vol. 63, p. 216; A. Wallach, *Thrust*, vol. 17, pp. 36–39.

23. J. Oakes, *Keeping Track: How Schools Structure Inequality* (New Haven, Conn.: Yale University Press, 1985), p. 211

24. J.I. Goodlad & J. Oakes, "We must offer equal access to knowledge," *Educational Leadership*, vol. 45, no. 5 (February 1988), p. 22. Copyrighted material used with permission from the Association for Supervision and Curriculum Development (ASCD).

25. J.H. Johnston & G.C. Markle, *What Research Says to the Middle Level Practitioner* (Columbus, Ohio: National Middle School Association, 1986), p. 59.

26. Oakes (1986b, 1986c). See also Oakes (1986a), p. 17.

27. J. Oakes, "Curriculum inequality and school reform," *Equity and Excellence*, vol. 23, nos. 1–2, (1987/1988), pp. 8–13; K.D. Trimble & R.L Sinclair, "On the wrong track: Ability grouping and the threat to equity," *Equity and Excellence*, vol. 23, nos. 1–2 (1987/1988), pp. 15–21, 20.

28. P.S. George, "Tracking and ability grouping: Which way for the

middle school?" *Middle School Journal*, vol. 20, no. 1 (September 1988a), pp. 24, 26, 27.

29. P.S. George, "Education 2000: Which way the middle school?" *Middle School Journal*, vol. 62, no. 1 (1988b), p. 14.

30. National Middle School Association, Resolution 88.3 (1988).

31. *Middle Level Education's Responsibility for Intellectual Development* (Reston, Va.: National Association of Secondary School Principals, 1989), p. 17.

32. *Turning Points: Preparing American Youth for the 21st Century* (Washington, D.C.: Carnegie Council on Adolescent Development, 1989), pp. 66, 49.

33. For example, see A. Jackson, "From knowledge to practice: Implementing the recommendations of *Turning Points*," *Middle School Journal*, vol. 21, no. 3 (January 1990), pp. 1–3; and C.F. Toepfer, "Implementing *Turning Points*: Major issues to be faced," *Middle School Journal*, vol. 21, no. 5 (May 1990), pp. 18–21.

34. P. Welsh, "Fast Track Trap: How Ability Grouping Hurts Our Schools, Kids, and Families," *Washington Post Outlook*, September 16, 1990, p. 1+.

35. J. O'Neil, "Gifted education," *ASCD Education Update* (October 1990), p. 7.

36. National Middle School Association annual conference program (1990), p. 128.

37. National Middle School Association annual conference program (1991), p. 93.

38. O'Neil (1990), p. 7.

39. See S.D. Allan, "Ability grouping research reviews: What do they say about grouping and the gifted?" *Educational Leadership*, vol. 48, no. 7 (April 1991), pp. 60–65; Feldhusen (1991), p. 66; J.A. Kulik, "Findings on grouping are often distorted: Response to Allan," *Educational Leadership*, vol. 48, no. 6 (March 1991), p. 67; R.E. Slavin, "Are cooperative learning and 'untracking' harmful to the gifted? Response to Allan," *Educational Leadership*, vol. 48, no. 6 (March 1991), pp. 68–71.

40. Hastings (1992), p. 14.

41. National Middle School Association annual conference program (1992), p. 58.

42. National Middle School Association annual conference program (1993), pp. 74, 68.

43. National Middle School Association annual conference program (1995), pp. 116, 127, 94.

44. T.O. Erb, "Encouraging gifted performance in middle schools," *Midpoints*, vol. 3, no. 1 (1992), p. 17. Copyrighted material used with permission from the National Middle School Association (NMSA).

45. R.A. Lotan, P.E. Swanson, & G.K. LeTendre, "Strategies for de-tracked middle schools: Curricular materials, instructional strategies, and

access to learning," *Middle School Journal*, vol. 24, no. 1 (September 1992), p. 4.

46. P.S. George, "Tracking and Ability Grouping in the Middle School: Ten Tentative Truths," *Middle School Journal*, vol. 24, no. 4 (March 1993), pp. 17–24.

47. C. Ascher, "Successful detracking in middle and senior high schools," *ERIC Digest*, no. 82 (October 1992).

48. R.E. Slavin & J.H. Braddock, "Ability grouping: On the wrong track," *College Board Review*, vol. 168 (1993), pp. 17–18.

49. A. Wheelock, "The Case for Untracking," *Educational Leadership*, vol. 50, no. 2 (October 1992), pp. 6–10.

50. *The Middle School and Beyond* (Alexandria, Va.: Association for Supervision and Curriculum Development, 1992), p. 75.

51. P.S. George, *How to Untrack Your School* (Alexandria, Va.: Association for Supervision and Curriculum Development, 1992), p. 9.

52. R.S. Marsh & M.A. Raywid, "How to make detracking work," *Phi Delta Kappan*, vol. 76, no. 4 (December 1994), p. 315.

53. See R.M. Jaeger & J.A. Hattie, "Detracking America's schools," *Phi Delta Kappan*, vol. 77, no. 3 (November 1995), pp. 218–219; R.E. Slavin, "Detracking and its detrackers," *Phi Delta Kappan*, vol. 77, no. 3 (November 1995), pp. 220–221; and R. Smith-Maddox & A. Wheelock, "Untracking and students' futures," *Phi Delta Kappan*, vol. 77, no. 3 (November 1995), pp. 222–228; J.J. Gallagher, "Comments on 'The reform without cost?' " *Phi Delta Kappan*, vol. 77, no. 3 (November 1995), pp. 216–217.

54. D.J. Brewer, D.I. Rees, & L.M. Argys, "Detracking America's schools: The reform without cost?" *Phi Delta Kappan*, vol. 77, no. 3 (November 1995), p. 214.

55. Slavin (1995), p. 221.

56. D.J. Brewer, D.I. Rees, & L.M. Argys, "The reform without cost: A reply to our critics," *Phi Delta Kappan*, vol. 77, no. 6 (February 1996), p. 444.

57. R.E. Slavin, "Mastery Learning Reconsidered," *Review of Educational Research*, vol. 57, no. 2 (1987a) pp. 206, 205–206, 206.

58. B.A. Sizemore, "The politics of curriculum, race, and class," *Journal of Negro Education*, vol. 59, no. 1 (1990), p. 83.

59. E.G. Cohen, "Teaching in multiculturally heterogeneous classrooms: Findings from a model program," *The McGill Journal of Education*, vol. 26 (1991), p. 21.

60. M. Sapon-Shevin, "Cooperative learning and middle schools: What would it take to really do it right?" *Theory into Practice*, vol. 33, no. 3 (1994b), p. 189.

61. V.E. Lee & J.B. Smith, "Effects of restructuring on the achievement and engagement of middle-grade students," *Sociology of Education*, vol. 66 (July 1993), p. 180.

62. R.E. Slavin, "Achievement effects of ability grouping in secondary

schools: A best-evidence synthesis," *Review of Educational Research*, vol. 60 (Fall 1990), p. 494.

63. C.A. Tomlinson, "Gifted education and the middle school movement: Two voices on teaching the academically talented," *Journal for the Education of the Gifted*, vol. 15, no. 3 (1992), p. 231.

64. Allan (1991), pp. 65, 62.

65. R. Scott, "Untracking advocates make incredible claims," *Educational Leadership*, vol. 51, no. 2 (October 1993), p. 79; and D.J. Cocking, "Ability grouping: Don't throw the baby out with the bathwater," *Gifted Child Today*, vol. 13, no. 3 (May/June 1990), p. 13.

66. K. Rogers, *The Relationship of Grouping Practices to the Education of the Gifted and Talented Learner*, The National Center on the Gifted and Talented Research Based Decision Making Series, No. 1 (Storrs: University of Connecticut, 1991), pp. 2, 4.

67. J. Kulik & C. Kulik, *Analysis of the Research on Ability Grouping: Historical and Contemporary Perspectives*, National Research Center on the Gifted and Talented Research-Based Decision Making Series, monograph no. 9204 (Storrs: University of Connecticut, 1982); and J. Kulik & C. Kulik, "Effects of ability grouping on student achievement," *Equity and Excellence*, vol. 23, nos. 1–2 (1987), pp. 22–29.

68. See A. Gamoran, "The stratification of high school learning opportunities," *Sociology of Education*, vol. 60 (1987), pp. 135–155; A. Gamoran, "How tracking affects achievement: Research and recommendations," *Newsletter of the National Center for Effective Schools*, vol. 5, no. 1 (1990), pp. 2–6; A. Gamoran & M. Berends, "The effects of stratification in secondary schools: Synthesis of survey and ethnographic research," *Review of Educational Research*, vol. 57, no. 4 (1987), pp. 415–435.

69. Allan (1991); J. Kulik & C. Kulik, "Ability grouping and gifted students," in N. Colangelo & G.A. Davis (Eds.), *Handbook of Gifted Education* (Boston: Allyn & Bacon, 1990), pp. 178–196; Rogers (1991).

70. J.F. Feldhusen, "Gifted students must have time together in learning activities at their level and pace," *Images*, vol. 5, no. 2 (1991b), p. 2.

71. D. Schunk, "Peer models and children's behavioral change," *Review of Educational Research*, vol. 57, no. 2 (1987), pp. 149–174.

72. See J.F. Feldhusen, "Why the public schools will continue to neglect the gifted," *Gifted Child Quarterly*, vol. 12, no. 2 (1989), pp. 55–59; J.F. Feldhusen & M.F. Sayler, "Special classes for academically gifted youth," *Roeper Review*, vol. 12, no. 4 (1990), pp. 244–249.

73. Feldhusen & Moon (1992). Copyrighted material used with permission from the National Association for Gifted Children (NAGC).

74. J.J. Gallagher, "Academic effectiveness or social reform? A response to Robert Slavin and Jomills H. Braddock III," *The College Board Review*, no. 168 (Summer 1993), p. 18. Copyright © 1993 by College En-

trance Examination Board. Reproduced with permission. All rights reserved. www.collegeboard.com.

75. J. VanTassel-Baska, *Planning Effective Curriculum for Gifted Learners* (Denver, Colo.: Love Publishing, 1992), p. 13.

76. Fiedler, Lange, & Winebrenner (1993), p. 4.

77. Over the past four decades, a number of major surveys have been conducted on middle-level practices. (It should be noted that a well-known middle school survey conducted by Gallagher, Coleman, and Nelson [1993a, 1993b, 1993c] is not included in this section, as it was strictly a survey of attitudes—not of practices. Also, the issue of peer tutoring was not addressed as an individual item on the survey questionnaires. As has been noted, it is often included within the topic of cooperative learning.) This series of surveys includes:

1965 Survey: *The Junior High School Principalship* set forth the results of a survey of 4,496 junior high principals, representing over half of all junior high and middle schools in existence at the time of the survey in 1965. D.A. Rock & J.K. Hemphill, *Report of the Junior High School Principalship* (Washington, D.C.: National Association of Secondary School Principals, 1966).

1980 Survey: *The Middle Level Principalship: A Survey of Middle Level Principals and Programs* was the report of a survey conducted with 1,413 middle-level principals sponsored by NASSP. J. Valentine, D.C. Clark, N.C. Nickerson, & J.W. Keefe, *The Middle Level Principalship* (Reston, Va.: National Association of Secondary School Principals, 1981). It was similar in content to the 1965 survey (above) that was sponsored by the same organization.

1988 Survey: A 1988 survey conducted by the Center for Research on Elementary and Middle Grades at Johns Hopkins University evaluated the responses from 2,400 middle school principals on the degree to which various recommended practices for middle-level education were being implemented in their schools. The results were disseminated in the February 1990 edition of *Phi Delta Kappan*, vol. 71, no. 6: J.L. Epstein, "What matters in the middle grades—Grade span or practices?" pp. 438–444; J.H. Braddock, "Tracking the middle grades: National patterns of grouping for instruction," pp. 445–449; H.J. Becker, "Curriculum and instruction in middle-grade schools," pp. 450–457; D.J. MacIver, "Meeting the needs of young adolescents: Advisory groups, interdisciplinary teaching teams, and school transition programs," pp. 458–464; and J.M. Mc-Partland, "Staffing decisions in the middle grades: Balancing quality instruction and teacher/student relations," pp. 465–469; the November 1990 edition of the *Middle School Journal*, vol. 22, no. 2: J.L. Epstein and D.J. MacIver, "National practices and trends in the middle grades," pp. 36–40; and in the book *Education in the Middle Grades: National Prac-*

tices and Trends by J.L. Epstein and D.J. MacIver (Macon, Ga.: Panaprint, 1990).

1989 Survey: The authors of this survey compared 93 middle schools identified as "Schools of Excellence" by the National Institute of Education with a control group of 154 non-identified schools on the basis of their degree of match with a list of ten components describing recommended middle school practice. N.A. Connors & J.L. Irvin, "Is 'middle-schoolness' an indicator of excellence?" *Middle School Journal*, vol. 20, no. 5 (May 1989), pp. 12–14. Copyrighted material used with permission from the National Middle School Association (NMSA).

1993 Survey: NASSP conducted a survey of middle-level principals, assistant principals, and leadership team members (lead teachers) during the winter of 1991–1992. A stratified sample of 2,000 middle schools was identified for participation, but only 570 principals, or 29 percent, responded. Results were published in J. W. Valentine, D.C. Clark, J.L. Irvin, J.W. Keefe, & G. Melton, *Leadership in Middle Level Education: A National Survey of Middle Level Leaders and Schools* (Reston, Va.: National Association of Secondary School Principals, 1993), as well as in the September 1994 issue (vol. 26, no. 1) of the *Middle School Journal*: J.L. Irvin, J.W. Valentine, & D.C. Clark, "Essential elements of a true middle school: What should be vs. what is," pp. 45–58; and J.L. Irvin, "Middle level research is coming of age," pp. 68–70. It should be noted that the authors' anti-gifted bias clearly shows, some of the findings lack internal consistency, and there are times when the authors' conclusions do not match their data.

1995 Survey: A study was conducted in 1995 by the National Research Center on Gifted and Talented to determine how current middle-level schools are addressing the needs of diverse learners, including gifted learners. The survey instrument was developed by gleaning principles and practices associated with middle-level education from a review of the related literature. It was administered to a stratified sample of middle schools throughout the nation, and 500 principals and 449 teachers responded. T. Moon, C.A. Tomlinson, & C.M. Callahan, *Academic Diversity in the Middle School: Results of a National Survey of Middle School Administrators and Teachers*, monograph no. 95124 (Charlottesville, VA: National Research Center on the Gifted and Talented, 1995).

2001 Survey: This study was conducted by the National Association of Secondary School Principals in the spring and summer of 2000. Although the authors claim that this is the first study to have sent surveys to all American middle schools, that distinction actually belongs to the 1965 survey by Rock and Hemphill (cited above). Responses were obtained from 1,423 middle-level principals. D. Clark, V. Petzko, S. Lucas, & J. Valentine, *Research Findings from the 2000 National Study of Leadership in*

Middle Level Schools, presented at the National Middle School Association annual convention, Washington, D.C., November 1, 2002.

78. Rock & Hemphill (1966), pp. 44, 6, 46, 47.

79. Valentine et al. (1981), pp. 70, 84.

80. Epstein & MacIver (1990), pp. 13, 14, 15.

81. Moon, Tomlinson, & Callahan (1995).

82. Clark et al. (2001).

83. V. Petzko, conference session tape for session #1836, NMSA annual conference (2001).

84. Ibid.

85. J. Valentine, conference session tape for session #1836, NMSA annual conference (2001).

86. Connors & Irvin (1989).

87. Valentine et al. (1993).

88. Connors & Irvin (1989), pp. 12, 13, 14.

89. Valentine et al. (1993), pp. 56, 57, 56, 70, 85, 109.

90. Ibid., pp. 58, 85, 109, 58–59.

91. See R. Mills, "Grouping students for instruction: Issues of equity and effectiveness," in Judith L. Irvin (Ed.), *What Current Research Says to the Middle Level Practitioner* (Columbus Ohio: National Middle School Association, 1997), pp. 87–94; and R. Mills, "Grouping students for instruction in middle school," *ERIC Digest* (June 1998), EDO-PS-98-4.

92. Oakes (1985).

93. S. Willis, "Mainstreaming the gifted," ASCD *Education Update,* vol. 37, no. 2 (February 1995), pp. 1, 4, 5.

94. C.A. Tomlinson, "Gifted learners and the middle school: Problem or promise?" in *Gifted Education and Middle Schools* (Reston, Va.: Council for Exceptional Children, 1995a), pp. 31–34; "Differentiating instruction in the mixed-ability middle school classroom" (Reston, Va.: Council for Exceptional Children, 1995b), pp. 35–36; and "Instructional and management strategies for differentiated, mixed-ability classrooms" (Reston, Va.: Council for Exceptional Children, 1995c) pp. 39–40.

95. P.S. George, "In balance: Gifted education and middle schools," video script (Reston, Va.: Council for Exceptional Children, 1995), p. 48.

96. See A.S. Wells & I. Serna, "The politics of culture: Understanding local political resistance to detracking in racially-mixed schools," *Harvard Educational Review,* vol. 66, no. 1 (1996), pp. 93–118; and R.S. Weinstein, "High standards in a tracked system of schooling: For which students and with what educational support? *Educational Researcher,* vol. 25, no. 8 (1996), pp. 16–19.

97. P. Schmidt, "Massachusetts leads mounting charge against ability grouping," *Education Week* (January 13, 1993), pp. 1, 22, 24.

98. S. Denny, "How Fairfax fails the 'normal' student," *Washington Post* (August 14, 1994).

99. J. Johnson & J. Immerwahr, *First Things First: What Americans Expect from the Public Schools* (New York: Public Agenda, 1994), p. 19.

100. S. Farkas & J. Johnson, *Given the Circumstances: Teachers Talk about Public Education Today* (New York: Public Agenda, 1996), p. 20. It should be noted that the way in which the question was stated might have been confusing: *"Now I'm going to read you some ideas for changing the way public schools teach. For each, I'd like you to tell me if you think it would improve kids' academic achievement. . . . How about: Mixing fast learners and slow learners in the same class so that slower kids learn from faster kids"* (Johnson & Immerwahr, 1994, p. 42; Farkas & Johnson, 1996, p. 41).

This question is problematic in several ways. First, it does not indicate *how* slower students are expected to learn. By example? By peer tutoring? Evidence suggests that neither of these practices are conducive to meeting the academic needs of gifted students. The mere presence of high ability students does not necessarily cause average and below average students to imitate them as "role models," as research has shown that children tend to model or imitate those of like ability (Schunk, 1987). And the practice of having high-achieving students "tutor" others, as often happens in cooperative learning groups, is highly controversial, being viewed by some as unfair exploitation of children of high potential (Matthews, 1992; Robinson, 1990; S. Willis, "Cooperative learning fallout? Some see 'exploitation' of gifted students in mixed ability groups," *ASCD Education Update* [October 1990], pp. 6, 8).

Second, it presupposes that slower students *do* learn from faster students, an idea disputed by many researchers (Allan, 1991; Rogers, 1991; Schunk, 1987). Third, the preface to the question alludes to improving academic achievement, but it is unclear if this means improving academic achievement only for slower children or for all children.

101. Allan (1991), p. 65.

102. Rogers (1991); Allan (1991).

103. For example, see Feldhusen (1989), pp. 55–59; J.F. Feldhusen & D.M. Kennedy, "Effects of honors classes on secondary students," *Roeper Review*, vol. 11, no. 3 (March 1989), pp. 153–156; and J.F. Feldhusen & M.F. Sayler, "Special classes for academically gifted youth," *Roeper Review*, vol. 12, no. 4 (June 1990), pp. 244–249.

104. Allan (1991).

105. R. Scott, "Untracking advocates make incredible claims," *Educational Leadership*, vol. 51, no. 2 (October 1993), p. 79.

106. S.F. Farkas, J. Johnson, & A. Duffett, *Different Drummers: How Teachers of Teachers View Public Education* (New York: Public Agenda, 1997), pp. 32, 36.

107. Ibid., p. 9.

108. Ibid., p. 7.

109. J.F. Feldhusen (1991), p. 66. See also A. Tannenbaum, "Pre-

Sputnik to post-Watergate concern about the gifted," in A.H. Possow (Ed.), *The Gifted and Talented: Their Education and Development*, The 78th Yearbook of the National Society for the Study of Education (Chicago: University of Chicago Press, 1979), p. 16.

110. Sapon-Shevin (1994a), p. 35.

111. Tannebaum (1979), p. 7.

112. Johnson & Immerwahr (1994), p. 19.

113. Sapon-Shevin (1994a), p. 46.

114. J.D. Jones, B.E. Vanfossen, & M.E. Ensminger, "Individual and organizational predictors of high school track placement," *Sociology of Education*, vol. 68 (October 1995), p. 295.

115. K.L. Nyberg, J.D. McMillin, N. O'Neill-Rood, & J.M. Florence, "Ethnic differences in academic retracking: A four-year longitudinal study," *Journal of Educational Research*, vol. 91, no. 1 (1997), p. 41.

116. For a more in-depth discussion of these two cases, see B. Grossen, "How should we group to achieve excellence with equity?" *Effective School Practices*, vol. 15, no. 2 (Spring 1996), pp. 2–16; and D. Reschley, R. Kicklighter, & P. McKee, "Recent placement litigation, Part I, regular education grouping: Comparison of Marshall (1984, 1985) and Hobson (1967, 1969)," *School Psychology Review*, vol. 17, no. 1 (1988), pp. 9–21.

117. Trial Opinion, pp. 18–19, as cited in Grossen (1996), p. 3.

118. *Marshall et al. v. Georgia*, U.S. District Court for the Southern District of Georgia, CV482—233, June 28, 1984; Affd (11th cir. No. 84-8771, October 29, 1985). Note: The Court of Appeals decision was published as *Georgia State Conference of Branches of NAACP v. State of Georgia*, p. 100; as cited in Grossen (1996), p. 3.

119. See R.C. Spear, "Teacher perceptions of ability grouping practices in middle level schools," *Research in Middle Level Education*, vol. 18 (1994), pp. 117–130; and Moon, Tomlinson, and Callahan (1995).

120. Ibid.

121. B. Clark, "Social ideologies and gifted education in today's schools," *Peabody Journal of Education*, vol. 74, nos. 3 & 4 (1997), p. 83.

122. C.A. Tomlinson, "Making middle school work for gifted kids," *Principal* (September 1994), p. 53.

123. R. Gomm, "Strong claims, weak evidence: A response to Troyna's 'Ethnicity and the organization of learning groups'," *Educational Research*, vol. 37, no. 1 (Spring 1995), pp. 79–86.

124. N. Resh, "Track placement: How the 'sorting machine' works in Israel," *American Journal of Education*, vol. 106, no. 3 (May 1998), pp. 416–438.

125. Conversations with Chan Jee Kun and Poon Chew Leng, officials with the Singapore Ministry of Education, September 9, 2002.

126. C.M. Broaded, "The limits and possibilities of tracking: Some ev-

idence from Taiwan," *Sociology of Education*, vol. 70, no. 1 (January 1997), pp. 39, 48–49.

127. T. Kariya & J.E. Rosenbaum, "Bright flight: Unintended consequences of detracking policy in Japan," *American Journal of Education*, vol. 107, no. 3 (May 1999), pp. 226, 227, 228, 225. Copyright © 1999 by the University of Chicago. Copyrighted material used with the permission of the University of Chicago.

128. Slavin, (1995), p. 221.

129. T. Loveless, "Will tracking reform promote social equity?" *Educational Leadership*, vol. 55, no. 7 (April 1999), p. 29. See also S. Lucas and A. Gamoran, "Race and track assignment: A reconsideration with course-based indicators," working paper, University of Wisconsin, Madison, 1993.

130. D. Figlio & M. Page, *School choice and the distributional effects of ability tracking: Does separation increase equality?* (National Bureau of Economic Research, Cambridge, Mass.: December 2000), pp. 3, 29. Material used with permission of the lead author.

131. E. Winner, "The miseducation of our gifted children," *Education Week* (October 16, 1996).

132. J. Lloyd, "Sacrificing kids on the altar of equality," *Wall Street Journal* (August 7, 1996).

133. D. Brockett, "School leaders, researchers, re-examining middle school reform," *School Board News* (November 10, 1998), p. 5.

134. "Blair turns on mixed-ability myth," *London Daily Mail* (June 7, 1996).

135. See, for example, C.S. Collier, "Collier comments on Mosteller," *Harvard Educational Review*, vol. 67, no. 3 (1997), pp. 603–605; and L.R. Marcus & T. Johnson, "New possibilities for teaching diverse populations in tomorrow's high school," *High School Journal*, vol. 79, no. 2 (December 1995/ January 1996), pp. 134–138.

136. See Figlio & Page (2000), p. 21.

137. Ibid., p. 15.

CHAPTER 5

Cooperative Learning

Many times, while working in groups, I tried to take the initiative to go off on my own. I was reprimanded by the teachers and was told that breaking away from the group was wrong. I was forced to work with the group, at their pace, or face disciplinary actions. I found that if I disagreed with the group, I could not voice my opinion or I would quickly be hushed. I was not allowed to do anything on my own, or take things into my own hands. The teachers were quick to "correct" me and forced me to work only for my group as a whole.

Seventh grade student in Minnesota, 1993[1]

THE ISSUE DEFINED

Cooperative learning is an instructional strategy that encourages the use of small student groups in the classroom for instructional purposes. All group members are supposed to be responsible for helping and encouraging others, and the development of social skills is emphasized.[2] According to one author, cooperative learning and the middle school plan appear to be a natural fit: "A close examination of the goals of modern middle schools and the foundations of cooperative learning reveal that the two are highly complementary."[3] There are many different models of cooperative learning, each of which varies in terms of style and degree of popularity.[4]

As with the issue of ability grouping, the instructional strategy known as cooperative learning has proponents among supporters of the middle school concept,[5] while advocates for gifted education question its effectiveness for gifted learners.[6]

EVOLUTION OF THE CONTROVERSY

1960s–1970s: From College to Middle School

Published reports using the term *cooperative learning* first appeared in the late 1960s and early 1970s within the context of suggested instructional strategies for college and university students.[7] It appears to have first been suggested as an approach specifically for the middle school in 1971,[8] and throughout the rest of the 1970s the Johns Hopkins University Center for Social Organization of Schools conducted pilot studies of various small-group approaches, resulting in the development of several models for classroom use, while other educators independently began to experiment with the implementation of cooperative learning in the classroom.[9]

Explicit support for the active implementation of cooperative learning specifically at the middle school level goes back to the mid-1970s when the Ford Foundation sponsored a series of conferences on adolescent growth and development. One of the recommendations to emerge from these meetings was that "schools should provide an opportunity for peer and community interaction. Youth educating other youth should be encouraged."[10] This theme was similar to a report from the Association for Supervision and Curriculum Development (ASCD), that promoted group work at the middle school level for socialization purposes.[11]

1980s: Explosive Growth

Evidence suggests that the practice of cooperative learning had not yet been officially endorsed by the National Middle School Association (NMSA) in the early 1980s, as it is not mentioned in the 1982 edition of their policy statement *This We Believe*. However, interest in the concept of cooperative learning accelerated in the mid-1980s when Robert Slavin[12] and David and Roger Johnson,[13] now the leading names in the field of cooperative learning, each produced over 20 studies or reports on the subject. By the middle to late 1980s the topic began to appear in reports on middle school education, including two reports by the National Association of Secondary School Principals (NASSP),[14] as well as in the *Turning Points* report mentioned in Chapter 2, which suggested cooperative learning as an alternative to ability grouping. According to *Turning Points*, middle school educators must "ensure success for all students through the elimination of tracking by achievement level and promotion of cooperative learning."[15]

The number of conference sessions on the topic of cooperative learning went from single to double digits in 1988 (Appendix I), and remained high through the mid-1990s, coinciding with the massive decline in sessions on gifted learners (Appendix E), as well as with the shift from an emphasis on academic diversity to cultural diversity that occurred from 1991 to 1998 (Appendix B). It should be noted that sessions addressing cooperative learning preceded those on heterogeneous (mixed-ability) grouping by two years, indicating that cooperative learning was being presented as a strategy before the impetus for eliminating same-ability grouping began. However, It didn't take long for cooperative learning supporters to begin to market the concept as an alternative to ability grouping.[16]

The 1990s began with the education journal *Phi Delta Kappan* declaring that cooperative learning was a viable alternative to ability grouping:

Cooperative learning—an approach that allows students to work in small, mixed-ability learning teams—is perhaps the most widely recommended and best-documented instructional strategy for addressing the problem of student diversity in heterogeneous [mixed-ability] classrooms.[17]

The increased popularity of cooperative learning appears to have paralleled the decline in the use of ability grouping, and it was noted that "the strongest supporters of cooperative learning also tend to be the most vocal critics of ability grouping."[18] (See Table 3 later in this chapter.)

1990s: "Here to Stay"

In 1990, Robert Slavin declared that cooperative learning, with its "excellent research base, many viable and successful forms, and hundreds of thousands of enthusiastic adherents" was "here to stay,"[19] and an article in the *Middle School Journal* cautions advocates to avoid allowing cooperative learning to become "a passing fad."[20] By 1990, middle school advocates were told that "the research is clear that CL [cooperative learning] methods can significantly increase academic achievement"[21] and that this was a "highly recommended and proven practice."[22]

A 1990 edition of *Educational Leadership*, a publication of ASCD, featured 16 articles on the topic.[23] It is evident that concerns over the impact of cooperative learning had already been raised by advocates for gifted learners, as the first article displayed the following headline: "Cooperative Learning Can Benefit All Students, Even Those Who Are Low Achieving, Gifted or Mainstreamed."[24]

During the 1990s, journal articles on cooperative learning often appeared hand-in-hand with articles on ability grouping. As noted in Chapter 4, *Educational Leadership* devoted nearly an entire issue to the subjects, in 1991 and again in 1992. The March 1991 issue featured a piece by Susan Allan addressing ability grouping and cooperative learning issues, followed by responses supporting her position and a response from Robert Slavin disputing her assertions. The October 1992 issue featured an article by Ann Wheelock advocating detracking and an interview with Jeannie Oakes, followed by two articles addressing cooperative learning.[25]

Further strengthening the appeal of cooperative learning were the attitudes of professors at schools of education. According to one comprehensive study, large numbers of education professors surveyed endorsed team work where students receive only a group grade, and an even larger number of those surveyed believe that schools should work to avoid any sort of competition.[26]

Cooperative Learning and Social Change

In large measure, the driving push for the widespread use of cooperative learning was the belief that instructional practices in the schools could be used to implement social changes. According to social scientist Mara Sapon-Shevin:

Our goal should be schools in which cooperative learning can function as a catalyst—forcing us to uncover and dismantle the structures that separate and damage children, and reinvent schools that embody social and educational equity and justice.[27]

She is quite specific in articulating her utopian vision that cooperative learning will "move classrooms and society toward social justice and more equitable distribution of resources." In fact, she asserts that the implementation of cooperative learning would result in a utopia where most contemporary social ills would be solved:

In proposing "caring work" and the creation of communities of care as an underlying paradigm for cooperative learning . . . we envision a society in which no one gets lost, structured so that each citizen has an active role. All people would be guaranteed access to the resources of the society, including food, housing, health care, educational opportunities at all levels, and meaningful, well-paid work. Unemployment, poverty, homelessness—and the legacies of such hopelessness such as drug addiction—would be unheard of. . . . Childcare would be available to all requesting families, community-based care to home-bound senior citizens, and affordable housing to all.

So while some saw cooperative learning as just another instructional practice, others were promoting it as a way to awaken the "social, ethical, and political understanding" of students, since "cooperatively structured learning embodies values and practices that have transformative potential for [both] schools and society."[28]

RESPONSE FROM ADVOCATES FOR GIFTED LEARNERS

In 1991, cooperative learning activist Robert Slavin declared that "educators of the gifted should be in the forefront of the cooperative learning movement."[29] This was definitely not going to happen, as by the late 1980s and early 1990s members of the gifted community were raising questions about the growing use of cooperative learning and its effect on gifted learners. Advocates for gifted students had begun to see that the goals of cooperative learning were not necessary academic ones, but in many instances were social goals. According to James Gallagher: "Mr. Slavin promotes a social agenda for the schools rather than an academic one. He tries to convince the reader that his social agenda can be obtained at no cost to academic performance."[30] In other words, the academic achievement implications of cooperative learning were not of primary importance to many advocates. James Gallagher and his associates noted that:

The middle schools were . . . a major movement in this country that predates the current reform movement but has now been incorporated into it. . . . [Both the middle school movement and cooperative learning] have an emphasis on "equity goals," which often emphasize social behavior rather than academic and cognitive excellence. Both of these approaches have come into real or potential conflict with educators of the gifted, who have stressed the educational goal of excellence.[31]

It appears that the most significant early protests against cooperative learning may have come not from professionals, but from parents of gifted students, since the first explicit defense of cooperative learning is directed at them. "What to Say to Parents of Gifted Students" appeared in the April 1989 edition of the *Cooperative Link*, a publication associated with Johnson and Johnson. This article, which lacks any references to research and does not list an author, was written as an instruction manual for teachers and administrators for use with parents of gifted learners, and suggests numerous persuasive techniques intended to calm parents' fears. Parents of gifted students are characterized as "hard to convince," and thus cooperative learning advocates are given answers to a list of possible parental questions. Advocates are told to impress upon parents that there are numerous academic advantages for gifted students in heterogeneous (mixed-ability) learning groups—such as teaching other students.

In an almost prescient way, two articles appeared in a 1990 edition of *Journal for the Education of the Gifted* which alerted the field to the clash between advocates for gifted education and proponents of the middle school movement. In "Where Do Gifted Students Fit? An Examination of the Middle School Philosophy as it Relates to Ability Grouping and the Gifted Learner," Pamela Sicola makes the case that there exists a disconnect between the implementation of the middle school philosophy and the needs of gifted learners:

The solutions proposed by middle school philosophers for meeting the developmental needs of young adolescents, a decreased academic focus in favor of an increased affective focus in a heterogeneous setting . . . is incongruent with the solutions proposed by experts in the field of gifted education.[32]

In "Cooperation or Exploitation? The Argument Against Cooperative Learning for Gifted Students," Anne Robinson notes that the omission of gifted students from the studies on the effectiveness of cooperative learning "has produced some unfortunate translations into the world of practice. Overgeneralization is one of them." The author's conclusion, while not dealing specifically with middle-level education, is nonetheless relevant due to the popularity of cooperative learning at the middle level:

With increasing frequency, districts assert that the needs of their talented students are best met by helping others through cooperative learning strategies in the heterogeneous classroom. On that basis and to cope with the politically sensitive issue of tracking in secondary schools, some districts have ceased to offer advanced courses. Such policies are implemented in the face of evidence that advanced classes which offer subject matter acceleration produce clear, consistent, positive effects for talented students.[33]

As early as 1991, it is apparent that both middle school and cooperative learning activists had shifted into a defensive position on this issue. Robert Slavin, one of the leading proponents of cooperative learning, declared:

In the case of both untracking and cooperative learning, opposition is now developing among members of the same group: researchers, educators, and parents concerned about the education of gifted children.[34]

A 1992 article by Johnson and Johnson, "What to Say to Advocates for the Gifted," appears to be a longer version of the unattributed piece that appeared earlier in the *Cooperative Link*:

You can always tell when it's coming. A parent, colleague, administrator, or school board member stands up with a shrug and a smile, and you brace yourself, once again, to hear: "I'm an advocate of cooperative learning, *but* isn't the academic progress of gifted students slowed down when they work with lower achieving classmates?"[35] (emphasis in the original)

The authors then proceed to "prove" why such a concern is unwarranted. In the same year, an article in the *Middle School Journal* listed five points as "the most common arguments for the use of cooperative learning." It is curious that *all* of these justifications, or "common arguments," address gifted students. Obviously, this was a propaganda piece intended to provide middle school and cooperative learning activists with ammunition to use against those who were raising concerns over the impact of the widespread use of cooperative learning.

The "common arguments" were:

1. Gifted students will engage in greater information processing by explaining material to others;
2. Gifted students will learn how to work with others, how to communicate effectively, how to form productive relationships, how to share leadership and how to resolve conflicts;
3. Gifted students will enrich their self-esteem by being a major contributor to the group;
4. Gifted students will gain an acceptance of individual differences;
5. Gifted students will develop improved attitudes toward school because they will form closer peer affiliations.[36]

This list is followed by the assertion that "these are reasonable outcomes and they argue convincingly for the use of cooperative learning." This article is problematic in a number of ways. First, the list of "common arguments" is based upon false premises, implying that gifted students *will* learn more by teaching, *do* have the need to develop social skills, *do* have poor self-esteem, and *do* possess negative attitudes toward school. But what is more, this implies that the reason cooperative learning was developed was to meet the needs of gifted learners, an assertion one will find nowhere in the literature on cooperative learning. Interestingly, another issue actually raised by Johnson and Johnson is whether "group dependency upon the gifted student constitutes unfair exploitation." In spite of research evidence, the authors conclude that this question "remains unanswered."[37]

An exchange in the *Journal for the Education of the Gifted* between gifted advocate Ann Robinson and cooperative learning activist Robert Slavin summarized the arguments of both sides. Robinson identified the disadvantages of cooperative learning and noted that research studies found no student achievement differences that could be attributed to cooperative learning. Furthermore, she pointed out that in studies used by advocates of cooperative learning to support their position, students had demonstrated increases in basic skills, but not higher-level skills, and that the results were inaccurate due to a statistical phenomenon known as the "ceiling effect."[38] She called for caution in the "misuse and overuse" of cooperative learning with gifted students, and concluded:

Cooperative learning researchers and practitioners need to take responsibility for not being particularly interested in academically talented students. They are within their rights to devote their efforts elsewhere. However, citing literature with limited focus on talented students as justification for educational practices that directly affect them is incautious. These researchers need to acknowledge the limitations in their literature or cease to cite it as applicable.[39]

Advocates for cooperative learning did not agree. In a statement unsupported by citations, Slavin professed that "the best reason to use cooperative learning with gifted students is that they learn better in cooperative than in traditional classes."[40] However, Robinson responded:

If students are spending their time learning basic skills at a modest pace or are spending the majority of their time reviewing and teaching these skills to others, they will not have time to engage in other kinds of instructional experiences which are important to their development.[41]

Advocates for the gifted made the point that Slavin's research on the achievement effects of cooperative learning did not include effects on gifted children.[42] This would not be problematic if the omission had not produced a blanket overgeneralization and "unfortunate translations into the world of practice," a sentiment expressed by Robinson and echoed by researcher Susan Allan.[43] These "unfortunate translations" had real world results:

Gifted programs are being eroded by the increasing popularity of cooperative learning, and gifted students are being exploited in cooperative groups. . . . In the mistaken belief that heterogeneous cooperative learning groups benefit *all* students, schools are curtailing separate programs for the gifted. . . . In many middle schools, the trend to adopt cooperative learning has threatened to wipe out the entire [gifted] program.[44] (emphasis in the original)

More current research continues to give credence to the concerns expressed by advocates for gifted learners. One study reports the frustrations felt by high ability students who are forced to work in groups:

It is easy to understand why repetition of skills already mastered . . . evokes impatience with the pace of instruction—perhaps even boredom. . . . Most reformers sell cooperative learning as a means to enhance academic achievement; these same reformers urge educators to recruit their best students to serve as mentors for those who have not mastered the material. . . . Before such a vision is translated into a call for massive restructuring of our nation's schools, a great deal more needs to be learned about how cooperative learning affects academically able students—especially how such children feel about heterogeneous [mixed-ability] grouping and their obligation to instruct less able peers.[45]

Gifted Students Speak

What do gifted and high ability students themselves have to say about cooperative learning? In several studies on the use of cooperative learning, researchers found that "gifted students report feeling used, resentful, and frustrated by group work with students of lower ability,"[46] and that "when doing group work in a regular class, most of the time the gifted student ends up doing all the work and the others get all the credit." Gifted middle-level students in one study noted that they "spend a great deal of time teaching other students or checking their work,"[47] a practice leading to the conclusion that "when they are held to the level and pace of average students, gifted students are hurt academically, socially, and probably motivationally."[48]

Marian Matthews of Eastern New Mexico University is one of the best-known researchers on the effects of cooperative learning groups on gifted learners. Her 1992 interviews with gifted learners on their experiences in heterogeneous (mixed-ability) cooperative groups reveal that they "resent having to explain the material to students who won't listen to them" and "resent the time taken away from their own learning to work with uncooperative students." She states that gifted students often find that they must "do all the work," resulting in negative attitudes toward other group members. However, when working in homogeneous (like-ability) cooperative groups, gifted students "tend to develop the positive attitudes and gain the benefits" that cooperative learning supporters assert are the results of this approach.[49] Matthews' findings are similar to those of others which revealed "the intensity of [gifted students'] feelings when they have been obligated to spend extended periods of time in age-peer cooperative learning groups."[50]

In an extensive follow-up study in 1994, Matthews' initial results were replicated. She surveyed nearly 900 middle and high school students across the country and received comments such as the following:

A sixth grade female from Connecticut: I don't like working in groups because I always end up doing all the work. I do like working in groups that contain all gifted children or [those] willing to partake of the work. Our teachers *always* puts the gifted children with the troubled kids and expect us to help and improve *plus teach* them! The teachers don't care who is in your cooperative learning group and [they] don't try to change them. One or two smart kids end up doing 99.9 percent of the work, and get a slightly worse grade for not working together! (emphasis in the original)

A tenth grade female from Minnesota: The other students in the group will not help or try to get anything done or accept any kind of responsibility. Then, since no one cares about their grade and the group gets only one grade, I usually end up doing most or all of the work, and the others get an "A" because I did the project.

A sixth grade female from New York: Since I always end up doing everything, even when I try to get other people to do things, it is sort of like working by myself—except my teacher yells at me for doing everything and not giving anyone else a chance, which I did give (equal opportunity). It also takes longer because I have to wait for everyone to catch up to me.

An eleventh grade female from New York: I find that the attitudes of other students toward being smart, being "nerdy," eventually intimidates me into not even contributing. I feel like we accomplish nothing, and if we do, I end up doing most of the work. It is a generally frustrating, useless experience.[51]

These students had strong and poignant opinions on how cooperative learning had impacted their lives. However, Matthews' research results were distorted by social activist Mara Sapon-Shevin, who described the students' comments as expressions of "their distaste for having to work with students less capable," "their discomfort with other students," and "their reluctance to trust other, less-gifted students."[52] Both Sapon-Shevin and others believe that anything less than blissful acceptance of cooperative learning by gifted students is selfish, and such activists continue to be blithely convinced that heterogeneous (mixed-ability) groups are wonderful for all students:

Stronger students find working with and helping weaker ones intellectually stimulating and enriching. Their academic achievement continues to increase as they engage in the process of explaining the material to their team mates.[53]

Current studies echoing the findings of Matthews have come from researchers such as James Gallagher and his associates. According to one student in the Gallagher study: "Group work is usually unproductive because I am put as the leader to teach the others who could care less, and I end up doing all the work myself."[54]

In spite of Matthews' initial study and other evidence at that time,[55] in 1992 a leader in the middle school movement wrote: "Nowhere could I find in the gifted literature anything that suggested that cooperative groups were inherently bad for the gifted."[56] Although the peer review process can take up to two years or more, articles in the leading journals for gifted education appeared as though in response to the challenge. In 1992 and 1993, both *Gifted Child Quarterly* and *Roeper Review* published articles addressing the negative effects of cooperative learning on gifted students.[57]

"Social Loafing"

Why do gifted students resent working in heterogeneous (mixed-ability) groups? Are their claims of doing all the work exaggerated? The answer can be found by looking beyond the utopian pipedreams of social activists and extreme middle school proponents and examining the field of social psychology.

The problem of a reduction in individual effort when individuals are working in a group is so common that it even has a name—"social loafing." This phenomenon has been recognized by researchers for some time, being first described by Max Ringelmann in 1913.[58] In his discussion on individual versus group performance, he gave the example of motivational loss in a situation where a group provided power for a flour mill:

The result was mediocre because after only a little while, each man, trusting in his neighbor to furnish the desired effort, contented himself by merely following the movement of the crank, and sometimes even let himself be carried along by it.[59]

Social loafers don't care about evenly distributing the workload in a group project, choosing instead to let others do the work for them. It has been documented in numerous studies that individuals tend to put forth far less effort when working in groups than when working alone,[60] and it makes no difference if the task is important or trivial.[61]

The term *social loafing*, first introduced by Bibb Latané in 1979,[62] has since become an umbrella term that covers more specific types of social loafing. These have been identified as the "free rider effect" and the "sucker effect."[63]

The "free rider effect" occurs when group members recognize that the ability of a capable group member can guarantee the success of the group without their personal efforts. In other words, they see their contributions as unnecessary, since they will be able to partake in the group reward or outcome regardless of either the quality or quantity of their efforts. According to Norbert L. Kerr, a prominent researcher in this field, individuals he studied both "recognized and exploited . . . this opportunity to free ride, [thus] reducing their level of effort."[64] This reality is quite different from the naively utopian vision of Sapon-Shevin, who asserts that "an ethic of care pervades their group as students pay sensitive attention to each other. They give help when asked for it, and are always generous with encouragement and support."[65]

The "sucker effect" describes the role of any group member who is capable of carrying the "free rider"—but chooses not to. (This actually makes the term "sucker effect" a misnomer—the individual is choosing *not* to be a sucker.) A capable group member who recognizes that other group members are getting a free ride is faced with two choices. He or she can either: (1) work to the best of his or her ability, thus letting others have a free ride—with little or no contributions coming from the free riders; or (2) reduce the contributions and efforts of which he or she is personally capable in order to avoid both present and future attempts at exploitation by the group. According to Kerr, capable and responsible individuals who reduce their efforts in group situations are exhibiting the "sucker effect," because they see the situation as inequitable because "one contributes more to the group than others, but is not rewarded more than others," and they refuse to be exploited in this way. Kerr continues: "Apparently, the feelings of exploitation aroused by a free-riding partner are aversive enough to deflect subjects from the rational strategy; under certain conditions, people would apparently rather fail than carry a free rider."[66]

An example of this can be seen in the quote cited earlier from an eleventh grade female in Matthews' study, who stated that, while in cooperative learning groups, she is "eventually intimidate[d] . . . into not even contributing."[67] Obviously, though, most high ability students have a vested interest in maintaining their grades, so they avoid the "sucker effect" (that is, diminished efforts on their own part), and instead carry the load of the group for the free riders. This is congruent with the findings of two researchers who have identified a relationship between ability and the tendency to be a social loafer, finding that less-able group members are far more likely to engage in free-riding.[68]

Interestingly, some middle school activists actually *support* making gifted learners carry the responsibility for a group product. Writing in the *Middle School Journal*, Rachel Lotan and other middle school activists approve of the following teacher interaction: "Who is the facilitator in this group? Alicia? I want to remind you that it is your job to see that everyone in the group gets the help they need to understand the task."[69]

How can the effects of social loafing be eliminated, or at least controlled? Research indicates that when group members know that their work can be individually identified, social loafing (by both free riders and suckers) is lessened.[70] The reality of individual evaluation provides an incentive for individuals to strive for peak performance.

Although social loafing has been identified (if not by name at least by description) for nearly a century, cooperative learning enthusiasts act as though it doesn't exist. In their zeal for widespread implementation of cooperative learning, they have turned a deaf ear to a century of research by eminent social scientists who have studied group dynamics in depth. The leader in this field, Bibb Latané, sent forth this warning:

We suspect that the effects of social loafing have far-reaching and pro-found consequences both in our culture and in other cultures ... we must confess that we think social loafing can be regarded as a kind of social disease. It is a "disease" in that it has negative consequences for individuals, social institutions, and societies.[71]

The drive for using the middle schools as vehicles for social engineering has caused activists to ignore established scientific facts. The phenomenon of social loafing, the fraud of brain per-iodization—such facts are inconvenient to those who seek to jus-tify instructional practices they believe will lead to fundamental egalitarian social change.

Parents and Teachers Speak

In her 1994 survey on the response of gifted learners to coop-erative learning, Marian Matthews received the following feed-back from a teacher:

In regards to your survey (which I am thrilled to see you are doing!), I have received a great deal of feedback from parents and students. The students are grateful to have finally been asked how they feel and the parents are shocked to discover the intensity of *negative* feelings their children have that have been pent up inside them.[72] (emphasis in the original)

Around the same time, James Gallagher, Mary Ruth Coleman, and Suzanne Nelson, three advocates for gifted education, con-ducted a survey of attitudes among two groups: educators of the gifted and cooperative learning advocates. Issues which revealed strong differences between the two groups included whether the curriculum used with cooperative learning is appropriately chal-lenging for gifted students; whether enough evaluation has been conducted on the impact of cooperative learning on gifted stu-dents; and that gifted students express resentment toward being the "junior teacher."[73]

Sample quotes from teachers of gifted learners include:

[Cooperative learning] must be used with care for the gifted, or we are putting an artificial ceiling on their learning.

A main concern of these students now is that the regular classroom holds them back. This [cooperative learning] indicates a further impediment.

I feel [cooperative learning] grouping could work well if gifted students are frequently in the same group.

It is very wasteful to think that the best academic and intellectual ideas emerge from groups. They don't, and learning has got to have the major emphasis on personal effort.

It appears that the major objective of group practices is to reduce differences rather than adapt to differences.

The idea [of cooperative learning] and the reality are often very different.[74]

The survey results indicate that attitudes of teachers in both gifted and middle level education reflect the attitudes of the leaders of their respective groups, as expressed in both practitioner and research journal articles. The authors state that "a major gulf exists between the perceptions of these key groups of educators."[75]

Parents have also expressed frustration with cooperative learning. One parent, in recalling her daughter's middle school experience with cooperative learning, had this to say:

Parents spent hours shuttling students between houses, trying to coordinate the schedules of these pre-teens so everyone could meet at the same time. Invariably, it would be the same students who took on the majority of the workload to see that the job was done, because the whole group received the same grade. This cooperative grouping, intended to help slower students and to make leaders of faster students, in fact caused resentment when reality hit that not everyone carries the same load.[76]

Advocates for the gifted are not calling for a blanket rejection of all cooperative learning, but believe that there should not be a wholesale embrace of the concept until more research indicates how it can be best implemented. As stated by Marian Matthews:

Wholesale acceptance and advocacy of cooperative learning when we do not have a complete understanding of the learning process at work is at best unjustified and at worse immoral, especially when it is at the expense of gifted programming.[77]

SURVEY RESULTS ON COOPERATIVE LEARNING

Cooperative learning is addressed in some of the surveys that were discussed in Chapter 4.[78] In the 1988 survey of middle school principals, cooperative learning was listed as one of the "least used practices," with only 20 percent of schools reporting regular use. However, an additional 30 percent of principals surveyed noted that they intended to introduce the practice in the near future.[79] By 1995, 67 percent of the principals surveyed indicated that cooperative learning was used in schools at least weekly, a response that was consistent with the figure of 63 percent that was reported by teachers. Overall, 53 percent of the principals surveyed indicated that classes at their schools were organized for cooperative learning[80] (see Table 3).

It is obvious from the survey data that the growth of cooperative learning parallels the decline in the use of ability grouping, and it is now practiced as commonly as flexible ability grouping was over 30 years ago.

CONCLUSION

The position of cooperative learning enthusiasts has not changed over time. They consistently deny that cooperative learning has any negative academic impact on the education of gifted learners. Consider the following assertions:

Middle School Journal: Although some teachers and parents fear that cooperative groups in a heterogeneous [mixed-ability] class would tend to "water down" the curriculum, this has not been our experience.[81]

Robert Slavin: Sometimes a concern is expressed that cooperative learning will hold back high achievers. The research provides absolutely no support for this claim: high achievers gain from cooperative learning (relative to high achievers in traditional classes) just as much as do low and average achievers.[82]

Table 3
Ability Grouping and Cooperative Learning at the Middle School
Level: Practices Reported by Principals* (Reported in Percentages)

	1965	1980	1988	1995	2001
Tracking at all or some grade levels	20	11	26	9	N/A
Ability grouping used for certain subjects	68	74	56	10	72**
No ability grouping or tracking	9	11	18	73	15
Use of cooperative learning	N/A	N/A	20	53/67***	N/A

*Those surveys with noted interpretive problems as discussed in Chapter 4 are not included (Connors & Irvin, 1989; Valentine et al., 1993).

**This survey also reported that teachers grouped by ability within classrooms in 13 percent of schools responding.

***53 percent reported that classes were organized for cooperative learning; 67 percent reported that cooperative learning took place at least weekly.

As noted in Chapter 4, it is ironic to consider that, in 1987, Robert Slavin himself proclaimed that the achievement of high ability students suffers when they are held to the pace of their less-able classmates, a phenomenon that he christened the "Robin Hood Effect."[83] He has received stinging criticism for his denial that high-achieving students are held back, as well as for his unbridled promotion of cooperative learning. Again, according to James Gallagher:

Mr. Slavin promotes a social agenda for the schools rather than an academic one. He tries to convince the reader that his social agenda can be obtained at no cost to academic performance. That is a hard sell. Mr. Slavin points out that "Untracking must never be—or appear to be—taking from high achievers to give to low achievers." Yet that seems to be precisely what is happening out there in the countryside, with school systems abandoning honors courses and programs for gifted students—and citing Robert Slavin as their authority for doing so.[84]

As with the related issue of ability grouping, the attitudes of middle school advocates who support wholesale cooperative learning remain entrenched. If anything, their resolve may have been strengthened over time by the widespread use of this practice. The growth in the popularity of cooperative learning during the late 1980s is reflected in the number of NMSA conference sessions on the topic (Appendix I), and parallels the decline in the use of ability grouping. Cooperative learning, and the related practice of peer tutoring, are clearly the instructional groupings of choice for middle school activists.

Recent data continue to provide evidence that the widespread use of cooperative learning is having a detrimental effect on learning, at least in math. The 2000 National Assessment of Education Progress (NAEP) assessed math achievement among American students in grades 4, 8, and 12. Students in grades 4 and 8 who worked with other students to solve their math problems on a daily or weekly basis posted lower math achievement than those who did so on a monthly basis. The report concludes that students "generally seem to perform best when certain classroom activities were engaged in on a moderate basis, rather than on a daily basis."[85]

In addition, a major study on teacher training in math found that professional development courses for teachers that emphasize subject matter knowledge as opposed to special issues workshops such as "workshops in techniques for cooperative learning" resulted in higher academic achievement in math.[86]

A number of core beliefs driving the push for cooperative learning will be discussed in more detail in Chapter 7. As is the case with the efforts to eliminate ability grouping, these include the belief in equality of outcomes through the leveling of achievement, the belief in questioning the value of individuals, the belief in the supremacy of the group, the belief that gifted learners should address the needs of others at the expense of their own academic needs, and the belief in the negative consequences of competition.

NOTES

1. Tiffany Yecke, the author's daughter, wrote this essay in 1993 describing her middle school experiences during the 1991–1992 school year.

2. D.W. Johnson & R.T. Johnson, "How can we put cooperative learning into practice?" *The Science Teacher*, vol. 54 (1987), pp. 46–48.

3. G. Jones, *Cognitive conflict and cooperative learning*, ERIC document no. ED 319 598 (Washington, D.C.: Office of Educational Research and Improvement, 1990), p. 12.

4. See Jones (1990); R.E. Slavin, "Synthesis of research on cooperative learning," *Educational Leadership*, vol. 48, no. 5 (February 1991), pp. 71–82; R.E. Slavin, "Cooperative learning and student achievement," *Educational Leadership*, vol. 46, no. 2 (October 1988), pp. 31–33; K.D. Wood, "Meeting the social needs of adolescents through cooperative learning," *Middle School Journal*, vol. 20, no. 1 (September 1988), pp. 32–34.

5. See J.H. Braddock, "Tracking the middle grades: National patterns of grouping for instruction," *Phi Delta Kappan*, vol. 71, no. 6 (February 1990), pp. 445–449; *Turning Points: Preparing American Youth for the 21st Century* (Washington, D.C.: Carnegie Council on Adolescent Development, 1989); Jones (1990); R.E. Slavin, "Ability grouping, cooperative learning, and the gifted," *Journal for the Education of the Gifted*, vol. 14, no. 1 (1990a), pp. 3–8; R.E. Slavin, "Learning together," *American School Board Journal*, vol. 177, no. 8 (1990b), pp. 22–23; R. Tyrrell, "What teachers are saying about cooperative learning," *Middle School Journal*, vol. 21, no. 3 (January 1990), pp. 16–19.

6. See S.D. Allan, "Ability grouping research reviews: What do they say about grouping and the gifted?" *Educational Leadership*, vol. 48, no. 7 (April 1991), pp. 60–65; P.R. Clinkenbeard, "Unfair expectations: A pilot study of middle school students' comparisons of gifted and regular classes," *Journal for the Education of the Gifted*, vol. 15, no. 1 (1991), pp. 56–63; C.J. Mills & W.G. Durden, "Cooperative learning and ability grouping: An issue of choice," *Gifted Child Quarterly*, vol. 36, no. 1 (1992), pp. 11–16; and A. Robinson, "Cooperation or exploitation? The argument against cooperative learning for talented students," *Journal for the Education of the Gifted*, vol. 14, no. 1 (1990), pp. 9–27. Copyrighted material used with the permission of Prufrock Press.

7. For example, see S. Cleland, "Internships are second best," *Liberal Education*, vol. 55, no. 3 (October 1969), pp. 421–432; D. Fader, "Shaping an English curriculum to fit the junior college student," *Junior College Research Review*, vol. 5, no. 10 (June 1971), ERIC document no. 049 734; M.D. Hardee & L.B. Mayhew, "Faculty advising in colleges and universities," ERIC document no. 041 326 (1970).

8. K. Taylor, *An approach to environmental education: A three stage program for intermediate grades*, ERIC document no. 080 290 (1971).

9. See W.M. Alexander & P.S. George, *The Exemplary Middle School* (New York: Holt, Rinehart & Winston, 1981). B.K. Bryant, "The educational context for the study of cooperation and helpful concern for others," paper presented at the annual meeting of the American Educational Research Association (Chicago, April 1974), ERIC document no. 091 315; S. Calvert, "On cooperative learning with teachers as facilitators," *A Review of General Semantics*, vol. 29, no. 2 (June 1972), pp. 206–209; E. Conrad, *Peer Tutoring: A Cooperative Learning Experience* (Tucson: Arizona University Center for Educational Research and Development, 1974), ERIC document no. ED 108 747; C.H. Postma, "Student and teacher af-

fective perception of stimulation-gaming as a pedagogical technique," paper presented at the annual conference of the American Educational Research Association (Chicago, April 1974), ERIC document no. 090 936.

10. J. Lipsitz (Ed.), *Barriers: A New Look at the Needs of Young Adolescents* (New York: The Ford Foundation, 1979), p. 49.

11. *Report of the Working Group on the Emergent Adolescent*, Association for Supervision and Curriculum Development (Alexandria, Va.: ASCD, 1975).

12. Articles published by R.E. Slavin in the 1980s include: "Combining cooperative learning and individualized instruction: Effects on student mathematics achievement, attitudes, behaviors," *The Elementary School Journal*, vol. 84 (1984a), pp. 408–422; "Effects of cooperative learning and individualized instruction on mainstreamed students," *Exceptional Children*, vol. 50 (1984b), pp. 434–443; "Students motivating students to excel: Cooperative incentives, cooperative tasks, and student achievement," *The Elementary School Journal*, vol. 85 (1984c), pp. 53–63; "Grouping for instruction: Equity and effectiveness," *Equity and Excellence*, vol. 23, no. 1 (1986), pp. 31–36; "Cooperative learning and individualized instruction," *Arithmetic Teacher*, vol. 35 (1987a), pp. 14–16; "Cooperative learning and the cooperative school," *Educational Leadership*, vol. 45 (1987b), pp. 7–13; "Cooperative learning: Can students help students learn?" *Instructor*, vol. 96 (1987c), pp. 74–76; "Cooperative learning: Where behavioral and humanistic approaches to classroom motivation meet," *The Elementary School Journal*, vol. 88 (1987d), pp. 29–37; "Mastery learning reconsidered," *Review of Educational Research*, vol. 57, no. 2 (1987e), pp. 175–213; "Accommodating student diversity in reading and writing instruction: A cooperative learning approach," *Remedial and Special Education*, vol. 9 (1988a), pp. 60–66; "Cooperative learning and individualized instruction," *Education Digest*, vol. 53 (1988b), pp. 23–25; "Cooperative learning and student achievement," *Educational Leadership*, vol. 46, no. 2 (October 1988c), pp. 31–33; "Synthesis of research on grouping in elementary and secondary schools," *Educational Leadership*, vol. 46, no. 1 (September 1988d), pp. 67–77; "The cooperative revolution in education," *The Education Digest*, vol. 54 (1988e), pp. 22–24; "Comprehensive cooperative learning models for heterogeneous classrooms," *Pointer*, vol. 33 (1989a), pp. 12–19; "Cooperative learning and student achievement," *The Education Digest*, vol. 54 (1989b), pp. 15–17; "Here to stay—or gone tomorrow?" *Educational Leadership*, vol. 47, no. 4 (December 1989/January 1990a), p. 3; "Research on cooperative learning: Consensus and controversy," *Educational Leadership*, vol. 47 (December 1989/January 1990b), pp. 52–54.

13. Articles published by D.W. Johnson and R.T. Johnson in the 1980s include: "Constructive peer relationships, social development, and cooperative learning experiences: Implications for the prevention of drug

abuse," *Journal of Drug Education*, vol. 10, no. 1 (1980a), pp. 7–24; "Effects of cooperative, competitive, and individualistic conditions on children's problem-solving performance," *American Educational Research Journal*, vol. 17, no. 1 (1980b), pp. 83–93; "Integrating handicapped students into the mainstream," *Exceptional Children*, vol. 47, no. 2 (1980c), pp. 90–98; "Effects of cooperative and individualistic learning experiences on interethnic interaction," *Journal of Educational Psychology*, vol. 73, no. 3 (1981a), pp. 444–449; "Effects of cooperative, competitive, and individualistic goal structures on achievement: A meta-analysis," *Psychological Bulletin*, vol. 89, no. 1 (1981b), pp. 47–62; "The integration of handicapped children into the regular classroom: Effects of cooperative and individualistic instruction," *Contemporary Educational Psychology*, vol. 6, no. 4 (1981c), pp. 344–353; "Student-student interaction: The neglected variable in education," *Educational Researcher*, vol. 10, no. 1 (1981d), pp. 5–10; "Building friendships between handicapped and nonhandicapped students: Effects of cooperative and individualistic instruction," *American Educational Research Journal*, vol. 18, no. 4 (1981e), pp. 415–423; "Effects of cooperative, competitive, and individualistic experiences on self-esteem of handicapped and nonhandicapped students," *Journal of Psychology*, vol. 108, no. 1 (1981f), pp. 31–34; "Are low achievers disliked in a cooperative situation? A test of rival theories in a mixed ethnic situation," *Contemporary Educational Psychology*, vol. 8, no. 2 (1983a), pp. 189–200; "Effects of cooperative, competitive, and individualistic learning experiences on social development," *Exceptional Children*, vol. 49, no. 4 (1983b), pp. 323–329; "Integrating severely handicapped seventh-grade students into constructive relationships with nonhandicapped peers in science class," *American Journal of Mental Deficiency*, vol. 8, no. 2 (1983c), pp. 189–200; "Cooperative small-group learning," *Curriculum Report*, vol. 14, no. 1 (1984a); *Circles of learning: Cooperation in the classroom* (Alexandria, Va.: ASCD, 1984b); "The effects of cooperative, competitive, and individualistic student interaction patterns on the achievement and attitudes of students learning the golf skill of putting," *Research Quarterly for Exercise and Sport*, vol. 55, no. 2 (1984c), pp. 139–134; "Classroom conflict: Controversy versus debate in learning groups," *American Educational Research Journal*, vol. 22 (1985a), pp. 237–256; "Oral discussion, group-to-individual transfer, and achievement in cooperative learning groups," *Journal of Educational Psychology*, vol. 77 (1985b), pp. 60–66; "The effect of cooperative and individualist learning experiences on positive and negative cross-handicap relationships," *Contemporary Educational Psychology*, vol. 10 (1985d), pp. 127–138; "Effects of cooperative, competitive, and individualistic goal structures on computer-assisted instruction," *Journal of Educational Psychology*, vol. 77, no. 6 (1985e), pp. 668–677; "Effects of single-sex and mixed-sex cooperative interaction on science achievement and attitudes and cross-handicap and cross-sex relationships," *Journal of*

Research in Science Teaching, vol. 22, no. 3 (1985f), pp. 207–220; "Student-student interaction: Powerful but ignored," *Journal of Teacher Education*, vol. 36, no. 4 (1985g), pp. 22–26; "Computer-assisted cooperative learning," *Educational Technology*, vol. 26 (1986a), pp. 12–18; "Different cooperative learning procedures and cross-handicap relationships," *Exceptional Children*, 53 (1986b), pp. 247–252; "Mainstreaming and cooperative learning strategies," *Exceptional Children*, vol. 52 (1986c), pp. 553–561; "What research says: Action research: Cooperative learning in the science classroom," *Science and Children*, vol. 24 (1986d), pp. 31–32; "How can we put cooperative learning into practice? *The Science Teacher*, vol. 54 (1987a), pp. 46–48; "Research shows the benefits of adult cooperation," *Educational Leadership*, vol. 45, no. 3 (November 1987b), pp. 27–30; "Cooperative learning in mathematics education," *Yearbook of the National Council of Teachers of Mathematics*, (1989a), pp. 234–245; "Cooperative learning: What special education teachers need to know," *Pointer*, vol. 33 (1989b), pp. 5–10; "Toward a cooperative effort: A response to Slavin," *Educational Leadership*, vol. 46, no. 7 (April 1989c), pp. 80–81; and "Social skills for successful groupwork," *Educational Leadership*, vol. 47, no. 4 (December 1989/January 1990), pp. 29–33.

14. *An Agenda for Excellence at the Middle Level*, National Association of Secondary School Principals (Reston, Va.: NASSP, 1985); *Middle Level Education's Responsibility for Intellectual Development* (Reston, Va.: NASSP, 1989).

15. *Turning Points* (1989), p. 9.

16. Braddock (1990); *Turning Points* (1989); Johnson & Johnson (1989a, 1989b); Jones (1990); Slavin (1990a, 1990b); Tyrrell (1990).

17. Braddock (1990), p. 449.

18. Mills & Durden (1992), p. 11.

19. Slavin (1990a), p. 3.

20. P. Evans, T. Gatewood, & G. Green, "Cooperative learning: Passing fad or long-term promise?" *Middle School Journal*, vol. 24, no. 3 (January 1993), pp. 3–7.

21. Tyrrell (1990), p. 16.

22. Braddock (1990), p. 449.

23. Articles on cooperative learning in the vol. 47, no. 4 (December/January 1990) edition of *Educational Leadership* include: D.K. Augustine, K.D. Gruber, & L.R. Hanson, "Cooperation works!" pp. 4–7; R. Brandt, "On cooperative learning: A conversation with Spencer Kagan," pp. 8–10; L. Carson & S. Hoyle, "Teaching social skills: A view from the classroom, pp. 31–32; C. Edwards & J. Stout, Cooperative learning: The first year," pp. 38–42; S.S. Ellis, "Introducing cooperative learning," pp. 34–37; T. Good, B.J. Reys, D.A. Grouws, & C.M. Mulryan, "Using workgroups in mathematics instruction," pp. 56–61; M.R. Hannigan, "Cooperative learning in elementary school science," pp. 25–26; D.W.

Johnson & R.T. Johnson, "Social skills for successful group work," pp. 29–33; S. Kagan, "The structural approach to cooperative learning," pp. 12–16; A. Ratzki & A. Fisher, "Life in a restructured school," pp. 46–51; M. Sapon-Shevin & N. Schniedewind, "Selling cooperative learning without selling it short," pp. 63–65; J.L. Schultz, "Cooperative learning: Refining the process," pp. 43–45; Y. Sharan & S. Sharan, "Group investigation expands cooperative learning," pp. 17–21; R.E. Slavin, "Here to stay or gone tomorrow?" p. 3; R.E. Slavin, N. Madden, & R.J. Stevens, "Cooperative learning models for the three R's," pp. 22–28; S. Totten & T.M. Sills, "Selected resources for using cooperative learning," pp. 66–67.

24. Augustine, Gruber, & Hanson (1990), p. 4.

25. D.W. Johnson & R.T. Johnson, "What to say to advocates for the gifted," *Educational Leadership*, vol. 50, no. 1 (October 1992), pp. 44–47; and M. Matthews, "Gifted students talk about cooperative learning," *Educational Leadership*, vol. 50, no. 1 (October 1992), pp. 48–50. Copyrighted material used with permission from the Association for Supervision and Curriculum Development (ASCD).

26. S. Farkas, J. Johnson, & A. Duffett, *Different Drummers: How Teachers of Teachers View Public Education* (New York: Public Agenda, 1997), p. 13.

27. M. Sapon-Shevin, "Cooperative learning and middle schools: What would it take to really do it right?" *Theory into Practice*, vol. 33, no. 3 (1994a), p. 189.

28. M. Sapon-Shevin & N. Schniedewind, "If cooperative learning's the answer, what are the questions?" *Boston University Journal of Education*, vol. 174, no. 2 (1992), pp. 20, 21–22; 14, 21. Material used with permission of the lead author.

29. Slavin (1991), p. 70.

30. For example, see J.J. Gallagher, "Academic effectiveness or social reform? A response to Robert Slavin and Jomills H. Braddock III," *The College Board Review*, no. 168 (Summer 1993), p. 18. Copyright © 1993 by College Entrance Examination Board. Reproduced with permission. All rights reserved. www.collegeboard.com.

31. J.J. Gallagher, M.R. Coleman, & S. Nelson, "Perceptions of educational reform by educators representing middle schools, cooperative learning, and gifted education," *Gifted Child Quarterly*, vol. 39, no. 2 (Spring 1995), pp. 66–67. Copyrighted material used with permission from the National Association for Gifted Children (NAGC).

32. P.K. Sicola, "Where do gifted students fit? An examination of middle school philosophy as it relates to ability grouping and the gifted learner," *Journal for the Education of the Gifted*, vol. 14, no. 1 (1990), p. 40. Copyrighted material used with the permission of Prufrock Press.

33. Robinson (1990), pp. 11, 11–12.

34. Slavin (1991), p. 68.

35. D.W. Johnson & R.T. Johnson, "What to say to parents of the gifted," *Educational Leadership,* vol. 50, no. 2 (October 1992), p. 44, emphasis in the original. Copyrighted material used with permission from the Association for Supervision and Curriculum Development (ASCD).

36. J.H. Johnston, G.C. Markle, A.A. Arth, L. Roh, D. Tonack, & P. Trawinski, "Gifted and talented education: Part II: Programs, curriculum and outcomes," *Middle School Journal,* vol. 23, no. 4 (March 1992), p. 56. Copyrighted material used with permission from the National Middle School Association (NMSA).

37. Ibid.

38. Ceiling effects occur when the achievement of students goes beyond the instrument used to measure their achievement. In other words, the measured learning gains are not accurate because the measuring instrument does not cover all ranges of ability.

39. Robinson (1990), pp. 22, 35–36.

40. Slavin (1990b), p. 6.

41. Robinson (1990), p. 34.

42. See Mills & Durden (1992); Robinson (1990).

43. See Allan (1991); Robinson (1990), p. 11.

44. S. Willis, "Cooperative learning fallout? Some see 'exploitation' of gifted students in mixed-ability groups," *ASCD Education Update* (October 1990), p. 6. Copyrighted material used with permission from the Association for Supervision and Curriculum Development (ASCD).

45. S. Ramsay & H. Richards, "Cooperative learning environments: Effects on academic attitudes of gifted students," *Gifted Child Quarterly,* vol. 41, no. 4 (Fall 1997), pp. 166–167.

46. Willis (1990), p. 9.

47. Clinkenbeard (1991), pp. 59, 62.

48. Willis (1990), p. 9.

49. Matthews (1992), p. 48.

50. P. Ellett, "Cooperative learning and gifted education," *Roeper Review,* vol. 16, no. 2 (1992), p. 116.

51. M. Matthews, "Gifted students respond to cooperative learning," paper presented to the National Association for Gifted Children (November 1994), pp. 4–5, 4, 5, 7. Material used with permission of the author.

52. Sapon-Shevin (1994a), p. 188.

53. Tyrrell (1990), p. 16.

54. J.J. Gallagher, C.C. Harradine, & M.R. Coleman, "Challenge or boredom? Gifted students' views on their schooling," *Roeper Review,* vol. 19, no. 3 (March 1997), p. 136.

55. Allan (1991); Clinkenbeard (1991); Mills & Durden (1992); and Robinson (1990).

56. T.O. Erb, "Encouraging gifted performance in middle schools," *Midpoints*, vol. 3, no. 1 (1992), p. 17.

57. Ellett (1992); J.F. Feldhusen & S. Moon, "Grouping gifted students: Issues and concerns," *Gifted Child Quarterly*, vol. 36, no. 2 (1992), pp. 63–67; E.D. Fiedler, R.E. Lange, & S. Winebrenner, "In search of reality: Unraveling the myths about tracking, ability grouping, and the gifted," *Roeper Review*, vol. 16, no. 1 (September 1993), pp. 4–7; Mills & Durden (1992).

58. Max Ringelmann was a French agricultural engineer who published an analysis of data he collected on human workers performing various tasks from 1882–1887. See D. Kravitz & B. Martin, "Ringelmann rediscovered: The original article," *Journal of Personality and Social Psychology*, vol. 50, no. 5 (1986), pp. 936–941. Note that Kravitz and Martin state that Ringelmann's work "may be considered the first social psychological experiment . . ." (p. 937).

59. M. Ringelmann, "Recherches sur les moteurs animes: Travail de l'homme [Research on animate sources of power: The work of man]," *Annales de l'Institut National Agronomique, 2e serie-tome XII*, 1913, 1–40, as cited in D. Kravitz & B. Martin, "Ringelmann rediscovered: The original article," *Journal of Personality and Social Psychology*, vol. 50, no. 5 (1986), p. 938.

60. See Kravitz & Martin (1986), pp. 936–941; S. Harkins, "Social loafing and social facilitation," *Journal of Experimental Social Psychology*, vol. 23 (1987), pp. 1–18; S. Harkins, B. Latané, & K. Williams, "Social loafing: Allocating effort or taking it easy?" *Journal of Experimental Social Psychology*, vol. 16 (1980), pp. 457–465; N. Kerr, "Motivation losses in small groups: A social dilemma analysis," *Journal of Personality and Social Psychology*, vol. 45, no. 4 (1983), pp. 819–828; B. Latané, K. Williams, & S. Harkins, "Many hands make light the work: The causes and consequences of social loafing," *Journal of Personality and Social Psychology*, vol. 37, no. 6 (1979), pp. 822–832.

61. C.J. Hardy & B. Latané, "Social loafing in cheerleaders: Effects of team membership and competition," *Journal of Sport and Exercise Psychology*, vol. 10 (1988), pp. 109–114,

62. Latané, Williams, & Harkins (1979), p. 831.

63. See Harkins (1987); and C.J. Hardy, "Social loafing: Motivational losses in collective performance," *International Journal of Sport Psychology*, vol. 21 (1990), pp. 305–327; Kerr (1983), pp. 819–828; and J. Orbell and R. Dawes, "Social dilemmas," in G. Stephenson and J.H. Davis (Eds.), *Progress in Applied Psychology*, vol. 1 (Chichester, England: Wiley, 1981).

64. Kerr (1983), p. 826.

65. Sapon-Shevin & Schniedewind (1992), p. 21.

66. Kerr (1983), pp. 820, 827.

67. Matthews (1994), p. 7.

68. C.J. Hardy & R.K. Crace, "The effects of task structure and teammate competence on social loafing," *Journal of Sport and Exercise Psychology*, vol. 13 (1991), pp. 372–381.

69. R. Lotan, P. Swanson, & G. LeTendre, "Strategies for detracked middle schools: Curricular materials, instructional strategies, and access to learning," *Middle School Journal*, vol. 24, no. 1 (September 1992), p. 8.

70. See Harkins (1987), pp. 1–18.

71. Latané, Williams, & Harkins, (1979), p. 831.

72. Matthews (1994), p. 2. Material used with permission of the author.

73. The results were published in several articles, including J.J. Gallagher, M.R. Coleman, & S. Nelson, *Cooperative Learning as perceived by Educators of Gifted Students and Proponents of Cooperative Education*, ERIC document no. 355 675 (Chapel Hill North Carolina University, 1993a); *Cooperative Learning and Gifted Students: A National Survey*, ERIC document no. 359 717 (Chapel Hill: North Carolina University, 1993b); S.M. Nelson, J.J. Gallagher, & M.R. Coleman "Cooperative learning from two different perspectives," *Roeper Review*, vol. 16, no. 2 (December 1993c), pp. 117–121; and J.J. Gallagher, M.R. Coleman & S. Nelson, "Perceptions of educational reform by educators representing middle schools, cooperative learning, and gifted education," *Gifted Child Quarterly*, vol. 39, no. 2 (Spring 1995), pp. 66–76.

74. Nelson, Gallagher, & Coleman (1993a), pp. 12, 13, 14.

75. Gallagher, Coleman, & Nelson (1995), p. 72.

76. N. Granstrom, "A parent criticizes middle school theory," *Basic Education* (May 1999).

77. Matthews (1994), p. 10. Material used with permission of the author.

78. See Chapter 4, note 77 for a description of the surveys listed.

79. J.L. Epstein & D.J. MacIver, *Education in the Middle Grades* (Macon, Ga.: Panaprint, 1990), pp. 64, 66.

80. T. Moon, C.A. Tomlinson, & C.M. Callahan, *Academic Diversity in the Middle School: Results of a National Survey of Middle School Administrators and Teachers*, National Research Center on the Gifted and Talented, monograph number 95124 (1995), pp. 43, 67, 21.

81. Lotan, Swanson, & LeTendre (1992), p. 13.

82. R. Slavin, "Cooperative learning in middle and secondary schools," *The Clearing House*, vol. 69, no. 4 (March/April 1996), p. 202.

83. Slavin (1987e), p. 206.

84. J. Gallagher, "Academic effectiveness or social reform?" *The College Board Review*, no. 168 (Summer 1993), p. 18.

85. *The Nation's Report Card: Mathematics 2000* (Washington, D.C.: National Center for Education Statistics, NCES 2001–517, 2000), p. 156.

86. G.J. Whitehurst, "Research on Teacher Preparation and Professional Development," remarks for the White House Conference on Pre-

paring Tomorrow's Teachers (March 5, 2002), citing D.K. Cohen & H.C. Hill, "Instructional policy and classroom performance: The mathematics reform in California," *Teachers College Record*, vol. 102, no. 2 (February 2000), pp. 294–343.

CHAPTER 6

Peer Tutoring

I don't like working in groups because I always end up doing all the work. . . . Our teachers always put the gifted children with the troubled kids and expect us to help and improve plus teach them! The teachers don't care who is in your cooperative learning group and [they] don't try to change them. One or two smart kids end up doing 99.9 percent of the work, and get a slightly worse grade for not working together!

Sixth grade student in Connecticut, 1992[1]

THE ISSUE DEFINED

Data in journal articles and National Middle School Association (NMSA) conference sessions indicate that peer tutoring is a role that middle school activists believe gifted and high ability students should play. As with cooperative learning, peer tutoring enthusiasts do not hide their goal of using peer tutoring as a means to accomplish changes in society. According to some activists: "It is important to establish the extent to which peer tutoring can be used, especially as a technique for social change."[2]

It is not surprising that peer tutoring is often merged with the concept of cooperative learning, as it has been described as being very similar,[3] while also being treated as a separate, stand-alone instructional strategy.[4] Peer tutoring is sometimes referred to within the context of cooperative learning without being called peer tutoring when the cooperative learning group experience turns into a situation where one student has to teach the others.[5]

EVOLUTION OF THE CONCEPT

1970s–1980s: Assistance for Handicapped Children

Before the 1980s, peer tutoring went by other names, such as the buddy system or peer teaching.[6] By the late 1970s, "peer tutoring" began to emerge as the common term in the field.[7] It is defined as "a cooperative dyad composed of members of unequal status, in which the high status member is in a helping role."[8]

Its earliest use was as a strategy designed to meet the dual needs of providing assistance to handicapped children and providing socialization opportunities for them with non-handicapped students,[9] but then it evolved from a special education strategy to a general education strategy.[10] Peer tutoring addressed the problem of "large numbers of children in middle and junior high classrooms" that make it "difficult for the teacher to meet all the needs of every pupil in the class, especially those who are slow-learners or who experience emotional or learning problems."[11] In addition, a 1984 study of four different instructional interventions found that peer tutoring was the most cost-effective, a finding that continues to be cited as a reason to adopt this instructional strategy.[12]

An increase in the number of NMSA annual conference sessions on peer tutoring parallels the growth in cooperative learning (Appendix I), with both issues beginning a fairly steady period of growth around 1986 that lasted for nearly a decade. Since then, the practice of using gifted students as "junior teachers" has been more or less taken for granted. In 1989, *Turning Points* recommended the use of peer tutoring, declaring that it causes "high achievers to develop a sense of responsibility for those less advanced."[13] This is quite similar to the sentiments of social activist Mara Sapon-Shevin, who emphasized that gifted students are expected to develop "a sense of responsibility to their classmates,"[14] and activist Elizabeth Cohen, who stated that high ability students *must* provide help to others whenever asked.[15] A 1990 NMSA conference session program describes how participating in cooperative learning groups "allows students to be their own teacher and sets up a peer tutor situation,"[16] while the following year another session calls peer tutoring the next step "beyond cooperative learning."[17] Other sessions on peer tutoring describe its use in "fostering heightened self-esteem, role modeling and academic support."[18]

1980s–1990s: Linked with Mastery Learning

Peer tutoring is closely linked to mastery learning,[19] and as such can be seen as contributing to the leveling of student achievement. Mastery learning is an instructional practice that requires mastery of subject material before students can move on to new material. Such a practice sounds benign, but unfortunately, in many cases its implementation means that the entire class is made to wait until *all* students have learned the new material. In heterogeneous (mixed-ability) classrooms, this practice has serious consequences for faster learners. Both anecdotally and according to research in mastery learning situations it has been found that "faster students have to wait for slower students to catch up," resulting in "wasted time" for more able learners.[20]

As noted in Chapter 4, within the context of mastery learning, low-achieving students post gains at the expense of high achievers through a phenomenon known as "the Robin Hood Effect." Robert Slavin reviewed a number of studies on mastery learning, where students who did not reach mastery of the class subject matter were tutored by others who had already mastered the material, or by teachers. He concluded: "In several studies, positive effects were found for low-achievers only." Thus, the "Robin Hood Effect" occurs when the performance of low-achieving students rises as the achievement of high ability students falls, resulting in a leveling of performance.[21]

1990s: "Clerical Help"

Amazingly, another reason given for the use of peer tutoring is that tutors can be used to assist teachers with non-academic classroom duties. One NMSA conference session recommends that peer tutors can help teachers "with clerical and some non-instructional duties."[22] In other words, students who have completed their work can tutor others or perform clerical duties—but they cannot be allowed to work to the extent of their abilities and get ahead of the rest of the class. Limiting learning opportunities for high achievers will clearly result in a leveling of achievement.

RESPONSE FROM ADVOCATES FOR GIFTED LEARNERS

Advocates for the gifted have expressed concerns about whether it is ethical to use gifted children as junior teachers. Ann Robinson noted that student performance in cooperative learning groups often depends upon "the ability of a bright student to articulate explanations to team members on demand." She poses the question: "Does this dependency constitute exploitation?"[23] In a similar vein, a 1990 edition of *ASCD Education Update* carried a section with the subtitle: "Some See 'Exploitation' of Gifted Students in Mixed-Ability Groups."[24]

As noted in Chapter 5, Marian Matthews interviewed gifted students regarding their cooperative learning experiences and found that they often became peer tutors in those situations, reporting that they "resent having to explain the material to students who won't listen to them" and "resent time taken away from their own learning to work with uncooperative students."[25] Coleman and Gallagher report similar findings, indicating that in cooperative learning situations, "gifted students resent being the junior teacher,"[26] and that high ability students are often "turned off" by group learning experiences, as they end up "having to do all the work."[27] In all of these cases, the role of high ability students had become one of a peer tutor, not that of an equal group member.

In her follow-up study of nearly 900 middle school students, Marian Matthews again found that cooperative learning experiences instead often turn into peer tutoring. Of those students surveyed, 45 percent reported that they are often used as tutors, and only 9.6 percent would characterize their group work as challenging. Student comments reveal the frustration felt by many:

I find that the attitudes of other students towards being smart, being "nerdy," eventually intimidates me into not even contributing. I feel like we accomplish nothing, and if we do, I end up doing most of the work. It is a generally frustrating, useless experience.[28]

Similar frustrations have been expressed by parents:

Teachers want to use my son to help those who are less gifted, which is a laudable aim in itself. The problem with this forced redistribution of intellect is that it limits my son's educational opportunity and intellectual growth.[29]

CONCLUSION

Middle school activists, as well as social scientists, deny that harm will come to academically able students if they are regularly consigned to tutor others. Illogical and convoluted arguments, such as the one below, are used to support the use of peer tutoring in heterogeneous (mixed-ability) situations:

By educating the brightest and the best in the presence of those who are less able, no harm is done to students who are excellent if we develop pedagogical arrangements whereby excellent students can assist their less able classmates. . . . If we wish to motivate students to aspire to excellence, than we must provide more opportunities for them to help their less able peers.[30]

The author of a 1986 article in the *Middle School Journal* stated that "we will in the future undoubtedly hear more of peer tutoring."[31] However, questions have been raised about the ethical implications of its overuse, which is a popular component of the middle school concept, and these questions have gone unanswered by supporters of the practice.

The underlying beliefs supporting the widespread embrace of peer tutoring include the belief that high ability students have a moral responsibility to help their fellow students, that achievement should be leveled or equalized, and that academic competition must be eliminated (specifically, by holding back high ability students by forcing them to help their peers rather than moving ahead academically). These beliefs are discussed in more detail in Chapter 7.

NOTES

1. M. Matthews, "Gifted students talk about cooperative learning," *Educational Leadership*, vol. 50, no. 1 (October 1992), pp. 4–5. Copyrighted material used with permission from the Association for Supervision and Curriculum Development (ASCD).

2. E. Garcia-Vazquez & S.W. Ehly, "Peer tutoring effects on students who are perceived as not socially accepted," *Psychology in the Schools*, vol. 29, no. 3 (1992), p. 256.

3. See J. Cohen, "Theoretical considerations of peer tutoring," *Psychology in the Schools*, vol. 23, no. 1 (1986), pp. 175–186; T. Thorkildsen, "Some ethical implications of communal and competitive approaches to gifted education," *Roeper Review*, vol. 17, no. 1 (September 1994), pp. 54–57; T.O. Erb, "Encouraging gifted performance in middle schools," *Midpoints*, vol. 3, no. 1 (1992); and Matthews (1992), pp. 48–50.

4. D. Berliner, "The case for peer tutoring," *Instructor*, vol. 99 (1990), pp. 16–17; Cohen (1986), pp. 175–186; J.R. Jenkins & L.M. Jenkins, "Making peer tutoring work," *Educational Leadership*, vol. 44, no. 1 (September 1987), pp. 64–68.

5. Matthews (1992).

6. D. Fader, *The New Hooked on Books* (New York: Berkeley Publishing, 1976); and R.D. Strom, "Play and peer teaching," *Elementary School Journal*, vol. 79, no. 2 (1978), pp. 74–80.

7. M.E. Dale, "Peer-tutoring: Children helping children," *The Exceptional Parent*, vol. 9, no. 4 (1979), pp. 26–27; L.G. Thomas & J.E. Brophy, *Educational Psychology: A Realistic Approach* (New York: Holt, Rinehart, & Winston, 1977).

8. Cohen (1986), p. 180.

9. T. Apolloni, S.A. Cooke, & T.P. Cooke, "Establishing a non-retarded peer as a behavioral model for retarded youngsters," unpublished paper (Sonoma: California State College, 1975); M. Ballard, L. Corman, J. Gottlieb, & M.J. Kaufman, "Improving the social status of mainstreamed retarded children," *Journal of Educational Psychology*, vol. 69 (1977), pp. 605–607; B. Chaing, H.W. Thorpe, & C.B. Darch, "Effects of cross-age tutoring on word recognition performance of learning disabled students," *Learning Disability Quarterly*, vol. 3, no. 4 (1980), pp. 11–19; Dale (1979); D. Donder & J. Nietupski, "Nonhandicapped adolescents teaching playground skills to their mentally retarded peers: Toward a less restrictive middle school environment," *Education and Training of the Mentally Retarded* (December 1981), pp. 270–276; J. Harris & J. Aldridge, "Ten reasons why peer tutors won't work," *Academic Therapy*, vol. 19, no. 1 (1983), p. 46; P. Wagner & M. Sternlicht, "Retarded persons as 'teachers': Retarded adolescents tutoring retarded children," *American Journal of Mental Deficiency*, vol. 79 (1975), pp. 674–679.

10. N. Bar-Eli & A. Raviv, "Underachievers as tutors," *Journal of Educational Research*, vol. 75, no. 3 (1982), pp. 139–143; C.R. Greenwood, G. Dinwiddie, B. Terry, L. Wade, S. Stanley, S. Thibadeau, & J. Delquadri, "Teacher versus peer-mediated instruction: An eco-behavioral analysis of achievement outcomes," *Journal of Applied Behavior Analysis*, vol. 17 (1984), pp. 521–538; T.R. King, "Learning for a pal," *The Reading Teacher*, vol. 35 (1982), pp. 682–684; L. Maheady & D.M. Sainato, "The effects of peer tutoring upon the social status and social interaction patterns of high and low status elementary school students," *Education and Treatment*

of Children, vol. 8, no. 1 (1985), pp. 51–65; M. Mandoll, P. Mandoll, & T.F. McLaughlin, "Effect of same-age peer tutoring on the spelling performance of a mainstreamed elementary LD student," *Learning Disability Quarterly,* vol. 5, no. 2 (1982), pp. 185–189; H.E. Piggott, J.W. Fantuzzo, & P.W. Clement, "The effects of reciprocal peer tutoring and group contingencies on the academic performance of elementary school children," *Journal of Applied Behavior Analysis,* vol. 19, no. 1 (1986), pp. 93–98; T. Russell & D.F. Ford, "Effectiveness of peer tutors vs. resource teachers," *Psychology in the Schools,* vol. 20, no. 4 (1983), pp. 436–441; and Thomas & Brophy (1977).

11. M. Bowermaster, "Peer tutoring," *Middle School Journal,* vol. 18, no. 1 (November 1986), p. 20.

12. H. Levin, G. Glass, & C. Meister, *Cost Effectiveness of Four Educational Interventions* (Stanford, Calif.: Stanford University Press, 1984); and Berliner (1990), p. 16.

13. *Turning Points: Preparing American Youth for the 21st Century* (Washington, D.C.: Carnegie Council on Adolescent Development, 1989), p. 52.

14. M. Sapon-Shevin, "Giftedness as a social construct," *Teachers College Record,* vol. 89, no. 1 (1987), p. 50.

15. E.G. Cohen, "Teaching in multiculturally heterogeneous classrooms: Findings from a model program," *The McGill Journal of Education,* vol. 26 (1991), pp. 7–23.

16. National Middle School Association annual conference program (1990), p. 116.

17. National Middle School Association annual conference program (1991), p. 40.

18. National Middle School Association annual conference program (1993), p. 90.

19. Jenkins & Jenkins (1987); National Middle School Association annual conference program (1990), p. 59.

20. M. Arlin & J. Webster, "Time costs of mastery learning," *Journal of Educational Psychology,* vol. 75, no. 2 (1983), p. 187.

21. R.E. Slavin, "Mastery learning reconsidered," *Review of Educational Research,* vol. 57, no. 2 (1987), pp. 175–213, 176, 206, 205–206.

22. National Middle School Association annual conference program (1991), p. 128.

23. A. Robinson, "Cooperation or exploitation? The argument against cooperative learning for talented students," *Journal for the Education of the Gifted,* vol. 14, no. 1 (1990), p. 18.

24. S. Willis, "Cooperative learning fallout? Some see 'exploitation' of gifted students in mixed-ability groups," *ASCD Education Update* (October 1990), p. 6.

25. Matthews (1992), p. 48.

26. M.R. Coleman, J.J. Gallagher, & S. Nelson, "Cooperative learning

and gifted students: A national survey," Gifted Education Policy Studies Program (Chapel Hill: North Carolina University, June 1993), ERIC document no. 359 717, p. 2; and J.J. Gallagher, M.R. Coleman, & S. Nelson, "Perception of educational reform by educators representing middle schools, cooperative learning, and gifted education," *Gifted Child Quarterly*, vol. 39, no. 2 (Spring 1995), p. 71.

27. J. Gallagher, C.C. Harradine, & M.R. Coleman, "Challenge or boredom? Gifted students' views on their schooling," *Roeper Review*, vol. 19, no. 3 (March 1997), p. 136.

28. M. Matthews, "Gifted students respond to cooperative learning," paper presented to the National Association for Gifted Children (November 1994), p. 5. Material used with permission of the author.

29. A.H. Bloom, "What are you teaching my son?" *Educational Leadership*, vol. 53, no. 7 (April 1996), p. 83. Copyrighted material used with permission from the Association for Supervision and Curriculum Development (ASCD).

30. C.V. Willie, "When excellence and equity complement each other," *Harvard Educational Review*, vol. 57 (May 1987), p. 207.

31. Bowermaster (1986), p. 21.

CHAPTER 7

Analysis of Beliefs and Driving Convictions

The year was 2081, and everybody was finally equal. They weren't only equal before God and the law. They were equal every which way. Nobody was smarter than anybody else. Nobody was better looking than anybody else. Nobody was stronger or quicker than anybody else. All this equality was due to the 211th, 212th, and 213th Amendments to the Constitution, and to the unceasing vigilance of the United States Handicapper General.

Kurt Vonnegut, Jr., 1961[1]

An analysis of the beliefs that appear to undergird the instructional practices discussed in previous chapters provides a detailed view of the driving convictions behind the calls for change that are influencing classroom behaviors. Social scientists describe a belief as a deeply held value or sentiment that ultimately results in specific opinions, attitudes, and behaviors.[2] The classroom practices discussed in the previous chapters are thus *behaviors* that are driven by *beliefs*. The nature of these underlying beliefs can be inferred from the actions and words of those who are striving to reduce the rigor of the middle school curriculum, eliminate ability grouping, and increase the use of cooperative learning and peer tutoring. Five distinct beliefs can be identified, and all of them are driving anti-gifted practices in a number of middle school classrooms:

1. Belief in the equality of outcomes, as manifested by the decrease in rigor of the middle school curriculum, the calls to eliminate ability grouping, and the increased use of cooperative learning and peer tutoring, all of which result in the leveling of achievement.[3]

2. Belief in questioning the value of individualism, as manifested in the drive for eliminating ability grouping (which focuses on individual effort) in favor of cooperative learning.[4]

3. Belief in the supremacy of the group over the individual, as manifested in the drive for eliminating ability grouping (which focuses on individual effort) and increasing the use of cooperative learning and peer tutoring.[5]

4. Belief that advanced students have a duty to help others at the expense of their own needs,[6] as manifested in the increased use of both peer tutoring and cooperative learning.

5. Belief that competition is negative and must be eliminated, as manifested in the drive for eliminating ability grouping (which focuses on individual effort) in favor of cooperative learning and peer tutoring.[7]

As can be seen, there is a great deal of overlap among these five beliefs. Taking this into account, they can be categorized into three fundamental convictions: radical equity, group rights, and coercive egalitarianism.

Radical equity is a type of equity that demands not equality of opportunity, but rather, equality of outcomes. As will be seen, the word *equity* can be defined in many different ways, and as such it is often miscast in the context of the "equity vs. excellence" debate when, as we shall see, it would be more appropriately addressed in the context of *radical equity vs. radical elitism*. Beliefs underlying this principle include equality of outcomes through the leveling of achievement, along with the elimination of competition.

Group rights is a conviction based upon the belief in the supremacy of the group over the individual, and can be discussed in the context of *group rights vs. individual rights*. Beliefs underlying this conviction include the questioning of individualism, the supremacy of the group, and that advanced students have a duty to help others at the expense of their own educational needs.

Coercive egalitarianism is a conviction based on the belief in forced equality, as evidenced by the expressed desire to level achievement and eliminate competition. It can be discussed within the context of *apex excellence vs. mediocrity*. Underlying beliefs include the notion that advanced students have a responsibility to help others to their own detriment, belief in the equality of outcomes and the leveling of achievement, and belief in the elimination of competition.

RADICAL EQUITY

The root word for the term *equity*—equal—presupposes that a comparison of some type will be made. When used in the context of education, *equity* has been defined in many different ways to reflect different types of comparisons. For example: equal treatment, regardless of individual differences;[8] equal treatment of those who have similar needs, also called horizontal equity;[9] equal degrees of treatment, based upon diagnosed need, also known as vertical equity;[10] equality of funding;[11] equal distribution of resources;[12] equal outcomes;[13] and equality of opportunity.[14] Thus, qualifiers can be added to the term *equity* in order to distinguish finer and more specific meanings. Without such qualifiers or explicit contextual details, one can only attempt to infer which of the many types of equity is meant when the term is used.

It appears that when the term *equity* is used by middle school and social activists, it has come to take on a meaning that is vastly different from the meaning inferred by advocates for gifted learners—that is, equality of opportunity.[15] Belief in reaching "equity" by producing equality of outcomes through the leveling of achievement appears to be the sort of equity embraced by radical proponents of the middle school movement. This is driving the move for the excessive use of cooperative learning and peer tutoring, as well as the unquestioning embrace of the theory of brain periodization and the watered-down academics that accompany it. Middle school activists promote these practices as a way to gain what they call "equity." I propose that this type of equity should be called *radical equity*, meaning equality of outcomes.

The idea of equality of outcomes is a by-product of the 1960s, and holds that excellence is relative, not objective. As such there can never be an absolute standard for excellence. Charles Reich described this in 1970 as he wrote of a new utopia that he called "Consciousness III":

Consciousness III rejects the whole concept of excellence and comparative merit. . . . It refuses to evaluate people by general standards, it refuses to classify people, or analyze them. Each person has his own individuality, not to be compared to that of anyone else. Someone may be a brilliant thinker, but he is not "better" at thinking than anyone else, he simply possesses his own excellence. A person who thinks very poorly is still excellent in his own way. . . . Because there are no governing standards, no one is rejected.[16]

According to Reich, there must be no standards and thus no judgments, because all personal qualities are relative. Absolute standards are rejected and true excellence is denigrated so that all will be viewed as "equal."

Equality of Outcomes through the Leveling of Achievement

The theory of brain periodization gave middle school activists the excuse to dumb-down academic offerings at the middle school, resulting in a widespread leveling of achievement and thus a movement toward equality of outcomes. This is what is meant by social scientist Jeanne Oakes when she declares that "more limited reforms should be attempted to help *equalize the effects of schooling*"[17] (emphasis added).

"Equalizing the effects of schooling" clearly means raising the achievement of some students while lowering it for others. Diluting the level of academic rigor clearly harms the achievement levels of all children, especially the gifted—but nonetheless, this is the stated goal of some prominent middle-level activists. Consider this statement from middle school activist Paul George: "What I would like to do is to start everybody from the starting line, and let the—to use the old example—the level playing field determine who gets what. And so my interest is equity."[18] He desires equality of outcomes but, curiously, uses a sports metaphor to describe his goal. Clearly, equality of outcomes is incongruent with the field of sports (at least for now).

The general theme of equity also appears in the arguments calling for the elimination of ability grouping and the increased use of cooperative learning. Opponents identify ability grouping as: (1) an impediment to social justice, and thus an impediment to equity;[19] (2) undermining democratic values, assumed to include equity;[20] (3) responsible for disparate social consequences, or social inequities;[21] and (4) responsible for perpetuating notions of classism and a stratified society, or inequitable opportunities.[22]

However, the move toward more heterogeneous (mixed-ability) classes and the increased use of cooperative learning complicate the goal of leveling achievement, since high ability students often dominate group interactions. Social activist Elizabeth Cohen, among others, declares that teachers must implement strategies to *prevent* such dominance by high-achieving students in order to promote "the process of status generalization"—in other words, to ensure *equality of outcomes*:

Teachers must be trained in the use of several status treatments designed to prevent the domination of high-status students in the groups. . . . It requires a fundamental understanding of the status processes in the classroom so that the process of status generalization can be recognized and treated.[23]

She is saying that the actions naturally demonstrated by high ability students (called "high status" students by Cohen) should be actively and deliberately discouraged by classroom teachers. In her view, demonstrations of ability by high-achieving students need to be "treated," as one would treat a disease.

Consider the reaction of one middle school student upon her move into such a "reform-minded" middle school:

Tabitha reported the emotional pain she endured by being ostracized by the majority of the students. . . . The climate of her new school disparaged academic achievement. Although Tabitha had always loved school and began the school year eagerly, in a matter of days she was begging to stay home. The work was far too easy, and she reported that any display of intelligence was ridiculed by many of the other students. "First I wasn't accepted [by other students] simply for not being from there, and then, having academic pursuits sort of added to the—I don't want to say segregation, but do you know what I mean?"[24]

Clearly, some schools have taken to heart and diligently implemented practices recommended by middle school activists to promote equality of outcomes. Their goal is to "create less differentiated learning experiences (especially by ability)"[25] in order to force egalitarianism by "promot[ing] social equity in achievement among students."[26]

The NMSA remains resolute in its determination to produce

equal outcomes by leveling achievement. A recent NMSA research summary on academic achievement declares that a priority aim of the middle school movement is "equitable high achievement for all types of learners."[27] Just what is that supposed to mean? An NMSA position statement on ability grouping, issued in 2001, appears to provide the answer. Rather than addressing the issue of ability grouping, the statement pronounces that middle schools have an obligation to "work deliberately to diminish disparities in students' learning and achievement."[28] That this is not confined to closing the historic academic achievement gap between the races is quite clear, as further on the statement reminds middle schools of their "non-negotiable" commitment to non-academic aims.

Elimination of Competition

The desire to eliminate competition is a leveler as well. As stated above, Cohen recommends that teachers discourage high-dominance students, and cooperative learning activists Johnson and Johnson agree. They even proclaim that the performance of advanced or gifted students has negative consequences:

High ability students who defy peer pressure against excelling academically, in effect, make classmates look like losers in the teacher's eyes. They also set a standard of performance that increases the effort classmates have to put into schoolwork.[29]

Amazingly, their message is that high ability students should succumb to peer pressure and strive *not* to achieve, or they will risk making their classmates look bad—and their actions might even go so far as to force these non-motivated students to work harder!

One education researcher even advises teachers and students to question the ethical implications of competitive learning situations. The reason? "By stressing fairness, students and teachers will be encouraged to reflect on the political and moral workings of social institutions."[30]

What opponents of competition fail to realize is that many students, especially gifted ones, are motivated by competition to do their best. This can be illustrated with a sports analogy:

Olympic swimmers do not simply swim as fast as they can; they sometimes swim against the clock, against the records of others. And it is generally agreed that they need to swim against the competition to assess their real achievement.[31]

Nonetheless, many so-called reformers continue to insist that competition is counterproductive for all children, and that rewards or recognition are not motivating—but toxic. They assume that rewards (good grades) are available only in a very limited supply, and that competition is a devious way to ensure that some students are rewarded while others are not.[32] This point can be seen in the words of one prominent opponent of competition, Alfie Kohn, who narrowly defines competition as "mutually exclusive goal attainment, an arrangement in which one person succeeds only if others fail—or, in the stronger variety, only by actively making others fail."[33]

Such a narrow definition does not align with the positive reality of the competitive spirit in American society. A report on the personal characteristics of the men who thwarted the hijacking of United Flight 93 on September 11, 2001 makes this point. *U.S. News and World Report* interviewed the friends and family members of these men, and in four of five cases, the men were described as highly competitive. Todd Beamer, whose famous line "Let's roll" epitomizes the determination of these heroes, was described by his wife as "very competitive." Jeremy Glick's father-in-law used the same phrase to describe his daughter's husband. Another of these brave men, Mark Bingham, was described as "fiercely competitive, even in a game of Scrabble," and a friend described Tom Burnett as "exceptionally bright, driven and competitive."[34]

A competitive spirit drove these men to overpower the hijackers. Yes, they cooperated in doing so, but it was a spontaneous cooperation driven by necessity, not a contrived cooperation aimed at ensuring that everyone was equal in the fight. Yet, radical middle school activists seem intent on breeding a sense of competition *out of* the next generation of Americans. Imagine how different the fate of Flight 93 would have been without the powerful driving force of competitiveness among the passengers.

Competition is a necessary component in the will to succeed, but social activists fail to see this. Instead, they are vigorously campaigning to eliminate the competitive spirit and do not hide this fact. From working to eliminate spelling bees and academic honor rolls to striving to eliminate high school valedictorians, activists seem determined to place our children in a contrived world where academic excellence is neither recognized nor rewarded. Not content to remove competition from the academic arena, activists are also campaigning to do away with competitive sports and games. Activist Alfie Kohn openly proclaims that one of the goals of cooperative learning is to "subvert efforts to teach children to accept competition."[35]

This belief is reflected in the attitudes of many education school professors. According to a recent survey, "the majority of education professors dislike academic competition [and] think schools should avoid competition." This is alarming in that, as the survey authors point out, "assuming they are at least reasonably effective, what education professors teach about learning and schools shapes the goals, expectations, and priorities of the nation's teaching corps."[36]

Radical Equity vs. Elitism

In the past, the issue of "equity" has often been addressed within the context of the "equity vs. excellence" debate. Unfortunately, this inherently presupposes a dichotomous relationship: "Equity vs. excellence" implies that the issues are mutually exclusive. Thus, the groundwork for an adversarial relationship between supporters and opponents of one or the other view is laid out before the first syllable of discourse has been uttered. It is logical to assume that two concepts placed at opposite sides of a debate would be the opposite of one another. If the issue is equity (in any one of its many permutations), what would be the opposite? That would depend upon the type of equity under consideration.

In the case of equity meaning the forced equality of outcomes, the opposite would be the deliberate *in*equality of outcomes—which can be brought about by special treatment for some and denied opportunities for others. In other words, this is not *excellence*, but *elitism*. As with the term *equity*, the term *excellence* carries a meaning that is different for middle school activists than it is for advocates for gifted learners. Advocates for gifted learners define educational excellence as meaning a range of performance at the highest levels of any endeavor.[37] Middle school activists, however, disparage educational excellence as a type of elitism. It has been called an "excluding policy" that results in "arrogance."[38] In the opinion of one educator:

When we isolate gifted and talented children from the mainstream—by separate schools, tracks, courses, grouping—we run the risk of contributing to an elitism that does not reflect a true democracy.[39]

In this context, middle school advocates who argue for equity are fighting against what they perceive as elitism and the special treatment that it may entail.[40] Rightfully so, there is a fervent dislike for special treatment that sets any child or group of children apart as the recipients of special favors at the expense of others. Consequently, middle school advocates criticize educational practices that they perceive as elitist, such as the perceived over-allocation of resources toward gifted programs and "membership in a private club"[41]—that is, the assignment of children to gifted programs. Ability grouping is viewed as a threat to equity because it is seen as "contribut[ing] to a stratified society"[42] and "perpetuat[ing] notions of superior and inferior classes of citizens."[43] Even though there is scant evidence that such conclusions are justified, activists use this strident rhetoric to gain support for their cause.

Conversely, advocates for gifted students argue that ability grouping or differentiated instruction are not necessarily elitist, and schools that treat gifted children as "the anointed few" are doing such children, and the field, a disservice. Classroom practices such as ability grouping are seen simply as ways to meet the needs of these students:

Equality of opportunity and equality of treatment in education, however, are not the same—nor should they be. In any profession, the client's needs dictate the nature of the prescription. High-quality services should be available to all, but the nature and organization of those services should vary based on diagnosed need. Education can ill-afford to level its services lest the pill of mediocrity be absorbed into the blood stream of all our students.[44]

Radical equity promotes equality of outcomes, while *radical elitism* prevents equality by elevating some individuals above all others, denying opportunities to all but the anointed few. Both are extreme views, thus fitting the dichotomous nature of an "X versus X" debate much better than the more nebulous terms *equity* and *excellence*.

The belief in radical equity, as expressed by activist proponents of the middle school concept, drives their dual calls for change in the classroom as well as for change in society at large.[45] Practices such as cooperative learning and the elimination of ability grouping are promoted as ways to attain a general sort of equity, since such actions are viewed as a "commitment to the values underlying American democracy."[46] By demonizing gifted programs as "elitist," middle school activists manipulate individuals into supporting their goal for radical equity—equality of outcomes—and the classroom practices that support it.

In separating from Britain, our founding fathers declared that all men had the right to the *pursuit* of happiness. It is important to note that there was no guarantee of *attaining* happiness. To guarantee the attainment of happiness is to guarantee equality of outcomes—and this is clearly not the American way. Individuals, through their desires, aspirations, efforts and motivations, can strive to attain happiness and personal fulfillment, and must be assured of access to opportunities to do so. Equality of opportunity is a fundamental right in our society—but to demand equality of outcomes is nothing more than a thinly veiled attempt at imposing a socialist utopia.

It has been postulated that *equity* becomes the focus in educational policy and practice when the pressing national issue is perceived to be social inequality, and is addressed with the ascendancy of a more socialist-leaning political philosophy.[47] Thus, the radical strivings that began in the 1960s spilled over into education and helped to drive policy there. It remains to be seen whether a shift in national priorities post–September 11, 2001 will change this focus.

SUPREMACY OF THE GROUP

The conviction that the rights of groups should trump the rights of individuals is supported by beliefs that question individualism,[48] stress the supremacy of the group over that of the individual,[49] and assert that advanced students are duty-bound to help fellow group members.[50]

Questioning Individualism and Elevating the Supremacy of the Group

In 1971, the education journal *Phi Delta Kappan* published an article which stated that "American children do not grow up by accident, chance or default. They are socialized into becoming egocentric individualists" and that "egocentric individualism or egocentric self-reliance" constitute the "core value that contributes directly to characteristic American social behavior."[51] Most people would characterize this negative portrayal of what it is to be an American as an extreme view.

Even those who disparage individualism acknowledge that it is part of American culture, much to their dismay.[52] This belief is reflected in middle school activists who instruct teachers to move "from individualism to a communitarian ethic."[53] However, activists such as Johnson and Johnson cloak their socialist-leaning agenda in a patriotic theme. "It is time to recognize the relationship between cooperative learning [groups] and a commitment to the values underlying American democracy."[54] So we have a strange situation in that those who would fundamentally alter American society claim that their radical changes are really the true values of our culture.

Middle school activists such as Paul George also criticize the American spirit of individualism and likewise use this as a justification for the increased use of cooperative learning: "A society beset by individualism run rampant requires a system of schooling in which cooperation and interdependence are exemplified."[55] He returns to this theme over a dozen years after his original statement when he criticizes ability grouping as "unjustifiably emphasiz[ing] the centrality of individual student ability."[56] Cooperative learning activists Johnson and Johnson continued with this same theme, stating that a focus on the individual "results in a strict self-centeredness while ignoring the plight of others."[57] In the minds of such radical middle school activists, then, the heroism of the Americans on United Flight 93 must be hard to comprehend.

The goal of promoting "group identity" is pervasive in the middle school literature. The *Middle School Journal* even published an article titled "Curriculum for identity: A middle level educational obligation," which claims that "school now offers the best possibilities of assisting increasing numbers of students to deal with developing identity needs. . . . Identity development must become a major middle level education curriculum goal."[58] A NMSA conference session expanded upon this theme by stating that, through the use of cooperative learning, "Competition is directed away from individual performance and toward a group identity."[59] Activist Paul George stated that students must be encouraged to "see themselves as important parts of positive and varied groups." Furthermore, he emphasized that for middle school students, group membership *"must be their focus of identification"*[60] (emphasis added). Cooperative learning is promoted as a way to move the focus away from the individual to a "whole-group identity," and strategies have been articulated in how to best make this happen.[61] Students are thus encouraged to sublimate their individualism for the sake of the group.

Many school social workers have also shifted their focus, and are encouraged to target their efforts on groups as opposed to "reactive treatment of an individual."[62] What they fail to consider, however, is that the needs of a group and expending efforts on that group, as opposed to an individual child, stereotypes all children with socio-economic or racial similarities as having similar needs across the board.

One ninth grade girl used an essay on the Ayn Rand novel *Anthem* to articulate a middle school group experience. It should be noted that the experience recounted took place two years before the essay was written, but it obviously still provoked strong emotions:

"It is a sin to write like this. It is a sin to think words no others think. . . ." So writes Equality 7-2521 as he sits in the subway tunnel from the Unmentionable Times. Equality 7-2521 has grown up in a world where the individual no longer exists, and free will has been obliterated. It is an age where individualism has been done away with, and the needs of the group dictate all actions. No one was to be different from the others, let alone rise above them. Yet Equality 7-2521 did just that—and knew he would have to face the consequences.

I, too, have lived in such a system, under a new educational program called Outcome-Based Education (OBE).[63] Collectivism is forced into every aspect of the learning process. Many times, while working in groups, I tried to take the initiative to go off on my own. I was reprimanded by the teachers and was told that breaking away from the group was wrong. I was forced to work with the group, at their pace, or face disciplinary actions. I found that if I disagreed with the group, I could not voice my opinion or I would quickly be hushed. I was not allowed to do anything on my own, or take things into my own hands. The teachers were quick to "correct" me and forced me to work only for my group as a whole.

When my school did away with the honor roll because it acknowledged the accomplishments of individuals, I wrote an article against it. However, when I submitted it to the school newspaper, the teacher in charge repeatedly badgered me to change what I had written. Even after I had changed it slightly and returned it to her, it appeared in the newspaper altered and watered-down. Later, I discovered that this particular teacher had been one of the leaders in the local OBE movement.

While unity is necessary for a nation to survive, there must be a line drawn as to where voluntary unity ends and compulsory unity, which denies individualism, begins. *Anthem* gives us a terrifying picture of what the future may be like if collectivism slowly invades our society and personal achievement is belittled and eventually denied. It is our duty to ensure that this work of fiction does not become a reality.[64]

Advanced Students Must Help Others

The movement to place the rights of groups above the rights of individuals is also expressed in the belief that advanced students must be responsible for helping others.

As early as 1987, Mara Sapon-Shevin noted that teachers had a duty to help gifted students to develop "a sense of responsibility to one's classmates," and that they should look at their talents "in terms of how they might be important to others" in order to serve "greater societal justice." According to her point of view, the only value to be attached to advanced achievement is the value it gives to the group: "Within such a structure, a child who is academically advanced *could* in fact be valued for this difference if that child's performance were helpful to the entire group."[65] In other words, abilities are to be valued only so far as they contribute to the needs of the group.

Echoing this, in 1989 *Turning Points* stated that peer tutoring was an important educational tool, in part because "high achievers develop a sense of responsibility for those less advanced."[66] Cooperative learning enthusiasts Johnson and Johnson agreed, stating that "Group membership carries an obligation to respond to others' needs with empathy and support."[67] Others argue for "a curriculum that empowers all gifted children to work toward social justice" which must involve adding "group advocacy" and "processes for effecting change" to the school curriculum.[68]

A similar theme is expressed by social activist Elizabeth Cohen, who stated that in classrooms utilizing cooperative learning and peer tutoring, "behavior is governed by a new set of norms" which include: "You have the duty to assist anyone who asks for help." She stresses this point by advising that this must be "explicitly taught to students."[69] The new set of norms to which Cohen refers may be those articulated by Johnson and Johnson, who declared that high ability students *"don't understand that personal fulfillment cannot exist without responsibility for others' well-being"*[70] (emphasis added). The goal is clear: The self is to be sublimated for the good of the group.

Individual Rights vs. Group Rights

The supremacy of group rights over the rights of individuals appears to be part of historical shift occurring in society at large.

The 1982 Supreme Court decision in *Board of Education of the Hendrick Hudson Central School District v. Rowley* ruled that although handicapped children must have individualized educational programs, the state was not required to provide a particular level of service or opportunities.[71] However, some interpretations of the arguments in favor of *Rowley* saw it as a shift of focus away from the individual and toward the group.[72] The needs of Amy Rowley, the handicapped student, were described not as the needs of an individual, but rather, as the needs of a group (her classmates) to be involved in an inclusive learning experience.[73] It is apparent that this new argument on the preeminence of the group accelerated attempts to implement such a view in the classroom.

The desire among middle school reformers to shift emphasis away from the individual to the group can be seen as early as 1970, when a vision for middle level education was articulated to include having teachers "discourage any emphasis upon working independently," as "social cooperation [is] a major goal."[74] A decade later, middle school activists Johnston and Markle continued this theme, noting the importance of "group norms and rules, group expectations, and group cohesiveness" and how they "may be influenced by the teacher." They also pointed out the use of groups in fostering change:

Groups are among the most powerful forces influencing our intellectual, emotional, and social lives. In fact, we live our lives in relatively small groups that have a demonstrated impact on our perceptions, attitudes, and behavior. The group can solidify positions we already hold or change our positions completely.... Such an influential force, given proper attention, can become a powerful ally in the learning process.[75]

Continuing with this theme, in the 1990s Mara Sapon-Shevin wrote that the responsibility of educators was to "structur[e] and arrang[e] educational and social environments to promote positive group interdependence" through the use of heterogeneous cooperative learning groups. She stated that students who participate in cooperative learning experiences will experience conflict "between the good of the group and the good of the individual," an experience that will help teachers "reinvent schools that embody social and educational equity and justice."[76]

As discussed in previous chapters, it is well known that the achievement of individuals is being sacrificed for that of the group when group-based mastery learning is used in the classroom. This phenomenon, called "the Robin Hood Effect," occurs when the performance of low achieving students rises as the achievement of high ability students falls.[77] Some individuals have rightly questioned whether this constitutes exploitation of high ability children.[78] Consider the remarks of one parent:

The problem with this forced redistribution of intellect is that it limits my son's educational opportunity and intellectual growth. Advocates of collaborative learning argue that it's more important to encourage socially desirable aspirations than to develop individual students' knowledge base and intellectual skills. I disagree.[79]

In a different angle on group rights, one NMSA session describes middle school students as members of a minority group who are victims of society's injustices, and recommends that the middle school curriculum be used not to improve their academic achievement, but rather, to empower their fight for justice:

In many ways, young adolescents in our society constitute a minority group. They have been neglected, stereotyped, and at times exploited. ... Like all minority groups, young adolescents need to be empowered. This session will examine our distorted views of young adolescents and suggest ways in which curriculum can begin to liberate and empower them.[80]

Parallels in Society

By the mid- to late 1990s, it was being postulated that America had gone from a nation of individuals to one of groups, where the rights of groups take precedence over the rights of individuals.[81] Evidence in support of this point can be seen in the observation that the American Civil Liberties Union (ACLU) has switched its civil rights focus from the defense of individual rights to that of groups.[82] This view is consistent with the viewpoint which notes that the issue of group rights vs. individual rights has now become an issue in American law:

In the middle 1960s, with the passage of the Civil Rights Act of 1964 and the Immigration Act of 1965, which eliminated all references to race and all quotas on the basis of nationality, it seemed as if the individual rights ideal had triumphed. But then, as we saw, the equation came up of how to achieve practical equality, and we began to slide again toward group definition, this time for purposes of correction and benefit, rather than for purposes of discrimination and segregation.[83]

It is quite curious that one of the fundamental principles that drove the founding of this nation, the protection of individual rights, is now giving way to devaluing the rights of individuals in favor of the rights of groups. The rhetoric of middle school activists suggests that practices implemented in many middle schools that favor groups over individuals mirror the growth of this phenomenon within the culture at large.

COERCIVE EGALITARIANISM

The term *coercive egalitarianism* was first introduced by Stephen Schroeder-Davis, an advocate for gifted learners, and is defined as "forced equalization through neglect and/or compulsion; forced regression toward the mean."[84] Another author, Stanley Schmidt, refers to the same concept as "wishful egalitarianism," since he concludes that many educators would prefer to pretend that academic differences among students do not exist rather than address the very real intellectual differences among children. He condemns educators who are "determined to inflict on real children a system [of education] based on a wishful premise [egalitarianism]."[85] Other educators concur, noting that reform enthusiasts need to "come to grips with the fact that life was no fairer in doling out academic ability than it was with athletic, artistic, musical, or manual ability."[86]

As articulated by Schroeder-Davis, coercive egalitarianism can occur either deliberately or through negligence. The "coercive" nature of this sort of egalitarianism is manifested in a number of ways. *Peer pressure* may play a role, as when the culture of a school is such that academic achievement is disparaged, resulting in "resentment of and hostility toward academically able children."[87] An example of this can be seen in the words of a high school student: "I have been spit upon, ostracized, and verbally abused for doing my homework on a regular basis, for raising my hand in class, and particularly for receiving outstanding grades."[88] That this is not an isolated incident can be seen in data collected in the 1998 National Assessment of Educational Progress. Researchers report that between 23 and 29 percent of eighth grade students agree or strongly agree with the statement: "My friends make fun of people who try to do well in school."[89] Philosopher C.S. Lewis stated that in a culture wed to egalitarianism, "All incentives to learn and all penalties for not learning will vanish. The few who might want to learn will be prevented—who are they to overtop their fellows?"[90]

Group dynamics likewise play a role, such as when capable individuals reduce their efforts in group situations, thus exhibiting the "sucker effect," as they see the group situation as inequitable in terms of the necessary commitment of effort and refuse to be exploited in this way. As noted by C.S. Lewis, when a society accepts egalitarianism, "those who are in any or every way inferior can labor more wholeheartedly and successfully than ever before to pull down everyone else to their own level."[91]

The *desire to conform* can be coercive as well. Consider the words of a gifted elementary school student: "My teacher normally wants us to stay with the rest of the group and not go ahead. I am an obeying student so I do what she says."[92]

Finally, coercion can also be the result of *deliberate actions* by adults in authority. C.S. Lewis noted that to make egalitarianism succeed, adults have to ensure that underachievers "must not be made to feel inferior to intelligent and industrious pupils. The differences between pupils . . . must be disguised."[93] Activist Elizabeth Cohen puts this into action by recommending that teachers should actively and deliberately discourage high ability students from exhibiting leadership characteristics. As noted earlier, she believes that demonstrations of ability by high-achieving students need to be "treated," as one would treat a disease. One teacher stated: "I, for one, do not believe the so-called research that indicates that these children have educational needs other children do not. . . . They need to learn discipline and to *fit in*"[94] (emphasis added).

Beliefs supporting the conviction of coercive egalitarianism fall into three categories: the belief in equality of outcomes through the leveling of achievement,[95] the belief in the elimination of competition,[96] and the belief that advanced students have a duty to help others.[97]

Equality of Outcomes through the Leveling of Achievement

As is the case in the area of radical equity, an underlying belief supporting coercive egalitarianism is the belief in equality of outcomes. An example of a strategy used to reach this goal by leveling achievement can be seen in the early days of the middle school movement, when activist Paul George presented an NMSA conference session in 1979 denouncing individualized instruction. The session was titled "The Myths of Individualized Instruction: Research and Practice," and the text description noted that the presenter had "significant findings which unveil the myths of individualized instruction."[98] In other words, he was stating that no accommodations should be made to address the unique and specific needs of individual students, but rather, that all students at all ability levels should receive identical instruction.

Evidence of this belief can also be seen in a study published in 1993, where researchers described how the restructuring of middle schools is aimed at specific goals, including the creation of "less differentiated learning experiences (especially by ability)."[99] Another study, also focused on middle school students, presented the assumption that the results of differentiated instruction are negative, because "differentiated instruction may lead to unequal results for students."[100] This fear of "unequal results" reveals the desire to level achievement, for this is how equal outcomes can be achieved.

Improving academic achievement, be it for gifted children or for all others, is not much of an issue to prominent middle school activists. Conrad Toepfer, a proponent of the brain periodization theory, ridicules what he perceives as the "contemporary infatuation with improving performance in academic achievement,"[101] and one NMSA conference session illogically laments that "high student achievement" is "an Achilles heel when it comes to educational innovation."[102] Statements such as these, which endorse a move away from academic rigor and support the "Robin Hood Effect," display more evidence of the desire to level achievement.

Several prominent researchers have noted that "social equality in achievement" is promoted by middle school instructional and grouping practices.[103] Middle school activists Johnston and Markle declare that "teachers must be aware that it may not be productive to require students to behave in ways that are at variance with group norms,"[104] indicating the encouragement for leveling of behavior, be it academic or otherwise. These statements support the recommendation by Jeanne Oakes that "reforms should be attempted to help equalize the effects of schooling."[105] To "equalize the effects of schooling" and to achieve "social equality in achievement" both indicate the leveling of academic performance, and as Gallagher points out, this is clearly a social aim:

If this call for heterogeneous grouping was matched with calls of equal fervor for additional educational preparation for these general education teachers so that they would have at their disposal strategies or ways of modifying content appropriately for their bright students, then one could feel more sympathy for this position, but such calls are rarely heard. This silence encourages the conclusions that there are some other reasons for this call for bringing gifted students back to the regular classroom that has little to do with the needs of gifted students. . . . [These are] policies that were really designed to foster a type of social equity.[106]

Gallagher sees the challenge facing teachers as a lack of training to meet the needs of gifted learners. However, it is interesting to note that some proponents of the leveling of achievement view as the greatest challenge to be overcome the natural abilities of high-performing students:

Efforts to offset economic and social barriers to cognitive development will succeed in equalizing academic aptitude only to a certain degree: Some students will still learn faster than others, even if the discrepancy between the most and least rapid learners is decreased.[107]

James Gallagher and his associates demonstrate that the leveling of performance ("reducing differences") is not a mere by-product of middle school polices, but a goal. In their study of the effects of cooperative learning on gifted students, one teacher expressed the view that "it appears that the major objective of grouping practices is to *reduce* differences rather than *adapt* to them"[108] (emphasis added).

The goal to change society through actions initiated in the middle school remains firmly entrenched among middle school activists. The mission to level student achievement is mentioned more than once in the 2001 NMSA policy statement, with middle schools being called upon to "deliberately work to reduce disparities in educational attainment." Middle schools are reminded to "support their commitment to social equity," and that "heterogeneous assignment of students is the norm."[109] In essence, the NMSA position statement is merely a condensed version of the radical rhetoric of the 1990s.

As is the case with the growing preeminence of group rights over individual rights, data suggest that larger social movements have also attempted to support equal outcomes. For example, one researcher noted that "the ACLU switched its civil rights focus from equality of opportunity to equality of results."[110]

Elimination of Competition

As noted earlier, the desire to eliminate competition is also a leveler of sorts. As early as 1979, the Ford Foundation advocated that activities for middle school students should "de-emphasize competition."[111] In 1985, the National Association of Secondary School Principals (NASSP) also recommended that teachers eliminate opportunities for competition, replacing them instead with cooperative learning.[112] A decade later, Johnson and Johnson were still criticizing competition as a by-product of individualism, calling it "strict self-centeredness" that "ignor[es] the plight of others."[113] Social activist Nell Noddings even advises teachers to "get rid of competitive grading."[114]

References to academic competition are often presented in tandem with references to athletics. For example, a 1987 NMSA conference session titled "A Philosophy [sic] Dilemma: What to Do about Competition and Awards in Academics, Sports, and the Arts?" addressed "issues related to competition" that "may impede the effectiveness of middle level education."[115] Another NMSA conference session titled "All Must Play" described "guidelines where students could develop and exhibit skills to the best of their abilities without pressures to determine individual or group superiority," while another session called for a " 'no-cut' student eligibility process," the goal of which was "equalizing team membership."[116] The stated goal for middle school physical education was to eliminate comparisons and competitions,[117] and academic competition and related issues were seen as "impede[ing] the effectiveness of middle level education."[118]

It would be interesting to speculate how the radical opponents of competition would analyze and evaluate the personal characteristics of the heroes of Flight 93 on September 11, 2001, as mentioned earlier.

Advanced Students Must Help Others

The use of peer tutoring and widespread cooperative learning can also be seen as manifestations of the conviction of coercive egalitarianism. Studies of reactions to the practices of peer tutoring and cooperative learning make the "coercive" portion of the term clear. As noted in previous chapters, Marian Matthews found that gifted students "resent having to explain the material to students who won't listen to them" and "resent time taken away from their own learning to work with uncooperative students."[119] Coleman and Gallagher had similar findings, indicating that "gifted students resent being the junior teacher."[120] However, NMSA conference sessions echo the words of social activist Sapon-Shevin and demonstrate the expectation that teachers ensure that advanced students help others: "All students are implicitly responsible for being promotive of each others' literacy."[121]

Also mentioned earlier is the study of nearly 900 middle school students and their reactions toward group work in cooperative learning/peer tutoring situations. Matthews reports the frustration felt by many gifted students and the resulting coercive egalitarianism. Note that, in this case, the actions of others forces the gifted student to become like them: "I find that the attitudes of other students towards being smart, being 'nerdy,' eventually intimidates me into not even contributing."[122]

Apex Excellence vs. Mediocrity

As discussed earlier, the logic underlying the proverbial "equity vs. excellence" debate is flawed in that *equity* has multiple meanings. Likewise, the term *excellence* has come to have multiple definitions. Middle school activists prefer definitions that are relative and subjective: "when all are learning what they need to become all they are capable of becoming,"[123] or "performing on the boundary of individual limits."[124]

Consider the thoughts of one activist who typifies the call for a "re-creation" of the definition of excellence from an objective standard to a subjective one:

Once again, the classical image portrays the embodiment of excellence—an excellence reflecting fairly narrow definitions of achievement and potential . . . traditionally defined by a rather small group of people in our society. This portrayal may fit comfortably with those students who have been raised with the same values and traditions as the setters of the definition. It may not, however, match the wide range of students who are not the progeny of those who have historically defined the parameters of excellence.[125]

The "values and traditions" referred to are those that have defined the American character for over 200 years. During that time, the standard of excellence has been objective and absolute. Americans of all backgrounds and traditions can aspire toward this standard of excellence. Unfortunately, middle school activists and social reformers actively strive to inhibit the desire for excellence, as well as its attainment. In contrast, gifted advocates define excellence as a "range of performance which describes and challenges the highest levels of expectation in any endeavor,"[126] a definition that presupposes an absolute standard.

Unfortunately, the commonly accepted definition of excellence, which sets forth a standard toward which students could both aspire and strive, has given way to more subjective meanings from those who would call for the elimination of an absolute standard.

Just as it was necessary to provide a qualifier for the term *equity* (to denote radical equity), so it is necessary to add a qualifier to *excellence* so as to make clear the reference to an absolute standard. I propose that an appropriate phrase to describe performance at the highest levels of any endeavor is *apex excellence,* a term coined by gifted advocate Carol Tomlinson.[127] Those who argue for apex excellence are not fighting against equity—they are fighting against mediocrity, or woefully inadequate attainment.[128] Mediocrity has been described as a characteristic of an egalitarian environment that "relentlessly lowers the general standards . . . to levels the weak ones can meet."[129] Thus, *apex excellence vs. mediocrity* represents two extremes on the continuum of performance.

Proponents of apex excellence support the nurturing and encouragement of talent so that students can aspire to challenges larger than themselves:

People are indeed all equal in terms of political and social rights and should have equal opportunities; but they do not necessarily avail themselves equally of these opportunities and hence do not get rewarded equally for their accomplishments. People are rewarded for what they accomplish, given equal opportunity, rather than for what they might have, should have, or could have accomplished.[130]

CONCLUSION

Convictions drive beliefs and beliefs drive behaviors. The beliefs detailed in this chapter undergird three convictions—radical equity, group rights, and coercive egalitarianism—and together they drive anti-gifted behaviors. These anti-gifted behaviors, as manifested in specific classroom practices, have not occurred by accident or as an afterthought—they have been implemented deliberately, and with great zeal. The next chapter addresses the activist nature of this implementation.

NOTES

1. Kurt Vonnegut, Jr., "Harrison Bergeron," in *Welcome to the Monkey House* (New York: Bantam Doubleday Dell Publishing Group, 1961).

2. B. Berelson & G.A. Steiner, *Human Behavior* (New York: Harcourt, 1964); I. Azjen, "Attitudes, traits and actions: Dispositional prediction of behavior in personality and social psychology," in L. Berkowitz (Ed.),

Advances in Experimental Social Psychology, vol. 2 (New York: Academic Press, 1987), pp. 1–62; J. Cooper & R.T. Croyle, "Attitudes and attitude change," *Annual Review of Psychology*, vol. 35 (1984), pp. 395–426; R.H. Fazio, "How do attitudes guide behavior?" in R.M. Sorrentino & H.T. Higgins (Eds.), *The Handbook of motivation and cognition: Foundation of Social Behavior* (New York: Guilford Press, 1986), pp. 204–243; R.E. Petty & J.T. Cacioppo, "The elaboration likelihood model of persuasion," in L. Berkowitz (Ed.), *Advances in Experimental Social Psychology*, vol. 19 (New York: Academic Press, 1986), pp. 123–205; M. Rokeach, "Long-range experimental modification of values, attitudes and behaviors," *American Psychologist*, vol. 26, no. 5 (1971), pp. 453–459; H.C. Triandis, J. Adamopoulis, & D. Brinberg, "Perspectives and issues in the study of attitudes," in *Attitudes and Attitude Change in Special Education: Theory and Practice* (Reston, Va.: Council for Exceptional Children, 1984), pp. 21–40; M.P. Zanna & J.K. Rempel, "Attitudes: A new look at an old concept," in D. Bar-Tal & A. Kruganski (Eds.), *The Social Psychology of Knowledge* (New York: Cambridge University Press, 1988).

3. See J. Oakes, *Keeping Track: How Schools Structure Inequality* (New Haven, Conn.: Yale University Press, 1985), p. 211; P.S. George, "In balance: Gifted education and middle schools," video script, in *Gifted Education and Middle Schools* (Reston, Va.: Council for Exceptional Children, 1995), p. 48; *Turning Points: Preparing American Youth for the 21st Century* (Washington, D.C.: Carnegie Council on Adolescent Development, 1989); E.G. Cohen, "Teaching in multiculturally heterogeneous classrooms: Findings from a model program," *The McGill Journal of Education*, vol. 26 (1991), pp. 7–23; D.W. Johnson & R.T. Johnson, "What to say to parents of the gifted," *Educational Leadership*, vol. 50, no. 2 (October 1992), pp. 44–47; J.H. Johnston & G.C. Markle, *What Research Says to the Middle Level Practitioner* (Columbus, Ohio: National Middle School Association, 1986); C.B. Howley, A. Howley, & E.D. Pendarvis, *Out of Our Minds* (New York: Teachers College Press, 1995); V.E. Lee & J.B. Smith, "Effects of restructuring on the achievement and engagement of middle-grade students," *Sociology of Education*, vol. 66 (July 1993), pp. 164–187; Oakes (1985); J. Oakes, A.S. Wells, M. Jones, & A. Datnow, "Detracking: The social construction of ability, cultural politics, and resistance to reform," *Teachers College Record*, vol. 98, no. 3 (Spring 1997), pp. 482–510; M. Sapon-Shevin, "Cooperative learning and middle schools: What would it take to really do it right?" *Theory into Practice*, vol. 33, no. 3 (1994a), pp. 183–190; M. Sapon-Shevin, *Playing Favorites: Gifted Education and the Disruption of Community* (Albany: State University of New York Press, 1994b); R.E. Slavin, "Research on cooperative learning: Consensus and controversy," *Educational Leadership*, vol. 47, no. 4 (December 1989/January 1990), pp. 52–54; and C.F. Toepfer, "What to know about young adolescents," *Social Education*, vol. 52, no. 2 (1988), pp. 110–112.

4. R.T. Fruehling, "Socialization, contract, and interpersonal relations, *Phi Delta Kappan*, vol. 52, no. 10 (June 1971), pp. 622–624; J. Gavora, "The quota czars," *Policy Review* (May/June 1997), pp. 22–27; P.S. George, "The middle school century," *Principal* (1981), pp. 11–14; P.S. George, "Tracking and ability grouping: Which way for the middle school?" *Middle School Journal*, vol. 20, no. 1 (September 1988), pp. 21–28; P.S. George, "Tracking and ability grouping in the middle school: Ten tentative truths," *Middle School Journal*, vol. 24, no. 4 (March 1993), pp. 17–24; N. Glazer, "In search of excellence and equity in our nation's schools," *Harvard Educational Review*, vol. 57, no. 2 (1987); Johnston & Markle (1986); J. Oakes, K.H. Quartz, J. Gong, & M. Lipton, "Creating middle schools: Technical, normative, and political considerations," *Elementary School Journal*, vol. 93, no. 5 (1993), pp. 461–480.

5. D.K. Lipsky & A. Gartner, "Inclusion, school restructuring, and the remaking of American Society," *Harvard Educational Review*, vol. 66, no. 4 (1996), pp. 762–796; M. Minow, *Making All the Difference: Inclusion, Exclusion, and American Law* (Ithaca, N.Y.: Cornell University Press, 1990); Oakes (1985); P.D. Salins, *Assimilation, American Style* (New York: New Republic, 1997); M. Sapon-Shevin, "Giftedness as a social construct," *Teachers College Record*, vol. 89, no. 1 (1987), pp. 39–53; Sapon-Shevin (1994a, 1994b); C.V. Willie, "When excellence and equity complement each other," *Harvard Educational Review*, vol. 57, no. 2 (May 1987), pp. 205–207.

6. *Turning Points* (1989); Cohen (1991); M.K. Kitano, "A multicultural educational perspective on serving the culturally diverse gifted," *Journal for the Education of the Gifted*, vol. 15, no. 1 (1991), pp. 4–19; Sapon-Shevin (1987).

7. Cohen (1991); Howley, Howley, & Pendarvis (1995); N. Noddings, "A morally defensible mission for schools in the 21st century," *Phi Delta Kappan*, vol. 76, no. 5 (January 1995), pp. 365–368.

8. Glazer (1987).

9. N.J. Salkind, "Equity and excellence: The case for mandating services for gifted children," *Journal for the Education of the Gifted*, vol. 12, no. 1 (1988), pp. 4–13.

10. Ibid.

11. H. Howe, "Remarks on equity and excellence in education," *Harvard Educational Review*, vol. 57 (1987), pp. 199–202.

12. Willie (1987).

13. Howley, Howley, & Pendarvis (1995).

14. M.D. Fantini, "Defining excellence: An equation of modern times," *Equity and Excellence*, vol. 22 (1986), pp. 32–42; J.F. Feldhusen & S. Moon, "Grouping gifted students: Issues and concerns," *Gifted Child Quarterly*, vol. 36, no. 2 (1992), pp. 63–67; Salkind (1988); R. Sternberg, "Neither elitism nor egalitarianism: Gifted education as a third force in

American education," *Roeper Review*, vol. 18, no. 4 (1996), pp. 261–263; J. VanTassel-Baska, *Planning Effective Curriculum for Gifted Learners* (Denver, Colo.: Love Publishing, 1992).

15. Fantini (1986); Feldhusen & Moon (1992); Salkind (1988); Sternberg (1996); VanTassel-Baska (1992).

16. C.A. Reich, *The Greening of America* (New York: Random House, 1970), p. 226.

17. Oakes (1985), p. 211.

18. George (1995), p. 48.

19. Cohen (1991); George (1988); Oakes (1985); Sapon-Shevin (1984).

20. D.W. Johnson & R.T. Johnson, "Cooperative learning and traditional American values: An appreciation," *Bulletin*, vol. 80, no. 579 (1996), pp. 63–65; Oakes (1985); R.E. Slavin & J.H. Braddock, "Ability grouping: On the wrong track," *The College Board Review*, vol. 168 (1993), pp. 11–18.

21. Oakes (1985); Sapon-Shevin (1984); Slavin & Braddock (1993).

22. Johnston & Markle (1986); Slavin & Braddock (1993).

23. Cohen (1991), p. 18.

24. J.A. Plucker & C.P. Yecke, "The effect of relocation on gifted students," *Gifted Child Quarterly*, vol. 43, no. 2 (Spring 1999), p. 100. Copyrighted material used with permission from the National Association for Gifted Children (NAGC).

25. V.E. Lee & J.B. Smith, "Effects of school restructuring on the achievement and engagement of middle-grade students," *Sociology of Education*, vol. 66 (July 1993), p. 181.

26. J.L. Irvin, "Middle level research is coming of age," *Middle School Journal* (September 1994), p. 69.

27. NMSA Research Summary #12: *Academic Achievement*, National Middle School Association (1997), p. 3.

28. NMSA Position Statement: *Ability Grouping*, National Middle School Association (January 2001), p. 1.

29. Johnson & Johnson (1992), p. 46.

30. T.A. Thorkildsen, "Some ethical implications of communal and competitive approaches to gifted education," *Roeper Review*, vol. 17, no. 1 (September 1994), p. 57.

31. C. Callahan, *The Performance of High Ability Students in the United States on National and International Tests* (Washington, D.C.: National Association for Gifted Children, 1993), p. 19.

32. See A. Kohn, "Group grade grubbing versus cooperative learning," *Educational Leadership*, vol. 48, no. 5 (February 1991), pp. 83–87; and N. Noddings, "A morally defensible mission for schools in the 21st century," *Phi Delta Kappan*, vol. 76, no. 5 (January 1995), pp. 365–368.

33. A. Kohn, "Resistance to cooperative learning: Making sense of its deletion and dilution," *Journal of Education*, vol. 174, no. 2 (1992), p. 45.

34. A. Cannon, "Final words from Flight 93," *U.S. News and World Report* (October 29, 2001), p. 32.

35. Kohn (1992), p. 46.

36. S. Farkas, J. Johnson, & A. Duffett, *Different Drummers: How Teachers of Teachers View Public Education* (New York: Public Agenda, 1997), pp. 13, 7.

37. C. Tomlinson, "The easy lie and the role of gifted education in school excellence," *Roeper Review*, vol. 16, no. 4 (June 1994), pp. 258–259.

38. Willie (1987), p. 205.

39. T.R. McDaniel, "Mainstreaming the gifted: Historical perspectives on excellence and equity," *Roeper Review*, vol. 11, no. 3 (1989), p. 171.

40. T.O. Erb, "Middle schools require the principles of quality to carry out their mission," *Middle School Journal*, vol. 27, no. 2 (1992), pp. 2–11; George (1993, 1995); Johnston & Markle (1986); Slavin & Braddock (1993).

41. See Erb (1992), p. 92; George (1993, 1995); Johnston & Markle (1986); Slavin & Braddock (1993); and National Middle School Association annual conference program (1993), p. 95.

42. Slavin & Braddock (1993).

43. Johnston & Markle (1986), p. 59.

44. VanTassel-Baska (1992), p. 13.

45. See Cohen (1991); *Turning Points* (1989); George (1988); A.G. Hilliard, "Conceptual confusion and the persistence of group oppression through education," *Equity and Excellence*, vol. 24, no. 1 (1988), pp. 36–43; Howley, Howley, & Pendarvis (1995); Noddings (1995); Oakes (1985, 1997); J. Oakes, "Curriculum inequality and school reform," *Equity and Excellence*, vol. 23, no. 1 (1987/1988), pp. 8–13; M. Sapon-Shevin, "Mainstreaming the handicapped, segregating the gifted: Theoretical and pragmatic concerns," paper presented at the annual meeting of the Educational Research Association, ERIC document no. ED 218 835 (1984); Sapon-Shevin (1994a, 1994b); R.E. Slavin, "Ability grouping in the middle grades: Achievement effects and alternatives," *Elementary School Journal*, vol. 93 (1993), pp. 535–552; Slavin & Braddock (1993); L.P. Stowell, J.E. McDaniels, & F.A. Rios, "Fostering change for democratic middle schools through teacher education," *Middle School Journal*, vol. 26, no. 5 (May 1995), pp. 3–10.

46. Johnson & Johnson (1996), p. 63.

47. See J.J. Gallagher, "Equity vs. excellence: An educational drama," *Roeper Review*, vol. 8, no. 4 (1986a), pp. 233–235; and McDaniel (1989).

48. Fruehling (1971), p. 622; Oakes et al. (1993), p. 468; George (1981), p. 14; George (1993), p. 18; Johnson & Johnson (1996), p. 64.

49. Johnson & Johnson (1996) p. 64; George (1988), p. 27.

50. Cohen (1991), p. 10; George (1993), p. 18; Johnson & Johnson (1992), p. 46; Johnson & Johnson (1996), p. 64; Sapon-Shevin (1987), p. 50; *Turning Points* (1989), p. 52.

51. Fruehling (1971), p. 622.

52. See A. Kohn, "Resistance to cooperative learning: Making sense of its deletion and dilution," *Journal of Education*, vol. 174, no. 2 (1992), pp. 38–58.

53. Oakes et al. (1993), p. 468.

54. Johnson & Johnson (1996), p. 64.

55. George (1981), p. 14.

56. George (1993), p. 18.

57. Johnson & Johnson, 1996 (p. 64).

58. C. Toepfer, "Curriculum for identity: A middle level educational obligation," *Middle School Journal*, vol. 22, no. 3 (January 1992), p. 8.

59. National Middle School Association annual conference program (1987), p. 69.

60. George (1988), p. 27.

61. L.N. Graves, "Cooperative learning communities: Context for a new vision of education and society," *Journal of Education*, vol. 174, no. 2 (1992), p. 69.

62. L.A. Furr, "Curriculum tracking: A new arena for school social workers," *Social Work in Education*, vol. 15, no. 1 (January 1993), p. 42.

63. "Outcome-Based Education," or OBE, was an educational fad of the 1990s which relied heavily on both mastery learning and cooperative learning, despite denials by people such as Robert Slavin. See, for example, "Outcome based education is not mastery learning," *Educational Leadership*, vol. 51, no. 6 (March 1994).

64. Tiffany Yecke, the author's daughter, wrote this essay in 1993 describing her experiences in a Minnesota middle school during the 1991–1992 school year.

65. Sapon-Shevin (1987), p. 50; emphasis in the original.

66. *Turning Points* (1989), p. 52.

67. Johnson & Johnson (1996), p. 64.

68. Kitano (1991), p. 13.

69. Cohen (1991), pp. 10, 16.

70. Johnson & Johnson (1992), p. 46.

71. C.A. Broadwell & J.C. Walden, "Free and appropriate education after *Rowley*: An analysis of recent court decisions," *Journal of Law and Education*, vol. 17, no. 1 (1988), pp. 35–51; E.M. Gallegos, "Beyond *Board of Education v. Rowley*: Educational benefit for the handicapped?" *American Journal of Education*, vol. 97, no. 3 (1989), pp. 258–288; M.M. McCarthy, "The *Pennhurst* and *Rowley* decisions: Issues and implications," *Exceptional Children*, vol. 49, no. 6 (1983), pp. 517–522; B.P. Tucker, "*Board*

of Education of the Hendrick Hudson Valley Central School District v. Rowley: Utter chaos," *Journal of Law and Education*, vol. 12, no. 2 (1983), pp. 235–245.

72. Lipsky & Gartner (1996); Minow (1990).

73. Minow (1990), p. 84.

74. C. Midjaas, "The middle school: An opportunity for humanized education," speech delivered at Northern Michigan University, ERIC document number ED 046 110 (May 8, 1970), p. 6.

75. Johnston & Markle (1986), pp. 46, 49.

76. Sapon-Shevin (1994), pp. 188, 189.

77. R.E. Slavin, "Mastery learning reconsidered," *Review of Educational Research*, vol. 57, no. 2 (1987), pp. 175–213, 76, 206, 205–206.

78. M. Matthews, "Gifted students talk about cooperative learning," *Educational Leadership*, vol. 50, no. 1 (October 1992), pp. 48–50, copyrighted material used with permission from the Association for Supervision and Curriculum Development (ASCD); M. Matthews, "Gifted students respond to cooperative learning," paper presented to the National Association for Gifted Children (November 1994), material used with the permission of the author; A. Robinson, "Cooperation or exploitation? The argument against cooperative learning for talented students," *Journal for the Education of the Gifted*, vol. 14, no. 1 (1990), pp. 9–27.

79. A.H. Bloom, "What are you teaching my son?" *Educational Leadership*, vol. 53, no. 7 (April 1996), p. 83.

80. National Middle School Association annual conference program (1992), p. 77.

81. Salins (1997).

82. Gavora (1997), p. 24.

83. N. Glazer, *We Are All Multiculturalists Now* (Cambridge, Mass.: Harvard University Press, 1995), p. 136.

84. S. Schroeder-Davis, *Coercive Egalitarianism: A Study of Discrimination against Gifted Children* (Manassas, Va.: Gifted Education Press, 1993), p. 1.

85. S. Schmidt, "Wishful egalitarianism," *Analog Science Fiction and Fact* (December 1994), reprinted in *MCGT News* (March/April 1995), p. 5.

86. C.S. Collier, "Collier comments on Mosteller," *Harvard Educational Review*, vol. 67, no. 3 (1997), p. 605.

87. Howley, Howley, & Pendarvis (1995), p. 83. See also J.J. Gallagher, C. Harradine, & M.R. Coleman, "Challenge or boredom? Gifted students' views on their schooling," *Roeper Review*, vol. 19, no. 3 (March 1997), p. 135.

88. P. Peters, "TAG student defends programs against critic" (Torrington, Conn.: *The Register Citizen*, July 1990), p. 10; cited in J. Renzulli and S. Reis, "The reform movement and the quiet crisis in gifted education," *Gifted Child Quarterly*, vol. 35, no. 1 (Winter 1991), p. 32.

89. K. Johnson, "The peer effect on academic achievement among public elementary school students" (Washington, D.C.: The Heritage Center for Data Analysis, no. 00–06, May 26, 2000), p. 5. Note that although the title refers to elementary schools, the data analysis covers grades four and eight.

90. Lewis (2001) p. 204.

91. Ibid., pp. 199–200.

92. Gallagher et al. (1997), p. 135.

93. Lewis (2001), p. 203.

94. B. Clark, "Social ideologies and gifted education in today's schools," *Peabody Journal of Education*, vol. 72, nos. 3–4 (1997), p. 83.

95. See Cohen (1991); Gavora (1997); Johnson & Johnson (1992); Johnston & Markle (1986); Howley, Howley, & Pendarvis (1995); Lee & Smith (1993); Oakes (1985); Toepfer (1988).

96. See Cohen (1991); Howley, Howley, & Pendarvis (1995); and Noddings (1995).

97. *Turning Points* (1989); Cohen (1991); Kitano (1991); Sapon-Shevin (1987).

98. P.S. George, National Middle School Association annual conference program (1979), p. 23.

99. Lee & Smith (1993), p. 181.

100. A. Gamoran, M. Nystrand, M. Berends, & P.C. Le Pore, "An organizational analysis of the effects of ability grouping," *American Educational Research Association*, vol. 32 (1995), p. 687.

101. Toepfer (1988), p. 10.

102. National Middle School Association annual conference program (1998), p. 77.

103. Cohen (1991); Lee & Smith (1993), p. 180.

104. Johnston & Markle (1986), p. 47.

105. Oakes (1985), p. 211.

106. J.J. Gallagher, "Least restrictive environment and gifted students," *Peabody Journal of Education*, vol. 72, nos. 3–4 (1997), pp. 159, 164.

107. Howley, Howley, & Pendarvis (1995), p. 208.

108. J.J. Gallagher, M.R. Coleman & S. Nelson, *Cooperative Learning as perceived by Educators of Gifted Students and Proponents of Cooperative Education*, ERIC document no. 355 675 (Chapel Hill: North Carolina University, 1993), p. 14.

109. *NMSA Position Statement: Ability Grouping*, endorsed by NMSA Board of Trustees (January 2001).

110. Gavora (1997), p. 25.

111. Lipsitz (1979), p. 49.

112. *An Agenda for Excellence at the Middle Level*, National Association of Secondary School Principals (Reston, Va.: NASSP, 1985).

113. Johnson & Johnson (1996), p. 64.

114. Noddings (1995), p. 368.

115. National Middle School Association annual conference program (1987), p. 83.

116. National Middle School Association annual conference program (1993), pp. 124, 110.

117. National Middle School Association annual conference program (1998), p. 115.

118. National Middle School Association annual conference program (1987), p. 83.

119. Matthews (1992), p. 48.

120. J.J. Gallagher, M.R. Coleman & S. Nelson, "Perceptions of educational reform by educators representing middle schools, cooperative learning, and gifted education," *Gifted Child Quarterly*, vol. 39, no. 2 (Spring 1995), p. 71.

121. National Middle School Association annual conference program (1996), p. 61.

122. Matthews (1994), p. 7.

123. Fantini (1986), p. 41.

124. *A Nation at Risk: The Imperative for Educational Reform*, National Commission on Excellence in Education (April 1983), p. 12 (available online at http://www.ed.gov/pubs/NatAtRisk/), as cited in M.D. Fantini, "Defining excellence: An equation for modern times," *Equity and Excellence*, vol. 22, nos. 4–6 (1986), p. 32.

125. S.L. Lightfoot, "On excellence and goodness," *Harvard Educational Review*, vol. 57, no. 2 (1987), p. 204.

126. C. Tomlinson, "The easy lie and the role of gifted education in school excellence," *Roeper Review*, vol. 16, no. 4 (June 1994), pp. 258–259.

127. Ibid.

128. Feldhusen & Moon (1992); J.J. Gallagher, "Education reform, values, and gifted students," *Gifted Child Quarterly*, vol. 35, no. 1 (1991), pp. 12–19; J.J. Gallagher, "Academic effectiveness or social reform: A response to Robert Slavin and Jomills H. Braddock, III," *The College Board Review*, vol. 168 (1993), pp. 18–34.

129. W.A. Henry, *In Defense of Elitism* (1994), cited in *Time* (August 29, 1994), p. 65.

130. Sternberg (1996), p. 263.

CHAPTER 8

Activist Implementation

We hope that our [student teachers] leave us as quiet revolutionaries. We are preparing them to challenge the status quo.

Middle School Journal, 1995[1]

Social psychologists have suggested that the strength of a belief, as well as the strength of its manifestation in attitudes and behaviors, is reflected in the level of intensity put forth to secure its implementation.[2] The most vocal efforts to implement anti-gifted practices at the middle level have been strongly activist in nature, representing a profound commitment to the beliefs and convictions driving these changes. An activist approach was used, and continues to be used, by radical advocates of the middle school concept in the move toward reducing the rigor of the middle school curriculum, eliminating ability grouping, and increasing the use of cooperative learning and peer tutoring.

As noted by Professor Stanley Pogrow of the University of Arizona, many educators are "seduced into pursuing" trendy reforms by "a reform/academic/research community that is largely out of touch with reality." He goes on to explain the strategies used by popular reformers to implement their goals, which include both the Hegelian principle and the driving force of beliefs:

The scenario goes like this: a sense of urgency is created, and a new terminology is coined; a national fellowship develops among the believers; stories of success appear in a journal such as this [*Phi Delta Kappan*]; and a massive national network of training is created. The advocacy is *driven largely by philosophy*, with only a smidgen of technique or research supporting the idea. The word then goes out that the technique is supported by research.[3] (emphasis added)

As evidence that a strong *belief* will even override *facts* as it drives behaviors, consider again the words of these educators:

Teacher: We represent all children and it is morally wrong to give different instruction to these gifted students. I, for one, *do not believe* the so-called research that indicates that these children have educational needs other children do not. If they are so smart they can find something useful to do with their time.[4] (emphasis added)

Principal: There exists a body of *philosophic absolutes* that should include this statement: The ability grouping of students for educational opportunities in a democratic society is ethically unacceptable. *We need not justify this with research*, for it is a statement of principle, not of science.[5] (emphasis added)

Some educators have clearly received the radical middle school message: The middle school plan is a noble mission with societal implications, and implementation is demanded with a sense of intensity and urgency.[6] This message permeates *Turning Points*, the seminal publication that helped to launch the contemporary middle school movement. Readers are told that "fundamental restructuring in existing educational policies and practices *must* occur" and "all states and communities *must* join in this effort." Time cannot be wasted, so states are instructed to "*immediately* convene task forces to review the recommendations in this report." An apathetic American society is blamed for all current social ills, as it "has not committed itself to addressing these serious and well-documented social problems." *Turning Points* concludes:

In short, *a large and activist constituency* for changing middle grade schools across the nation *must* be created if systemic improvement in the education of young adolescents is to occur.[7] (emphasis added)

As noted earlier, activist Paul George from the University of Florida at Gainesville declared that middle schools had become "the focus of societal experimentation, the vehicle for movement toward increased justice and equality in the society as a whole," and in reaction to criticism, ominously proclaimed that "we are in a race between the middle school concept and all the threats that peril its existence."[8] Information will be presented in this chapter to demonstrate the existence of an activist approach in the movement toward using the schools to promote social changes that the general public has neither asked for nor desires.

AN ACTIVIST VISION

In the early 1990s, Paul George and other middle school activists called upon educational leaders, such as school administrators, to doggedly pursue middle school goals by converting others to their point of view. The fervor of their words reflects a missionary-like intensity:

Beyond developing a common vision, school leaders need to help others understand why a change is necessary. They must explain the negative evidence that has accumulated from research and experience with regard to rigid ability grouping, often called tracking. In discussions and presentations to individuals, small groups, and learner audiences, school leaders should point out the flaws of ability grouping and provide information that favors a more inclusive school approach.[9]

By the late 1990s, the tone had not changed. In an article titled "Speaking with One Voice: A Manifesto for Middle-Grades Reform," the authors end with a "Call to Action" that declares: "If middle-level school reform fails, it will not be because it was misguided. It will be because the effort . . . was not sufficiently comprehensive, intense, or long-lasting."[10] They blame any potential future failure on educators who are not totally committed to the mission at hand.

As recently as 1998, a National Middle School Association (NMSA) conference session even asserted the need for radical change when it is clear that such change is not wanted by the community, an issue that will be discussed in greater detail in Chapter 9:

When the departmentalized structure in a well-established junior high school produces the results desired by the community—high student achievement—there is no mandate for change. Successful graduates and high student test scores may result in Blue Ribbon recognition, but can be an Achilles heel when it comes to educational innovation.[11]

If the purpose of public education is student academic achievement, then what sort of "educational innovation" would be necessary in a school where students already meet challenging academic goals? None—if that is the purpose of public education. However, as has been documented, middle school activists clearly see another role for the school. As expressed in the *Middle School Journal*:

The transformation [of middle schools] and the continuing commitment to quality starts at the top. It must take on a different sense of what the real purpose of schooling is, and it adopts this new sense of purpose as a mission.[12]

So, just what is "the real purpose of schooling?" According to social activist Nell Noddings, it should be a "moral one of producing caring people," but instead remains "a relentless—and as it turns out, hapless—drive for academic adequacy." She continues:

The traditional organization of schooling is intellectually and morally inadequate for contemporary society. We live in an age troubled by social problems that force us to reconsider what we do in schools.[13]

Notice the social activist thought process: today's social problems *"force us* to reconsider what we do in schools." In other words, there can be no other choice. This belief is quite similar to that of middle school activists. Consider again the statement of one of the founding fathers of the middle school movement, John Lounsbury:

Our educational practices have compounded the ethical decline problem [of society] by over-emphasizing the knowledge acquisition objective of education and virtually ignoring in any official way the more important behavioral objectives. . . . Schooling, it is widely assumed, is a matter of acquiring knowledge. . . . Human behavior, however, is much more driven by attitudes than by knowledge, by feelings rather than facts. . . . Public education now, *whether we like it or not*, has new responsibilities— life building, character forming, personal growth responsibilities—that cannot be effectively carried out in a system and by a curriculum that was designed for submitting prescribed knowledge. . . . Needed is universal acceptance by all constituencies on a few major beliefs and goals, a true mission. The needed shift from cognitive goals measured by test scores to behavioral ones will require a shift in the nature of the teachers' role. (emphasis added)

According to Lounsbury, the "real purpose of schooling" is clearly *not* academic—it is behavioral, and teachers are expected to play a key role in implementing this new vision. Again, it is implied that this "change of mission" is so necessary that the need for it is out of anyone's control—it must occur "whether we like it or not." Lounsbury continues, both in claiming that schools should serve as incubators of change for society and in advocating immediate action:

In education, change is universally recognized as a key virtue. But there comes a time when patience is no longer a virtue. In middle level education, now is such a time. . . . Restructuring is indeed, needed, but it must be the restructuring of attitudes and assumptions, not merely the manipulation of the organizational aspects of education. . . . 'Dare the school build a new social order?' George Counts asked in 1932. It was a proper question then and it is a proper one now. I, for one, believe the school does have a social and political responsibility to work toward change for the better in our larger society. . . . [There is a] key role that only middle schools can play in building better human beings.[14]

That his sentiments were echoed nearly a decade later in 1999 by another middle school leader, James Beane, shows that the commitment to social activism remains firm:

Under siege as middle schools are, perhaps now is the time for their advocates to supplement their important talk about young people with some thought about what kinds of social purposes they think they should promote.[15]

One would assume that the public would be invited to a dialogue regarding any reconsideration of the purpose of public schools, or in the words of Lounsbury, the need for "universal acceptance by all constituencies on a few major beliefs and goals," but this is not the case. In a 1996 *Middle School Journal* article, the title arrogantly informs parents of the new reality: " 'School' no longer means what you thought."[16] Furthermore, education critic Alfie Kohn proclaims that educators, not the community, know what is best for children and should have the final say:

Educators should do all they can to bring parents aboard, to persuade and inform and organize, but in the final analysis there are some principles that have to be affirmed and some practices that cannot be tolerated.[17]

This arrogance is a stark contrast to the views reported in a 1965 survey of middle school educators which found that, over 30 years ago, half of the principals surveyed felt that it was a matter of principle to secure the support of the community for major changes *before* such changes were implemented.[18]

What do parents see as the goal of schooling? In an extensive 1998 survey, researchers Farkas and Johnson found that almost *all* parents—both black and white—agreed that it was "absolutely essential" that schools ensure mastery of reading, writing, and arithmetic. There was also extraordinarily high support for having "teachers and a principal who push students to study hard and to excel academically," with a significant number of both black and white parents believing that this is "absolutely essential." Furthermore, black parents, by a "stunning margin," believe that "the higher priority for the nation's schools should be to raise academic standards and achievement" as opposed to the attainment of social goals such as "more diversity and integration." Both black and white parents also fear that too much of an emphasis on social goals will cause schools to be "distracted from academics."[19]

However, many middle school activists remain relentless in their drive to use the middle school to implement social goals, regardless of what the public may want. Position papers released by the NMSA (in 1982 and 1995) were titled *This We Believe*, but beginning in 1996, the NMSA introduced a new feature in the *Middle School Journal* called "This We Believe and Now We Must Act." The new journal feature is intended to encourage middle school practitioners to move beyond *belief* and into *action*, so as to ensure the implementation of social goals through the middle schools:

This shared vision [will require] fundamental changes. . . . The changes needed to make middle schools more effective require new attitudes and new understandings about the broader goals of education. Extensive professional development is also needed to equip teachers and other educators for success in the new endeavor.[20]

As we shall see, change agents external to education helped to provide the impetus for broadening the purpose of education, and the training of both pre-service teachers and in-service teachers is being used to equip them for this fight.

THE INFLUENCE OF EXTERNAL CHANGE AGENTS

The model of educational change articulated by Matthew B. Miles, former professor of Psychology and Education at Teachers College, Columbia University, states that educational change is most effectively begun by individuals and groups that are external to education.[21] Furthermore, a link between the declarations of external agents and changes in policy has been demonstrated.[22] According to Miles, external agents, or catalysts of change, begin their approach by criticizing or attacking current practices, and follow this by presenting suggested changes. This is reminiscent of the strategy known as the "Hegelian Principle," which drove the activist agenda in *Turning Points* as outlined in Chapter 2: (1) create a crisis, (2) publicize the problem, and (3) present the solution. In this way, activists can step in and provide the very solution that they wanted to implement before their "crisis" was invented.

Documentary evidence demonstrates that both external and internal agents appear to have influenced middle school advocates in their calls for change, and that this change was driven in large part by anti-gifted beliefs and egalitarian goals. External participants include individuals such as researchers, social commentators, social scientists, social activists, and policymakers outside of the specific arena being studied (in this case, middle schools). Internal agents—in this case, proponents of the middle school concept, including both advocates and practitioners—operationalize change by adopting and implementing the proposals of external change agents.[23]

To stimulate change in the classroom, external agents described what they perceived as a "crisis" in society. Consider again the words of Noddings:

The traditional organization of schooling is intellectually and morally inadequate for contemporary society. We live in an age troubled by social problems that force us to reconsider what we do in schools.[24]

According to Noddings, the "crisis" leaves educators with no choice—they must "reconsider" the purpose of public education. Social activist Jeanne Oakes both underscores and amplifies this message when she states that "any change in this area will require an intensity not commonly seen in school reform."[25]

THE INFLUENCE OF INTERNAL CHANGE AGENTS

Internal agents of change include practitioners (in-service teachers and principals) and aspiring practitioners (student teachers, also called pre-service teachers). The expressions of external activists cited earlier are congruent with those of internal activists who feel that teacher education programs have a responsibility "to cultivate teachers' attention to the covert aims of schooling" in order to ensure that teachers can express their "political voice."[26] It must be noted that not all teacher education schools or professors of education espouse such radical views, but in a number of notable instances, some left-wing educators are quite explicit in their vision of teachers as activist social engineers.

Training of Student (Pre-service) Teachers

While some activists have encouraged pre-service teachers to contemplate "their own complicity in perpetuating a system of social inequality,"[27] others express doubts as to whether "[new] teachers will work collectively to transform the culture of schooling, either by altering its intellectual focus or by reframing its social and political function." Nonetheless, activists support radical efforts designed to accomplish this task. Note the extremist language regarding the role of teachers in the text below:

Committed teachers can empower themselves by joining forces with like-minded colleagues in the project of reformulating curriculum, altering the nature of classroom discourse, and establishing alliances between schools and *oppositional political movements*. . . . Through these practices, teachers will be able to redefine their role, establishing credibility as teacher-scholars and also as *political activists* . . . this change has the power to *transform schools' fundamental mission.* Instead of emphasizing the technical distribution of information, schools under the stewardship of reflective, *politically engaged teachers* will cultivate personal and collective practices for making meaning and taking ethical action.[28] (emphasis added)

In 1995, the *Middle School Journal* published an article similar in tone. "Fostering Change for Democratic Middle Schools Through Teacher Education" describes a radical curriculum for pre-service teachers that encourages the empowering of students through "social justice classrooms" because "education is a political act:"[29]

The way to act on this knowledge is to become *change agents within the public education system* and one of our goals is to prepare our novice teachers for the realities of teaching while *changing that which they know is not in the best interests of children.* . . . We want our [student teachers] to have a vision for just and equitable schooling for all children as well as the passion and means to make a difference in their classrooms and schools. . . . *It is impossible to remain politically neutral in a classroom.* Schools and teachers can use education to empower and liberate children or they can use education to dominate and oppress children. . . . We want our student [teacher]s to understand that not every educational decision is made for the best interests of children and that they have a choice as to which kind of force they will be—liberating or oppressing. We want them to understand that each act they make as a teacher either contributes to or challenges the status quo. . . . *We hope that our [student teachers] leave us as quiet revolutionaries. We are preparing them to challenge the status quo.* Our political stance is that schools are not entirely accessible nor empowering to all students and *we are trying to change that one cohort of student teachers at a time.*[30] (emphasis added)

Again, we see the arrogance of those who proclaim that they know better than parents or the community what is in the best interest of children. Prospective teachers are being trained to be both "change agents within the public education system" and "quiet revolutionaries." They are actively being trained to "challenge the status quo." Even as recently as 1999, an NMSA conference session refers to "novice teachers as agents of reform in middle grades."[31]

And if parents do not agree, their desires are simply to be ignored and overridden. To repeat the words of Alfie Kohn: "Educators should do all they can to bring parents aboard, to persuade and inform and organize, but in the final analysis there are some principles that have to be affirmed and some practices that cannot be tolerated."[32]

Ignoring the wishes of parents and the public is not uncommon among some key internal change agents—namely, professors at many education schools. In a comprehensive survey of 900 education school professors, researchers Farkas and Johnson identified several startling disconnects between the public and education school professors:

Interestingly, professors of education are often quite aware that the public is focused on priorities different from their own. But they are not fazed by this gap, believing that the public is not up-to-date on findings from research or especially competent to judge good schooling. In fact, [over three-quarters] of these teachers of teachers say *"the general public has outmoded and mistaken beliefs about what good teaching means. . . ."* [Furthermore], other respondents voiced a different kind of wish—that the public simply stay out of the education business: *"What bothers me is for the public to make the decision of what I, the teacher, should do in the classroom. I really resent that."*[33] (emphasis added)

This level of arrogance is alarming in that the training of new teachers has typically been under the purview of schools of education—giving such schools a captive audience. Their influence cannot be underestimated. As noted earlier, in addressing the level of influence wielded by some education school professors, these researchers stated:

Their convictions and beliefs, it seems, should have particular significance since they are the source of a chain reaction. Assuming that they are at least reasonably effective, what education professors teach about learning and schools shapes the goals, expectations, and priorities of the nation's teacher corps.[34]

The major disconnect identified between the beliefs of many education professors and those held by other education stakeholders should be a source of serious concern. Furthermore, this disconnect appears to be driven by beliefs, and by "a mind set that is unquestioning in its conviction of its own rightness."[35] As stated by Farkas and Johnson:

Education professors often cite research when justifying their preferred pedagogical practices, but this study suggests that it may be their self-ascribed ideological loyalties that seem to partially explain their preferences.[36]

These "ideological loyalties" would obviously display themselves in a number of ways, which may account for the belief among education school professors in this study that "public education's mission is to redress . . . the nation's social problems." In other words, social activism is in, and support for excellence is out. Consistent with the discussion on beliefs and convictions articulated in Chapter 7, Farkas and Johnson found that "there is one group of students—those considered academically gifted—whose needs appear to carry less priority than other groups," and their study shows that significantly less time and energy are expended in teaching prospective teachers about the needs of this group of students.[37]

The researchers who conducted this survey were startled by their findings: "It is unusual to find disparities of this magnitude about such fundamental goals, and involving an issue—public education—that is so close to the public's heart." They conclude:

Professors of education hold a vision of public education that seems fundamentally at odds with that of public school teachers, students, and the public. While the public's priorities are discipline, basic skills, and good behavior in the classroom, teachers of teachers severely downplay such goals. . . . Education professors put the public's priorities squarely at the bottom of their list.[38]

Other sources have echoed the concerns raised in this survey. For example, a recent editorial in *USA Today* addresses the importance of improving teacher quality, but then declares that "many of the 1,200 colleges that teach teachers refuse to step up to the job." The editorial describes how "many education professors undermine state standards," that "education schools refuse to teach effective instruction techniques," and that they "dodge accountability." According to the authors, resistance at a number of education schools to providing meaningful support for state academic standards means that many new teachers "are more inclined to scorn the standards than embrace them."[39] Such harsh criticism from a mainstream source should lay to rest the myth that only members of the "far right" are critical of the extreme policies and practices that permeate many schools of education.

According to some individuals in the field of education, sometimes our colleges of education "offer chaotic courses often bereft of serious intellectual content, and embrace a bizarre collection of educational half-truths and simple falsities,"[40] and "what they *do* teach often cannot be trusted. It rests on a shaky scientific base . . . more apt to be rooted in fads, trends, and ideologies than in rigorous research."[41]

Furthermore, evidence may suggest that the more time individuals spend in American colleges of education, the less they care about gifted learners. As will be discussed in Chapter 10, survey data indicate that among policymakers, the least sympathetic group to the concerns of gifted learners are state superintendents—and at the same time, they are more likely than any other group of policymakers to hold a doctoral degree.[42]

Around half of the education schools in the United States are accredited through an organization called NCATE: the National Council on Accreditation of Teacher Education. This organization has established six standards by which schools of education will be evaluated—but instead of focusing on helping teachers to be effective educators, five of the six standards address some facet of multiculturalism.[43] In contrast, as noted in Chapter 2, parents, teachers and policymakers want a "color blind" approach to educating children:

It appears that policymakers, like practitioners and members of the public, choose to identify students by learning characteristics more so than by race or ethnicity. . . . It appears that both policymakers and practitioners see their students primarily as learners with specific academic strengths and weaknesses, and only secondarily as members of a specific ethnic group.[44]

Yet, according to a report on NCATE, we are told:

Diversity is *the* single yardstick NCATE will use above all to measure the work of teacher trainers. . . . The NCATE standards repeatedly emphasize the necessity for teacher trainers and future teachers to exhibit the correct "dispositions" with regard to diversity. What does that mean? . . . G. Pritchy Smith, an education professor at the University of North Florida, made the point more explicitly. . . . "We should hire people who are anti-racists and encourage them to create a new world order. Social justice is the way to close the achievement gap. This should be the central "disposition."[45]

It is a curious sort of logic that would see "social justice" and not a rigorous curriculum, challenging academic opportunities, a school culture that values achievement, and high academic expectations as the means for closing the achievement gap.

In addition to these sorts of politically correct requirements, NCATE places on teacher trainers are the requirements placed on the content of programs within many schools of education. One would expect an accrediting organization to have independently developed a comprehensive set of criteria for each individual program, but this is not the case. NCATE relies upon the criteria and standards developed by a number of special interest groups, many of which have a decidedly liberal slant. Included among these groups is the National Association for the Education of Young Children (NAEYC), authors of the early childhood education program standards; the National Council for Teachers of English (NCTE), authors of the English/language arts education; and the National Middle School Association (NMSA), authors of the middle level education standards.[46]

It is not easy for schools of education to avoid complying with what they may view as objectionable NCATE standards when accreditation by NCATE is often required by state law. Requirements such as this prevent schools of education that want to break out of politically correct restraints from doing so. Chester Finn, President of the Fordham Foundation, writes:

Ed schools are part of the cartel that restricts entry into public school teaching in America, seeks to force everyone through essentially the same homogenized preparation program in ever more alike institutions, and defies common sense about how to attract talented people.[47]

It is a hopeful sign that some quality options have entered the public arena, such as the Teacher Education Accreditation Council (TEAC) and the American Board for Certification of Teacher Excellence, a program of the National Council for Teacher Quality (NCTQ). This will allow schools of education that do not want to be bound by a left-wing ideological agenda to have other options.

However, the fact remains that entities such as the National Commission on Teaching and America's Future (NCTAF) want to require that all schools of education be accredited by NCATE[48]—in spite of the fact that at least one study has demonstrated that there is little or no difference between teacher graduates of NCATE and non-NCATE institutions on measures such as achievement on national teacher exams, percentage of teachers hired, and teacher salaries. The authors conclude: "This inspires little confidence that institutions accredited by NCATE offer superior training."[49]

In-Service Teachers as Change Agents

In a 1986 NMSA publication, middle school activists J. Howard Johnston and Glenn Markle declared that teachers need to learn how to be more active in inducing change, and recommended that they "intervene systematically in the change of student attitudes." They continued:

Middle school teachers need to have a clear perception of their role in the development of student attitudes if they are to provide youngsters significant help with this important task. . . . Social psychology and educational research provide useful suggestions for developing desired attitude changes among middle school students. . . . Attitude formation and change is possible in schools because attitudes are learned. . . . By systematically applying attitude change techniques, the chances of developing desirable attitudes among middle school students can be improved.[50]

Do parents actually send their children to school to have their attitudes changed? Who gave schools the permission to do this? Here again we see the arrogance of those who believe they know what is best for other people's children.

In 1988, multiple articles by leading middle school activists appeared in *Social Education*.[51] These went beyond the scope of earlier articles that dealt with education of early adolescents, addressing instead (as did the *Middle School Journal*) the school as a means of implementing social change. One author refers to middle school proponents as "middle-level activists,"[52] and another charges teachers with "mak[ing] their classrooms a forum for democratic action" by "challenging students with value-laden issues."[53] Another author cites Lounsbury, one of the founding fathers of the middle school movement, as saying that the middle school years are "the years during which one's value system, one's behavior code . . . are formed,"[54] and another holds that action should occur at the middle level because "adult value patterns are largely set during one's middle level school years." The justification is thus set for the imparting of a specific set of social ideals to middle school students: "Social and human rights, in particular, call for action at all levels of the public school social studies curriculum."[55]

Lounsbury himself impresses upon his readers the important role of teachers in the quest for implementing societal changes through the middle school:

It is *teachers* who are the only real change agents. Those of us above that level may do a fine job dealing with ideas, but we do not implement those ideas with kids. It takes a teacher to do that.[56] (emphasis in the original)

The Carnegie publication *Turning Points* also used language directed at inducing teachers to action. Teachers were encouraged to "bring their own special interests and expertise to their teaching," but to ensure that the reader did not limit this to mean the sharing of hobbies or favorite books, the authors continued:

Young people exposed to ideas about which teachers care deeply see course material not as isolated facts and abstract concepts, but as powerful forces that affect people's lives and arouse people's passions.

Teachers, then, are to take the lead in "a fundamental transformation of the education of young adolescents [which] is urgently required," in part because "fundamental societal change is needed."[57]

The move to awaken teachers to what some believe is a civic duty to transform society by transforming public middle schools can also be seen in NMSA annual conference sessions beginning in the early 1990s. One state's education reforms were identified as an attempt at "massive, systemic social reform,"[58] and another session chastised those educators who were not actively involved in promoting change:

What factors are suppressing reform in the middle grades? Why do many lay and professional people reject progressive education and abhor thoughts of social reconstruction? This session is designed for teachers seeking to exert greater influence within the school community in order to affect change in the social community.[59]

Another session gave examples of opportunities for political activism and provided resources such as the names of political advocacy groups and their Web sites, and stated that teachers would be instructed in how to "survive politically."[60]

A sense of urgency regarding the "appropriate" training of teachers, and the warning of dire consequences if this does not occur, was delivered in 1995 by Tom Erb, influential middle school leader and editor of the *Middle School Journal*:

If we do not take immediate steps to examine the processes and practices by which middle grade teachers are prepared for the work they do as proprietors of the "last best chance" institutions for youth in American society, then we very clearly run the risk of losing the public education system to those whose political agenda is to dismantle the public schools.[61]

This is a strange sort of logic, because the very practices being pushed by radical middle school activists—against parental and community wishes—are what have broken the trust between the public and its schools.

In addition to teachers, social workers were also encouraged to function as change agents in the schools. An "advocacy agenda" has been identified by leaders in the area of social work that includes "promoting the use of the school's infrastructure as a social services delivery system."[62] School social workers are admonished to "be aware of the 'hidden agenda' of education," that is, the organizational structures and policies that ostensibly subjugate children, and social workers are advised that they are "in an excellent position to become 'spiritual pedagogues' " for students.[63] It is made clear that a new goal of social workers is to "promote change within the schools and [promote] social policies."[64]

OTHER EVIDENCE OF NMSA ACTIVISM

At annual conferences, the NMSA strongly favors speakers and entertainers who are known for their left-wing political activism (see Appendix J). An analysis of NMSA conference programs shows that keynote speakers or entertainers at annual NMSA conferences included people such as liberal activist Marian Wright Edelman, the founder and president of the Children's Defense Fund (1995); 1960s musicians Peter, Paul, and Mary, "activists for social justice" (1996);[65] author Toni Morrison (1997); reform critic Alfie Kohn (1998); and left-wing activist Jesse Jackson (1999). Only three men have appeared twice as keynote speakers, and all of them can be characterized as among the most radical voices in the contemporary middle school movement: Paul George of the University of Florida at Gainesville, J. Howard Johnston, co-author of many seminal middle school writings, and Conrad Toepfer, brain periodization advocate. It should be noted that evidence could not be found to indicate that any political conservatives, as either keynote speakers or entertainers, have appeared at any NMSA conferences in the entire history of that organization.

This organization, which prides itself on inclusiveness and diversity, thus appears to not see the need for *ideological* diversity.

CONCLUSION

Many middle-level leaders are convinced of the necessity of activism, and consequently promote its use for both in-service teachers and pre-service teachers. This approach promotes implementation of classroom practices designed to foster social change—*without* full disclosure and community input.

A number of dedicated middle school teachers appear to question this approach. In a comprehensive survey conducted in communities across the country, parents in *every community* reported that when they questioned teachers regarding required school policies and practices, the teachers responded with a statement similar to: "I don't know why we do it. If it were up to me, I'd do it differently."[66]

Another recent survey indicates a disconnect between the goals of some instructional leaders and the desires of teachers. Seventy-six percent of middle school principals surveyed reported that they were concerned over "teacher inability/unwillingness to engage in developmentally appropriate instructional practices for young adolescents."[67] The authors of this study attribute this to a lack of training—but it could just as easily be speculated that many teachers may be resisting what they see as activist reforms.

Furthermore, even retired educators are speaking out against the extreme positions held by many education activists—especially those at American colleges of education:

I've never been surprised when education professionals turn facts upside down to support their anti-intellectual, pro-social engineering agendas. . . . Sadly . . . professors at our schools of education have given up on the transmittal of knowledge as their number one priority in favor of trying to develop a society sans-individualism, whether we want it or not. . . . The weakness of the arguments of opponents of [ability] grouping is indicated by their oft-used pejorative descriptive terms—immoral, un-American, elitist, and out-of-touch; terms most middle-class Americans find intimidating. Attacking the philosophies and methods of parents and other citizens is another strategy public school educators use to disqualify any dissenters from joining in a critical discussion of public school policies and techniques. . . . All these techniques are used as substitutes for rational and quantifiable arguments. With these emotional and political techniques, supporters of classroom organizations such as heterogeneous [mixed-ability] and multi-age groups have essentially abandoned trying to justify them on the basis of cognitive learning improvement, which can be measured. . . . They have shifted the burden of proof of the validity of their programs and methods to the public's having to prove its own validity and relevance. This is a foolproof recipe for vouchers, which I don't want to see happen. I sometimes think educators want to be martyrs more than anything else. It's time for our schools of education to get in touch with the American public concerning what it truly wants for its children.[68]

Nonetheless, middle school activists continue their crusade with a sense of zeal and self-righteousness. Are their actions ethical? And are they in the best interest of our children? Chapter 9 will address these concerns.

NOTES

1. L.P. Stowell, J.E. McDaniel, & F.A. Rios, "Fostering change for democratic middle schools through teacher education," *Middle School Journal*, vol. 26, no. 5 (May 1995), pp. 7–8. Copyrighted material used with permission from the National Middle School Association (NMSA).

2. M. Burgoon & G.R. Miller, "Prior attitude and language intensity as predictors of message style and attitude change," *Journal of Personality and Social Psychology*, vol. 20, no. 1 (1972), pp. 246–253; D.M. Haslett, "Distracting stimuli: Do they elicit or inhibit counterargumentation and attitude shift," *European Journal of Social Psychology*, vol. 6, no. 1 (1977), pp. 81–94; W. Woods, N. Rhodes, & M. Beik, "Working knowledge and

attitude strength: An information-processing analysis," in R.E. Petty and J.A. Krosnick (Eds.), *Attitude Strength: Antecedents and Consequences* (Mahwah, NJ: Lawrence Erlbaum Associates, 1995).

3. S. Pogrow, "Reforming the wannabe reformers: Why education reforms almost always end up making things worse," *Phi Delta Kappan*, vol. 77, no. 10 (1996), pp. 657–658.

4. B. Clark, "Social ideologies and gifted education in today's schools," *Peabody Journal of Education*, vol. 74, nos. 3 & 4 (1997), p. 83.

5. C. Hastings, "Ending ability grouping is a moral imperative," *Educational Leadership*, vol. 50, no. 2 (October 1992), p. 14. Copyrighted material used with permission from the Association for Supervision and Curriculum Development (ASCD).

6. See P.S. George, "Tracking and ability grouping: Which way for the middle school?" *Middle School Journal*, vol. 20, no. 1 (September 1988), pp. 21–28; P.S. George, *How to Untrack Your School*, Association for Supervision and Curriculum Development (Alexandria, Va.: ASCD, 1992); A.G. Hilliard, "Conceptual confusion and the persistence of group oppression through education," *Equity and Excellence*, vol. 24, no. 1 (1988), pp. 36–43; N. Noddings, "A morally defensible mission for schools in the 21st century," *Phi Delta Kappan* (January 1995), pp. 365–368; J. Oakes, "Curriculum inequality and school reform," *Equity and Excellence*, vol. 23, no. 1 (1987/1988), pp. 8–13; *Turning Points: Preparing American Youth for the 21st Century* (Washington, D.C.: Carnegie Council on Adolescent Development, 1989); George (1988).

7. *Turning Points* (1989), pp. 80, 81, 66, 85.

8. George (1988), pp. 14, 17.

9. George (1992), p. 5.

10. J. Lipsitz, M.H. Mizell, A.W. Jackson, & L.M. Austin, "Speaking with one voice: A manifesto for middle grades reform," *Phi Delta Kappan* (March 1997), pp. 539–540.

11. National Middle School Association annual conference program (1998), p. 77.

12. K. Jenkins & D. Jenkins, "Total quality education: Refining the middle school concept," *Middle School Journal*, vol. 27, no. 2 (November 1995), p. 11.

13. Noddings (1995), pp. 366, 368.

14. J. Lounsbury, "A fresh start for the middle school curriculum," *Middle School Journal*, vol. 23, no. 2 (November 1991), pp. 5, 6, 7. Copyrighted material used with permission from the National Middle School Association (NMSA).

15. J.A. Beane, "Middle schools under siege: Responding to the attack," *Middle School Journal*, vol. 30, no. 5 (May 1999), p. 6. Copyrighted material used with permission from the National Middle School Association (NMSA).

16. T.O. Erb, " 'School' no longer means what you thought," *Middle School Journal*, vol. 27, no. 4 (March 1996), p. 2.

17. A. Kohn, "Only for *my* kid: How privileged parents undermine school reform," *Phi Delta Kappan*, vol. 79, no. 8 (April 1998), p. 576.

18. D.A. Rock & J.K. Hemphill, *Report of the Junior High School Principalship* (Washington, D.C.: National Association of Secondary School Principals, 1966), p. 38.

19. S. Farkas & J. Johnson, *Time to Move On: African-American and White Parents Set an Agenda for Public Schools* (New York: Public Agenda, 1998), pp. 38, 32, 10, 25.

20. S. Swaim, "Developing and implementing a 'shared vision'," *Middle School Journal*, vol. 28, no. 1 (September 1996), p. 55.

21. M.B. Miles, *Innovation in Education* (New York: Teachers College Press, 1964).

22. M.A. Hamilton, J.E. Hunter, & M. Burgoon, "An empirical test of an axiomatic model of the relationship between language intensity and persuasion," *Journal of Language and Social Psychology*, vol. 9, no. 4 (1991), pp. 235–255; D.R. Leff, D.L. Protess, & S.C. Brooks, "Crusading journalism: Changing public attitudes and policy making agendas," *Public Opinion Quarterly*, vol. 50 (1986), pp. 300–315.

23. Miles (1964), pp. 422–423.

24. Noddings (1995), p. 368.

25. Oakes (1987/1988), p. 8.

26. C.B. Howley, A. Howley, & E.D. Pendarvis, *Out of Our Minds* (New York: Teachers College Press, 1995), p. 48.

27. N.O. Houser & M. Chevalier, "Multicultural self-development in the preservice classroom: Equity education for the dominant culture," *Equity and Excellence in Education*, vol. 28, no. 3 (1993), p. 11.

28. Howley, Howley, & Pendarvis (1995), pp. 49, 47.

29. L.P. Stowell, J.E. McDaniel, & F.A. Rios, "Fostering change for democratic middle schools through teacher education," *Middle School Journal*, vol. 26, no. 5 (May 1995), p. 6. Copyrighted material used with permission from the National Middle School Association (NMSA).

30. Ibid., pp. 7–8.

31. National Middle School Association annual conference program (1999), p. 81.

32. Kohn (1998), p. 576.

33. S. Farkas, J. Johnson, & A. Duffett, *Different Drummers: How Teachers of Teachers View Public Education* (New York: Public Agenda, 1997), p. 16.

34. Ibid., p. 7.

35. Ibid., p. 29.

36. Ibid., p. 23.

37. Ibid., p. 24.

38. Ibid., p. 15.

39. "Too many teacher colleges major in mediocrity," *USA Today* (March 18, 2002), available online at www.usatoday.com/news/comment/2002/03/18/nceditf.htm.

40. D.M. Steiner, "An apologia for ed schools," *Academic Questions,* vol. 14, no. 4 (Fall 2001), p. 50.

41. C.E. Finn, "Toward pluralism in education," *Academic Questions,* vol. 14, no. 1 (Fall 2001), p. 64.

42. C. Yecke, *Policymakers' Views on Issues at the Middle School Level,* doctoral dissertation, University of Virginia (2001), p. 89.

43. For an analysis of this issue, see R. Holland, "New teachers face NCATE litmus test on diversity: Educators must exhibit 'correct' attitudes toward race and lifestyles," *Education Matters,* vol. 8, no. 2 (February 2002).

44. Yecke (2001), p. 182. See also Farkas & Johnson (1998); J. Johnson & J. Immerwahr, *First Things First: What Americans Expect from the Public Schools* (New York: Public Agenda, 1994); and S. Farkas & J. Johnson, *Given the Circumstances: Teacher Talk about Public Education Today* (New York: Public Agenda, 1996).

45. Holland (2002).

46. *NCATE Program Standards,* available online at www.ncate.org/standard/programstds.htm.

47. Finn (2001), p. 65.

48. See Holland (2002).

49. D. Ballou & M. Podgursky, "Teacher training and licensure: A layman's guide," in M. Kanstoroom & C.E. Finn, Jr. (Eds.), *Better Teachers, Better Schools* (Washington, D.C.: The Thomas B. Fordham Foundation, 2000), p. 45.

50. J.H. Johnston & G.C. Markle, *What Research Says to the Middle Level Practitioner* (Columbus, Ohio: National Middle School Association, 1986), pp. 78, 79, 81.

51. The following articles appeared in volume 52, number 2 of *Social Education* (1988): W.M. Alexander, "Schools in the middle: Rhetoric and reality," pp. 107–109; M.G. Allen, "Middle grades social studies: A modest proposal," pp. 113–115; T. Levy, "Making a difference in the middle," pp. 104–106; C.F. Toepfer, "What to know about young adolescents," pp. 110–112.

52. Levy (1988), p. 105.

53. Allen (1988), p. 114.

54. Levy (1988), p. 105.

55. Toepfer (1988), pp. 110, 112.

56. Lounsbury (1991), p. 7.

57. *Turning Points* (1989), pp. 54, 54, 36, 66.

58. National Middle School Association annual conference program (1998), p. 84.

59. National Middle School Association annual conference program (1994), p. 67.

60. National Middle School Association annual conference program (1998), p. 147.

61. T.O. Erb, "Close them down or beef them up? Whither middle grades teacher education programs," *Middle School Journal*, vol. 26, no. 5 (May 1995), p. 2.

62. M. Gibelman, "School social workers, counselors, and psychologists in collaboration: A shared agenda," *Social Work in Education*, vol. 15, no. 1 (January 1993), p. 45.

63. L.A. Furr, "Curriculum tracking: A new arena for school social work," *Social Work in Education*, vol. 15, no. 1 (January 1993), p. 42.

64. Gibelman (1993), p. 48. See also R.S. Levine, P. Allen-Meares, & F. Easton, "Primary prevention and the educational preparation of school social workers," *Social Work in Education* (Spring 1987), pp. 145–158.

65. National Middle School Association annual conference program (1995), back cover.

66. J.H. Johnston & R.D. Williamson, "Listening to four communities: Parent and public concerns about middle level schools," *NASSP Bulletin* (April 1998), p. 6 (online version).

67. D. Clark, V. Petzko, S. Lucas, & J. Valentine, "Research findings from the 2000 National Study of Leadership in Middle Level Schools," paper presented at the National Middle School Association annual conference, Washington, D.C. (November 1, 2001), p. 6.

68. C.S. Collier, "Collier comments on Mosteller," *Harvard Educational Review*, vol. 67, no. 3 (1997), pp. 603–605.

CHAPTER 9

Ethical Considerations

> Advocates whose fieldwork is really a species of revolutionary agitation may be violating [ethical standards] if the host people are being used primarily as a means to gain the researcher's own revolutionary goals.... If the change is not desired by that group, then the effort is ethically questionable.
>
> Joan Cassell, leader in the field of research ethics, 1982[1]

The underlying convictions of radical equity, group rights, and coercive egalitarianism, and the behaviors they are driving, lead to a series of concerns. These include the ethical implications of the implementation of these beliefs through changes in policy and practice in public schools.

THE MIDDLE SCHOOL AS A VEHICLE FOR SOCIAL EXPERIMENTATION

As early as 1969, *The Emergent Middle School*, a book considered to be a classic in the field, noted the utilitarian nature of the middle school as a vehicle for change:

The justification of a middle school organization as a means of accelerating the change process in education ... is a very real factor in many school districts. The belief that it is easier to innovate in a new than in an old organization is widespread.[2]

Over two decades later, this argument was still being cited as one of the reasons to justify the middle school concept. It was believed that there would be less resistance to significant change if such changes appeared to naturally accompany a new organizational structure for schools. The middle school was seen as:

serv[ing] as an ideal setting for implementation of needed innovations. It was thought that perhaps it would be easier to make significant changes needed if the school was a new one in the school organizational plan.[3]

As has been previously noted, activist Paul George declared that middle schools "became the focus of social experimentation," and others followed his lead in proclaiming "the need for experimentation" at the middle school.[4] Another activist pointed out that the "Carnegie Corporation of New York and an increasing number of other foundations are supporting experimentation in the middle grade schools."[5] (It should be noted that all three of these references were published in the official NMSA publication, the *Middle School Journal*.) Indeed, the Carnegie publication that played a significant role as an impetus to the contemporary middle school movement in 1989 reported that "Several foundations are involved in supporting experimentation in middle grade schools."[6] There was even a book titled *The Middle School Experiment*.[7]

However, the following question must be raised: Does anyone have the right to use the public schools as laboratories for social experimentation? All educators and social scientists should be well aware of the ethical issues inherent to this issue. In response to unethical experiments which took place in the fields of biomedical, psychological, and the social sciences, the National Commission for the Protection of Human Subjects of Biomedical and Behavioral Research was created by Congress in the 1974 National Research Act. The commission was asked to "identify a set of ethical principles and then to recommend ways to ensure that research is conducted in accordance with those principles." After discussion and debate, the commission decided not to make separate recommendations for the areas of biomedical research and

social research, since harm to human subjects was considered ta-
boo regardless of the field in which it might take place.[8]

The requirement of voluntary informed consent was a central
recommendation of the commission, and has been reiterated and
supported by others in the field of research ethics,[9] as well as in
a set of guidelines published by the Brookings Panel on Social
Experimentation and Ethical Research in 1975.[10] The word *voluntary* denotes that a free choice has been made, and *informed* implies
that all of the possible consequences of the experimental treatment
have been presented.

How does this impact educational experiments? Federal regulations will only allow the use of children as subjects with parental
permission,[11] and according to Rivlin and Timpane:

The question of children as subjects is particularly critical in social policy
research. . . . For some experiments . . . the harms envisioned may be
greater than the benefits for the children. . . . If envisioned benefits for
the children appear to be less weighty than the envisioned harms [are]
serious, such research would be morally unacceptable.[12]

However, it appears that middle schools did not offer students
or their parents the choice of whether or not to participate in a
program designed as a massive social experiment, nor were they
informed of all of the research pointing to potentially negative
consequences related to specific reforms. It may be argued that
the claims of middle school proponents that describe the implementation of the middle school concept as an "experiment" are
hyperbole—that is, a rhetorical overstatement. This raises a
question: Is implementation of the middle school concept really
an experiment? If the answer is no, then one has to ask why its
proponents are identifying it as such. If the answer is yes, then
one has to question why proper ethical guidelines have not been
followed.

The national commission recommended compensation for in-
juries resulting from bio-medical experimentation, and the Brookings Panel on Social Experimentation and Ethical Research (1975)
recommended compensation for subjects who are injured in social
experiments, as well. It can be speculated that, in response to the
"middle school experiment," parent-initiated litigation may be
possible.

RADICAL ADVOCACY RESEARCH

How do middle school activists justify their use of schools for conducting social experiments? They have made it clear that facts do not matter to them—no amount of research will change their beliefs, as they see themselves on a moral crusade, declaring, "We need not justify this with research, for it is a statement of principle, not science."[13] However, Joan Cassell, a leader in the field of research ethics, criticizes this approach: "Unfortunately, when the language of ethics is used for political disputes, where one's opponents are labeled immoral rather than mistaken, more heat than illumination is generated."[14]

Joan Cassell has identified four separate and distinct types of fieldwork research involving direct contact with human subjects, and one of these, the advocacy model of fieldwork research, describes those researchers who believe they are on a moral mission. Advocacy researchers are defined as those who "are moved to intervene to help people improve or transform their destinies" because the researchers "wish to help those studied [to] gain power."

The author bases her ethical framework for judging fieldwork upon the Kantian categorical imperative, that is, "the fundamental principle that persons always be treated as ends in themselves, never merely as means":

When the categorical imperative is applied to advocacy research, it becomes clear that there are certain varieties of advocacy in which subjects may be used primarily as means rather than ends. In such cases, fieldworkers are promoting pre-determined goals for those studied, without examining indigenous values, goals, and lifeways. Thus, advocates whose fieldwork is really a species of *revolutionary agitation* may be violating the Kantian categorical imperative, if the *host people are being used primarily as a means to gain the researcher's own revolutionary goals.* Such fieldwork might be characterized as a kind of revolutionary "neocolonialism," in which *researchers are convinced not only that they know more than their hosts about what will benefit the subjects, but also that it is worthwhile to risk the well-being of their hosts in order to chance the making of a revolution.* . . . Thus, even if one agrees with a particular fieldworker in a particular effort to ameliorate or improve a group's situation, *if the change is not desired by that group, then the effort is ethically questionable.*[15] (emphasis added)

Previous chapters make it clear that radical middle school activists fit this description. They are promoting "a species of revolutionary agitation" by using middle school students "as a means to gain the researcher's own revolutionary goals." Their aim is to remake society to match their utopian vision of an egalitarian society, so their goals are social change. This observation holds true over time, and from a variety of sources. Consider these statements from previous chapters in light of the description of the advocacy model of fieldwork:

Middle School Journal, 1991: Restructuring is indeed, needed, but it must be the restructuring of attitudes and assumptions, not merely the manipulation of the organizational aspects of education.... "Dare the school build a new social order?" George Counts asked in 1932. It was a proper question then and it is a proper one now. I, for one, believe the school does have a social and political responsibility to work toward change for the better in our larger society.... [There is a] key role that only middle schools can play in building better human beings.[16]

McGill Journal of Education, 1991: What is at stake here is the attempt to undo the effects of inequality.... Social scientists have documented the ways in which classrooms tend to reproduce the inequalities of the larger society. Undoing these effects is an ambitious undertaking.[17]

Educational Leadership, 1992: There exists a body of philosophic absolutes that should include this statement: The ability grouping of students for educational opportunities in a democratic society is ethically unacceptable. We need not justify this with research, for it is a statement of principle, not of science. It should become a moral imperative along with the beliefs that slavery is immoral and that all people are created equal under the law.[18]

Boston University Journal of Education, 1992: [Cooperative learning will] move classrooms and society toward social justice and more equitable distribution of resources.... In proposing "caring work" and the creation of communities of care as an underlying paradigm for cooperative learning ... we envision a society in which no one gets lost, structured so that each citizen has an active role. All people would be guaranteed access to the resources of the society, including food, housing, health care, educational opportunities at all levels, and meaningful, well-paid work. Unemployment, poverty, homelessness—and the legacies of such hopelessness such as drug addiction—would be unheard of.... Childcare would be available to all requesting families, community-based care to home-bound senior citizens, and affordable housing to all.[19]

Theory into Practice, 1994: Our goal should be schools in which cooperative learning can function as a catalyst—forcing us to uncover and dismantle the structures that separate and damage children, and reinvent schools that embody social and educational equity and justice.[20]

Middle School Journal, 1996: This shared vision [will require] fundamental changes. . . . The changes needed to make middle schools more effective require new attitudes and new understandings about the broader goals of education.[21]

Middle School Journal, 1999: Under siege as middle schools are, perhaps now is the time for their advocates to supplement their important talk about young people with some thought about what kinds of social purposes they think they should promote.[22]

Furthermore, middle school activists, as is true with advocacy researchers, will often proceed with the changes they endorse and believe in even "if the change is not desired"—a fact that makes the action "ethically questionable." As noted earlier, a 1965 survey of middle school educators found that half of the principals surveyed felt that it was a matter of principle to secure the support of the community for major changes *before* they were implemented.[23] In less than 40 years, that implicit trust in the community has been replaced in many instances by bold arrogance. As noted earlier, education critic and social activist Alfie Kohn declares that educators, not the community or parents, know what is best for children and should have the final say.

The enthusiasm of reformers and the intensity with which they hold their beliefs appears to have driven some of them to act without sufficient consideration for either ethical issues or the potential consequences of their actions. According to experts in the field of research ethics:

In the ordinary world of experimentation, the danger may be that enthusiasts, interested primarily in their experiments or in the benefits that may result from the experiments if all goes well, may be too little attentive to some potential consequences to their subjects, or to the ethical interests of their own colleagues and of the larger society of which they are a part.[24]

CONCLUSION

Middle school activists have a vision of creating a brave new world by manipulating the instructional policies and practices in

American middle schools. The ethics of actively promoting and implementing this covert agenda should be questioned. After all, public schools belong to *the public*—those who support the schools through their tax dollars. Public schools were never meant to be the vehicle for massive social experiments aimed at achieving the questionable utopian goals of an elite few.

NOTES

1. J. Cassell, "Harms, benefits, wrongs and rights in fieldwork," in J.E. Sieber (Ed.), *The Ethics of Social Research: Fieldwork, Regulation and Publication* (New York: Springer-Verlag, 1982), pp. 19–20.

2. W.M. Alexander, E.L. Williams, M. Compton, V.A. Hines, & D. Prescott, *The Emergent Middle School* (New York: Holt, Rinehart & Winston, 1969), p. 17.

3. C.K. McEwin, "William M. Alexander: Father of the American Middle School," *Middle School Journal*, vol. 23, no. 5 (May 1992), p. 35.

4. L. McDonough, "Middle level curriculum: The search for self and social meaning," *Middle School Journal*, vol. 23, no. 2 (November 1991), p. 35.

5. A. Jackson, "From knowledge to practice: Implementing the recommendations of *Turning Points*," *Middle School Journal*, vol. 21, no. 3 (January 1990), p. 3.

6. *Turning Points: Preparing American Youth for the 21st Century* (Washington, D.C.: Carnegie Council on Adolescent Development, 1989), p. 84.

7. R. Edwards, *The Middle School Experiment* (London and Boston: Routledge and Kegan Paul, 1972).

8. M.L. Wax & J. Cassell, *Federal Regulations: Ethical Issues and Social Research* (Boulder, Colo.: Westview Press, 1979), pp. 46, 51.

9. Cassell (1982); A.M. Rivlin & P.M. Timpane, *Ethical and Legal Issues of Social Experimentation* (Washington, D.C.: Brookings Institute, 1975); J.E. Seiber, *The Ethics of Social Research: Surveys and Experiments* (New York: Springer-Verlag, 1982a); J.E. Seiber, *The Ethics of Social Research: Fieldwork, Regulation, and Publication* (New York: Springer-Verlag, 1982b); B.H. Stanley & J.E. Seiber, *Social Research on Children and Adolescents* (Newbury Park, Calif.: Sage Publications, 1992); B.H. Stanley, J.E. Seiber, & G.B. Melton, *Research Ethics: A Psychological Approach* (Lincoln: University of Nebraska Press, 1996).

10. Rivlin & Timpane (1975).

11. Stanley & Seiber (1992).

12. Rivlin & Timpane (1975), p. 43.

13. C. Hastings, "Ending ability grouping is a moral imperative," *Ed-

ucational Leadership, vol. 50, no. 2 (October 1992), p. 14. Copyrighted material used with permission from the Association for Supervision and Curriculum Development (ASCD).

14. Cassell (1982), p. 25.

15. Ibid., pp. 16, 14, 19–20.

16. J.H. Lounsbury, "A fresh start for the middle school curriculum," *Middle School Journal*, vol. 23, no. 2 (November 1991), p. 7.

17. E.G. Cohen, "Teaching in multiculturally heterogeneous classrooms: Findings from a model program," *The McGill Journal of Education*, vol. 26 (1991), p. 21.

18. Hastings (1992), p. 14.

19. M. Sapon-Shevin & N. Schniedewind, "If cooperative learning's the answer, what are the questions?" *Boston University Journal of Education*, vol. 174, no. 2 (1992), pp. 20, 21, 22. Material used with permission of the lead author.

20. M. Sapon-Shevin, "Cooperative learning and middle schools: What would it take to really do it right?" *Theory into Practice*, vol. 33, no. 3 (1994), p. 189.

21. S. Swaim, "Developing and implementing a 'shared vision'," *Middle School Journal*, vol. 28, no. 1 (September 1996), p. 55.

22. J.A. Beane, "Middle schools under siege: Responding to the attack," *Middle School Journal*, vol. 30, no. 5 (May 1999), p. 6. Copyrighted material used with permission from the National Middle School Association (NMSA).

23. D.A. Rock & J.K. Hemphill, *Report of the Junior High School Principalship* (Washington, D.C.: The National Association of Secondary School Principals, 1966), p. 38.

24. Rivlin & Timpane (1975), p. 178.

CHAPTER 10

Implications for the Twenty-First Century

If an unfriendly foreign power had attempted to impose on America the mediocre educational performance that exists today, we might well have viewed it as an act of war. As it stands, we have allowed this to happen to ourselves. We have even squandered the gains in student achievement made in the wake of the Sputnik challenge. Moreover, we have dismantled essential support systems which helped make those gains possible. We have, in effect, been committing an act of unthinking, unilateral educational disarmament.

A Nation at Risk, 1983[1]

In addition to the ethical implications regarding forced changes in middle school policies and practices, there are implications for our culture and our nation. Implicit in this discussion is the issue of the role of public trust, as well as an examination of policy changes necessary to undo the damage caused by the radical middle school movement.

IDEOLOGY AND THE PUBLIC TRUST

Those truly concerned with the quality of public education in this country—and with our nation's future—must place their focus on ensuring a quality academic education for American students, not on covertly imposing a social agenda or instigating ideological battles. As evidence, the best guide to educational success is often the study of that which has worked—or has *not* worked—elsewhere.

Lessons Learned

In the 1970s, Sweden implemented reforms which included the abolition of academic grading, claiming that giving students grades promoted competition over cooperation. (Sound familiar?) The school system pursued mass equality—but it did so at the expense of excellence. Although Sweden spent more on education per student than any other country in the world, student achievement fell into mediocrity.

The liberal Progressives were voted out of power in the fall of 1991, and one of the first changes to be instituted was a reform of the educational system. The new Education Minister, Beatrice Ask, proposed returning to a more traditional educational structure, reintroducing grades, academic competition, and the study of traditional ethics.

She contends that her country made a mistake in trying to use the public schools to deliver social services, eliminate competition, and promote liberal social changes: "Swedish schools have diluted the quality of education by trying to do too much," she declared. And she warned American educators to learn from Sweden's mistakes.[2]

As noted in Chapter 4, other nations—such as Great Britain, Japan, Taiwan, and Singapore—have likewise re-evaluated their levels of support for high ability learners and have made changes to ensure that their educational needs are being met. However, current evidence in America suggests the lessons learned from such countries have been lost on some American educators. In the late 1980s and 1990s, many state leaders, eager to improve their educational systems, were misled into believing that certain reforms and innovations had a proven academic track record. Worse yet, they often were unaware of the covert aims of such innovations. Trusting the activist rhetoric of "reform experts," some educators and policymakers allowed smooth talk and convincing presentations to mislead them into accepting innovations that served purposes other than academic ones.

Earlier warnings have gone unheeded. In an article with the

ominous title "The Age of Social Transformation," Peter Drucker states: "Making the school the organ of social polices has, without any doubt, severely impaired its capacity to do its own job."[3] And the result? A survey conducted by a non-partisan public policy institute proclaimed: "What has emerged is a deeply disturbing picture of an American public and community leadership frustrated and angered by the state of public education."[4]

Reaction to Criticism

Too often, those activists who promote and support many of the latest fads in education find they do not have facts and data to refute the arguments brought against their radical proposals. Since they cannot argue with the facts, they often resort to belittling anyone who disagrees with them. As a result, parents who question faddish practices often find themselves labeled as radical members of extreme "right-wing" fringe groups, or they are told they are the only ones who are complaining. Amazingly, manuals have been published and national conferences have even been held, sometimes at taxpayer expense, to advise administrators and educators on how to deal with the perceived "threat" from parents and citizens trying to express genuine concerns about their children's education.[5] Beginning in the mid-1990s and continuing to the present, numerous sessions at annual NMSA conferences presented strategies aimed at thwarting "right-wing" criticism or attacking perceived threats:

1994: The power and influence of the religious right with respect to education in this country is growing at a phenomenal pace. Many of the religious right's issues strike at the heart of the middle school movement.[6]

1995: Becoming right: Conservative critics of progressive curriculum. Not all parents who question the curriculum represent organized opposition. But when educators fail to offer reasonable responses, these parents may well join organized opposition.[7]

1996: Hot topics and their solutions, [including] the middle school and the extreme right.[8]

2000: Handling difficult parents: It's not your imagination. Parents are more demanding. That means having them breathe down your neck and question everything.[9]

2001: Middle school gains have been "washed away by the far right"; middle school policies have been "overpowered by arch-conservatives."[10]

Aside from eroding public trust and confidence in public education, branding critics as "the enemy" diverts attention from substantive issues and diminishes public cooperation and support. These confrontational stances tend to discredit serious researchers whose conclusions show either the shortcomings or true intentions of select current reforms. More often than not, a careful analysis of the effects of many current reforms validates that the concerns expressed by parents, community members, and conscientious educators are, indeed, legitimate.

An Issue of Trust

One of the foundations of American public education is that of trust between the parents and the schools. Parents have trusted that educators will do what is best for their children, but in too many cases that trust has been broken. There *are* some good education reforms among the bad, but this breech of trust has left many parents suspicious of all educational innovations. And can we blame them?

Without revealing their covert agenda to the American public, many middle school activists have striven to turn public middle schools into laboratories for producing students with "politically correct" attitudes in an attempt to remake American society. The way in which the middle school concept was promoted to the public did not reveal the non-academic and anti-intellectual intentions of middle school activists, who were driven more by ideology than by facts.

Here is just one example of how facts have been ignored. A study of nearly 9,000 eighth grade middle school students suggests that two components of the contemporary middle school concept (less departmentalization by subject area and more team teaching) are associated with higher levels of at-risk behavior among middle school students. Such behavior includes being involved in fights, being viewed as a troublemaker, and skipping school.[11] This study was published a decade ago, but it appears that no efforts were made to follow up on these disturbing results. While the study had other findings, the authors seemed to ignore their own data when they concluded that their results "lend empirical support" to continuing the middle school movement.[12]

As seen in previous chapters, it is not unusual for education researchers to ignore (or manipulate) their own data in order to pursue policies driven by a radical ideology. Is it any wonder, then, that many members of the public feel betrayed? The results of a Public Agenda survey of parents across America appear to confirm this observation:

Increasing numbers of educators and members of the public each believe the other has violated the unwritten contract long existing between them. Under this contract, educators agreed to educate America's children, and the public agreed to support them in their work. Today, neither group believes that the other is holding up its end of the bargain.[13]

WHICH WAY FOR GIFTED/HIGH ABILITY LEARNERS?

Many parents are coming to challenge school authorities regarding policies and practices they see as detrimental to students. As noted in the 2000 NMSA conference program, "parents are more demanding." It is interesting to see how very differently some school administrators respond to parental demands.

An Example of Successful Change

A parent who also served as a member of the Nashville, Tennessee school board, David Shearon produced a study that highlighted the need for a more rigorous curriculum for gifted/high ability middle school students in that district. Presented to the school board in January 1999, his initiative spurred the formation of a task force to study the problem and produce recommendations. The task force included a wide variety of stakeholders, including parents, teachers, principals, and administrators.[14]

Within five months, the task force recommendations evolved into plans set forth by both middle and high school principals to "step up their responsiveness" to the needs of gifted/high ability students by upgrading their course offerings for the 1999-2000 school year. Without asking for additional resources, these enterprising administrators were able to add 14 high school credit courses at their middle schools, and as a result, 18 of 23 middle schools were able to offer 3 courses for high school credit. At the high schools, 24 additional Advanced Placement (AP) courses were added.

The reaction in Nashville was supportive and enthusiastic. In fact, plans were drawn up to have all area middle schools offer 3 high school credit courses by the 2002-2003 school year.[15] According to David Shearon:

To lead, you have to ask the tough questions and be willing to listen when others ask them. I asked a tough question: "Why must my child go somewhere other than our local public middle school to get appropriate challenges?" By focusing on what some schools in our system were already doing, I was able to get the entire system to consider whether more schools couldn't do the same.[16]

Examples of Entrenched Resistance

The picture in many other districts is quite different from that of Nashville. Parents of gifted/high ability learners continue to be viewed by many middle school activists as obstacles to be overcome.[17] However, the fact is that if parents cannot find appropriate educational opportunities for their children within the public school setting, they will search for those choices elsewhere. This has become abundantly clear in some school districts.

For example, in 1996, parents and consultants evaluating the middle school program in Howard County, Maryland, protested the lack of opportunities for gifted/high ability students and recommended that, instead of across-the-board heterogeneous (mixed-ability) grouping, flexible ability grouping should be reinstated. In spite of this recommendation, and in spite of the fact that local survey results indicated that vast majorities of both teachers (66 percent) and parents (72 percent) favored such a move, the administration refused to listen. The result? The number of parents in Howard County who send their children to private schools or who homeschool them has increased by 50 percent over the last decade.[18]

In Wheeling, Illinois, parents who were frustrated with "middle school theorists" approached the local school board requesting that they be given the opportunity to choose more traditional instruction for their middle school children, and received "a resounding NO." The result? Several families chose to move out of the school district, while others enrolled their children in the local private school.[19]

Similar situations are occurring in places such as Los Angeles. An analysis there found that some schools deliberately avoid identifying gifted students "out of fear that the child will then transfer out [to district magnet schools] and lower the school's all-important test scores." Even the coordinator for the district's gifted and talented program admits that, as a result, "Minority parents, middle class parents, or anyone else who can, tend to send their children to private schools, and that's where the gifted are."[20]

Lessons Learned

Lessons such as these have been lost on many middle school activists, who recognized this issue as early as 1995, but who are strangely unaware that the very policies they continue to champion and force on the public schools are the root of this problem. Even middle school activist Paul George admits:

Nor can public education survive as anything other than pauper schooling if parents of gifted and talented students, frustrated in their attempts to secure the best the school has to offer, withdraw their children from the public schools and create a whole new system of private education.[21]

Fortunately, the manipulation of public middle schools by middle school activists is no longer going unchallenged. According to one parent, unless current policies change:

The exodus of the best and the brightest from the nation's public schools will only accelerate, and the widespread public perception that public schools are places of mediocrity rather than excellence will only deepen and, indeed, be confirmed. The public schools must stand for excellence, or they are finished, and American democracy will truly be the casualty.[22]

As noted earlier, international researchers concur:

The wide heterogeneity in de-tracked public schools may slow the coverage of curriculum. This slower pace may explain the decision of faster students to leave the public schools. . . . We conclude that the best-intentioned detracking reforms may not fix tracking problems. . . . If detracking lowers the achievement or engagement of faster students, it may drive them out of the public schools. . . . We hope American reformers can learn from this experience and avoid these outcomes.[23]

In a feeble and belated attempt to prevent the increasing exodus of gifted/high ability students from American middle schools, some activists have seemingly modified their positions. For example, in 1979 middle school activist Paul George promoted the goals of leveling achievement and producing equal academic outcomes by denouncing individualized instruction.[24] Amazingly, two decades later, he is actively *promoting* individualized instruction.[25] Such a move can be seen as blatant hypocrisy, as belated gestures will clearly not undo the damage wrought by several decades of vigorous activism on behalf of radical policies.

Options to Consider

Parents and educators of gifted/high ability students recognize that they are faced with at least four choices: (1) They can try to continue working within the framework of the middle school concept, as has been done for many years, although the hope that appropriate differentiation of instruction will occur may be questionable and attempts to obtain such accommodations can be frustrating; (2) They can recapture the intellectual mission of public education by fighting for appropriate services for gifted/high ability children that include options seen as anathema by middle school activists, as the citizens of Nashville did so successfully; (3) They can choose to leave the public school setting, as is occurring in places like Los Angeles and Howard County, Maryland, to find other instructional settings that appropriately meet the needs of their children; and/or (4) They can enter the policy arena with the hope of securing changes through that venue.

The option of working to foster change in the area of policy is worthy of serious consideration. Results of a recent survey indicate that certain policymakers may be more supportive of the needs of gifted students than others. Most significant are the differences between the beliefs of state legislators and state education commissioners regarding issues impacting gifted education.

Cooperative Learning and Peer Tutoring

Policymakers were asked to indicate their level of support for the following statement: "Cooperative learning, rather than grouping, should be used as a means of meeting the needs of students of varied levels of ability." The lowest level of agreement came from state legislators (53 percent), and the highest was expressed by gubernatorial policy advisors (92 percent) and state education commissioners (90 percent). Similar results were seen in response to the statement: "At the middle school level, students who have mastered course material should tutor those who have not." Again, gubernatorial policy advisors had the highest level of agreement (77 percent), closely followed by state education commissioners (71 percent).[26]

Ability Grouping

By far, the policymakers who hold the strongest beliefs against homogeneous (same-ability) grouping and the strongest in favor of heterogeneous (mixed-ability) grouping are state education commissioners. Ninety percent of the state education commissioners responding to the survey indicated support for heterogeneous grouping, with nearly half (48 percent) expressing strong support. Likewise, the level of support these same policymakers express for homogeneous (like-ability) grouping is the weakest of all policymakers, with 90 percent disagreeing with this practice. Conversely, state legislators express the strongest support for ability grouping, and half of them would also support allowing separate classes for gifted and talented students.[27]

The Needs of Gifted Learners

A statistically significant difference was found between state legislators and all other groups of policymakers (state and local school board members, state education commissioners, and gubernatorial advisors) in their rankings of the needs of gifted students, with state legislators ranking the needs of gifted students far higher than any other group. It should be noted, in contrast, that state education commissioners ranked the needs of gifted learners lower than any other group.[28]

Impact of Colleges of Education

Of additional interest is the fact that the policymakers who held the largest percentage of doctoral degrees were state education commissioners (60 percent), while the group with the smallest percentage of doctorates were state legislators (9 percent).[29] It is unknown whether state education commissioners received their doctorates at colleges of education, but such an assumption would not be unreasonable. This may suggest that the longer educators spend in schools of education, the more adverse they become toward the needs of gifted students.

This author concludes:

In view of their positions on ability grouping, cooperative learning and peer tutoring, it appears unlikely that state education commissioners as a group would be strong advocates for addressing the needs of advanced/gifted learners, and *may even work counter to those trying to address the needs of these students.*

On the issue of addressing the needs of advanced/gifted learners, state legislators were more likely to express beliefs aligned with practices more favorable to these students. . . . Although decisions on grouping practices are generally made at the local level, the power of state legislators has grown considerably over the past several years.[30] (emphasis added)

So advocates for advanced/gifted learners may find that focusing a significant portion of their lobbying efforts on state legislators, who appear to support practices favored by advocates for advanced/gifted learners, may prove to be an effective use of their time and resources.

WHICH WAY FOR THE MIDDLE SCHOOL?

Nearly a decade ago, gifted advocate Carol Tomlinson predicted that "if [the] middle school does not celebrate and extend the talent of high-end learners, it is at risk as an institution."[31] The growing backlash to what the public perceives as a watered-down curriculum, a hotbed of social engineering, and a lack of opportunities for gifted/high ability learners may indicate fulfillment of her prediction.

Public Discontent

The middle school as an institution is currently conflicted about its role. Precipitating this is a combination of factors, including public discontent with the middle school and the rise of the standards movement. As noted earlier, public discontent has been reported by a number of sources:

Education Week, 1998: Thirty years after districts began shifting away from junior versions of high school, the middle school model has come under attack for supplanting academic rigor with a focus on students' social, emotional, and physical needs.[32]

School Board News, 1998: Has the middle-school concept gone too far in catering to the social and emotional developmental needs of young adolescents at the expense of academic performance? That's exactly what some education experts and school leaders are charging.[33]

Teacher Magazine, 1998: After more than 30 years, the middle school reform movement has done little to improve the education young teenagers get.[34]

NMSA conference session, 1998: While the middle level movement has grown in terms of professional advocacy and school implementation, there is a growing criticism of middle schools and philosophy.[35]

Impact of the Standards Movement

The growth of the standards movement has jeopardized radical middle school goals. Since the early 1990s, all states have written new academic standards, and now are in various stages of implementing testing programs to support those standards and to hold schools accountable for student achievement.

A slight increase in interest among middle school leaders regarding standards and accountability can be seen in the late 1990s when the number of sessions addressing standards and testing at annual NMSA conferences increased from three sessions in 1998 to seven sessions in 2000. Although this is not a remarkable increase, it stands in contrast to the days when prominent middle school activists arrogantly ridiculed "the contemporary infatuation with improving performance in academic achievement."[36]

It should be noted, however, that the variety among these conference sessions has been limited. For example, one presenter made the same presentation every year for four years.[37] Furthermore, many of the presenters, when addressing testing, denigrate it rather than address its positive aspects. For example, the testing presentation by middle school activist Paul George at the 2000 NMSA conference ridicules a focus on measuring achievement:

Raise your students' achievement test scores—or else! Middle school educators are pressured as never before to respond to strident, threatening demands for increased academic achievement. What can school, classroom, and district leaders do?[38]

In 2000, the year that the number of sessions on standards and assessment peaked, the index of the NMSA annual conference program listed "Standards and Assessments" as a stand-alone topic category. However, this only lasted for one year, as it did not appear in later programs.

Widespread disagreement on the primary mission of public middle schools continues to grow among middle school proponents. It is apparent that social goals, not academic goals, remain a top priority for a number of middle school supporters. Consider that several NMSA conference sessions as recently as 2000 continued to advocate "practices that promote social justice," "revisioning the middle school around issues of social justice and equity," and teaching children how to become grassroots activists.[39]

Such a continuing cry for social aims makes it appear doubtful whether the contemporary middle school movement and the standards movement can successfully co-exist. Interestingly, many of the most vocal *supporters* of a dumbed-down middle school curriculum, cooperative learning, and peer tutoring are also among the most vocal *opponents* of standards and accountability. It can easily be speculated that the attacks by middle school activists and social reformers against standards, testing, and accountability are driven in large measure as a desperate attempt to retain control of the middle school as they envision it.

Alfie Kohn, a strong proponent of cooperative learning and a vehement foe of ability grouping and academic competition, is among such critics. He charges that testing is now a "national obsession" and that schools are in "a desperate quest to raise scores." He calls the use of standardized tests "nothing short of catastrophic," and claims that "unless we act to stop this, we will be facing a scenario that might be described without exaggeration as an educational ethnic cleansing."[40] (And yet parents who support ability grouping are the ones middle school activists call "extremists.")

Sessions at the NMSA annual conference in 2001 demonstrate profoundly differing views among middle school supporters regarding standards and accountability. Several session descriptions indicate positive attitudes toward standards and accountability, describing testing to measure high academic standards as "a useful tool to pinpoint student learning needs and carefully craft instruction on a schoolwide basis," and viewing such a move as a way to "enhance curricular rigor."[41]

Sadly, a much harsher tone predominates. One session identifies standards and accountability as unpleasantries that must be tolerated until they go away, stating that middle school educators must "find a balance between current political demands and doing what *Turning Points* and current reformers reference as best practices."[42] One prominent leader of the middle school movement, James Beane, spoke vehemently against the standards and accountability movement, repeatedly declaring that the middle school concept has been "overpowered by arch-conservatives," and that the gains made by middle school advocates have been "washed away by the far right." He bemoans what he views as the "betrayal" by middle school educators who dare to support standards and accountability. At one point he proclaimed: "Worse yet, too many so-called advocates are backpedaling as they try to reconcile middle school practices with standards and accountability." He concluded by saying that, without a concerted effort to reverse the present course, "I would claim that the middle school concept is essentially destroyed."[43]

His opinions have not changed much since he first offered them in 1999 in reaction to the impact of the standards and accountability movement. He is highly critical of anyone who would like to see middle schools maintain a traditional educational mission, and sees middle school advocates who support academic excellence as traitors to the cause:

Some middle school advocates already seem to have chosen a new direction, calling now for "academic excellence" as the slogan for a new phase of the middle school movement. . . . Are some "advocates" suddenly getting cold feet?[44]

Furthermore, he appears to be employing the "Hegelian Principle" to stir activists to action (see Chapter 2). He first declared a state of crisis—that the middle school is "under siege," and that "the social fabric of communities all over the country is already in shreds." He further lamented about what may happen should middle schools return to their traditional purpose of providing an academic education: "stripped of these [social aims], the middle school is left as an institution devoted to content coverage and bereft of any larger social meaning."[45] His solution to this self-declared crisis? To reclaim a social agenda for the middle school:

Under siege as middle schools are, perhaps now is the time for their advocates to supplement their important talk about young people with some thought about what kinds of social purposes they think they should promote.[46]

The same declaration of a crisis can be heard in the words of middle school activist Paul George at the 2001 NMSA conference. Note his exaggerated claims:

We've got controversial grouping strategies everywhere. We have tried desperately to get away from tracking—we have been unable to do so. The power of the gifted lobby has prevailed. There is no doubt about that. Middle school people have embraced heterogeneous [mixed-ability] grouping from the beginning. The National Forum on Middle Grades Education has made heterogeneous grouping its number one plank, and yet, visiting school after school after school after school after school [sic], I'd be willing to bet that at least 85 percent of Florida's middle school students experience a significant degree of ability grouping during their day. We want heterogeneous grouping. We have been politically unable to bring it to pass. The power of the gifted lobby is simply too strong.[47]

On one hand, George is fanning the fires as he sees the middle school flame being extinguished, but on the other hand, in the same presentation he makes an interesting and very telling admission regarding the middle school concept:

The full application and implementation of the middle school concept is likely to lead many students to the highest academic achievement they can reach. *We don't have the evidence to support that*—we need beyond the experience of individuals who are leaders and others. We need that kind of evidence.[48] (emphasis added)

So here we have a major voice in the middle school movement, the author of numerous articles, including "Tracking and Ability Grouping in the Middle School: Ten Tentative Truths," written nearly a decade ago—suddenly admitting that there are no "tentative truths" after all, because "we don't have the evidence." Since, by his own admission there is no evidence, then what have middle school policies been based on? Opinions? Anecdotes? Or perhaps . . . radical social agendas.

Options to Consider

Middle school proponents have several possible courses of action: (1) They can continue to ignore the concerns of members of the gifted community and focus exclusively on their radical agenda, knowing but not caring that they will face an ever-growing exodus of "the best and the brightest" from the public schools; or (2) They can acknowledge that the public wants an academic, not social activist, role for the middle school, and support flexible instructional arrangements, including ability grouping for specific subjects, in order to meet the educational needs of all children.

The former option is the route that middle school activists appear to be pursuing. The latter option is the only one that is compatible with the movement for standards and accountability.

The strident rhetoric from the 1990s is continuing in the new century, as activists are aware that the standards and accountability movement, by its very nature, is returning schools to a focus on academics. As a result, activists are struggling to justify the continued existence of the contemporary middle school according to their vision. For example, a new book (2001) titled *Reinventing the Middle School* is described as a road map to help the middle school return to its roots:

Many contemporary American middle schools are stuck in a state of "arrested development," failing to implement the original concept of the middle school to varying, though equally corruptive, degrees. To counter this situation, the contributors of *Reinventing the Middle School* propose that middle schools "reinvent" themselves by returning to the original concept of the middle school and implementing all aspects of it in an integrated fashion.[49]

This represents the intransigent stand of radical middle school proponents and their activist orientation, so it appears that the American public can expect little change from the leading advocates of the middle school concept—unless the standards and accountability movement succeeds in returning the middle schools to an academic mission.

One caution regarding the standards and accountability movement must be expressed, however. In some instances, educators have placed efforts exclusively on raising the skills and performance levels of low-achieving students, leaving high ability students to flounder. In some schools, administrators are requiring teachers to adhere to "pacing guides" which require all teachers to be on the same page of the same lesson on the same day. This is merely a repackaging of the damaging educational practice known as "Mastery Learning" which results in "the Robin Hood Effect," as discussed earlier.[50] When high ability students and faster learners are held to the pace of the slower students in the class, achievement of lower ability students may increase, but the cost is *declining* academic achievement among the others in the class. Such an approach undermines one of the underlying tenets of the standards and accountability movement: that *all* students should be challenged to the extent of their abilities. Ignoring the academic needs of gifted/high ability students was wrong before the rise of the standards movement—and it is still wrong now.

IMPLICATIONS FOR OUR CULTURE AND OUR NATION

E Pluribus Unum vs. the Supremacy of the Group

The embrace of non-academic categories of diversity, as demonstrated by the shifting priorities of the NMSA over time, is evidence of the conviction held by middle school activists of the supremacy of the group over the individual. Note that 1990 was the last year in which the number of sessions on academic diversity outnumbered that of cultural diversity, a trend that continued through 1998 (see Appendices B and C). Although the trend appears to have reversed in the last few years, this may have much more to do with the standards and accountability movement than with any philosophical change on the part of middle school activists, as will be seen.

The standards and accountability movement seeks to ensure that all children meet a set of academic standards. It is a challenge, given the problematic level of educational quality in many of our schools, to provide help to children who are struggling academically so they can meet state performance standards. Under the federal *No Child Left Behind* legislation, schools will be held accountable for academic results, so middle school educators must make time to attend to the *academic* needs of these children. This means that less time will be available for social goals—a fact which causes many middle school activists to view the standards and accountability movement with fear and disdain.

In spite of being faced with these new academic challenges, many middle-level activists are continuing in their ongoing desire to emphasize differences among children. The large numbers of NMSA conference sessions addressing non-academic differences conveys the belief that these differences are to be valued while differences in intellectual ability are to be ignored. This stands at odds with beliefs held by members of the public and policymakers. As articulated in Chapter 2, the public seems to be indicating the desire for a more inclusive and less divisive atmosphere in our public schools—in other words, more of a focus on "out of many, one," as opposed to the divisiveness of group identities. For example, the findings of a recent survey of over 800 parents suggest that an overwhelming majority of parents want their schools to emphasize to children that they are Americans, not members of various ethnic and cultural groups. The survey, conduced by a non-partisan organization, found that a large majority of parents agreed that "the best place for kids to learn to take pride in their ethnic or racial identity is at home—school is where they should be learning what it means to be an American."[51] And nearly all parents agreed with this statement: "There's too much attention paid these days to what separates racial and ethnic groups and not enough to what they have in common."[52] Another survey of over 1,000 public school teachers found very few teachers overall, and a similar percentage of black teachers, believe that schools should adapt to the backgrounds of students, "such as using street language to teach inner-city kids."[53]

Education policymakers are in agreement with the findings from national surveys that indicate the desire for a color-blind approach to educating children:

It appears that policymakers, like practitioners and members of the public, choose to identify students by learning characteristics more so than by race or ethnicity. . . . It appears that both policymakers and practitioners see their students primarily as learners with specific academic strengths and weaknesses, and only secondarily as members of a specific ethnic group.[54]

This is a very different attitude than the one we see among radical middle school activists, who continue to focus on group identities and the accompanying differences that serve only to divide.

American Values vs. Radical Equity

Traditional American values are given little emphasis in many of today's middle schools, a trend that has accelerated over time. A 1965 survey of middle-level principals indicated that "understanding values inherent to the American way of life" ranked third in a list of priorities for American middle schools.[55] Only acquisition of basic skills and acquisition of basic knowledge ranked higher. By 1980, however, that ranking had dropped to fifth place in the priorities for middle schools,[56] and by 1993 had plummeted to eighth place.[57]

This should come as no surprise, since most people tend to practice what they preach. American values such as rewarding individual effort, honoring individual achievement, and promoting healthy competition have given way to a capricious smorgasbord of liberal ideas that undermine these traditional values in many of our schools. Nonetheless, middle school activists try their best to camouflage their extreme ideas as being based on religious and patriotic principles, claiming that the middle school movement and all of its anti-gifted, anti-intellectual, social engineering policies and practices "has God and the U.S. Constitution on its side."[58]

Beliefs driving radical equity include the leveling of achievement and the desire for equality of outcomes. This is in stark contrast with the premise underlying our nation's founding principles. As mentioned in Chapter 7, the Declaration of Independence states that all people have the right to "life, liberty, and the *pursuit* of happiness." In other words, we are not guaranteed happiness—it is something we should be free to pursue, and its attainment is predicated upon our personal efforts and desires. Expecting (or demanding) equal outcomes for all serves to denigrate aspirations and individual initiative, and is decidedly at odds with the intent of America's founding fathers.

The simple fact is that traditional American history, and the values inherent in such lessons, have been relegated to an inferior status in many American schools. The result is a shocking lack of cultural and historical knowledge among American teenagers, who can recognize cartoon perverts Beavis and Butthead (99 percent) and rap star Snoop Doggie Dog (98 percent), but who cannot identify George Washington as the American general at Yorktown, or key passages from the Gettysburg Address. And it must be noted that these survey results do not represent the average American teenager, but students at our most elite colleges—those who possess high abilities and who we would expect to know their country's history.[59]

That American students have been exposed to a watered-down curriculum can be attributed to a number of causes, including the belief in the theory of brain periodization and the decreased use of ability grouping and concurrent rise in cooperative learning/ peer tutoring. Even in the standards and accountability movement, there is the chance that this dumbing-down will be maintained if educators attempt to "game the system" by bringing the achievement of high ability students down in order to make it appear as though the achievement gap is closing:

The newest trick on the block is a simple but potentially devastating one for almost all children. By dragging the nation's entire school achievement level down so low that group differences are minimized, it will appear as if at-risk students are closing the gap with their high scoring peers. If this accusation seems to border on the fanatical, consider the following two practices that are already underway in our schools: [the dumbing-down of the curriculum and the elimination of grouping].[60]

This stands in vivid contrast to the changes that came about in American education after the launch of Sputnik. Solid academic changes were made, but perhaps just as significant is the fact that they were accompanied by an altruistic sense of duty to one's country. Following Sputnik:

High scholastic standards and standing, academic advancement, studiousness, and career-mindedness were conspicuous themes in our schools. It became virtually unthinkable for a gifted child to bypass the tougher courses in favor of the less demanding ones. It certainly was no time for youth to do their own thing or to enjoy the privilege of doing nothing. Instead, they were brought up in a period of total talent mobilization, requiring the most able-minded to fulfill their potentials and submit their developed abilities for service to the nation.[61]

Will the tragedy of 9/11 result in a similar sense of duty to one's country among our young people? Education leaders can either inspire students to develop their talents and instill a sense of patriotic duty, or they can choose to criticize their patriotic aspirations. Only time will tell the direction American students will take.

America's Future vs. Coercive Egalitarianism

Around the time of Sputnik, the critical need for highly skilled professionals was evidenced by a lack of qualified workers in needed specialties:

Manpower statistics confirmed the existence of shortages in key professions. Again, the cause of this alarming situation was attributed to the commitment of schools to deal with mediocrity rather than superiority.[62]

Similar shortages exist now, but as highlighted in the report from the U.S. Commission on National Security/21st Century, their consequences are far more ominous:

The American educational system does not appear ready for such challenges. . . . There will not be enough qualified American citizens to perform the new jobs being created today—including technical jobs crucial to the maintenance of national security. Already the United States must search abroad for experts and technicians to fill positions in the U.S. domestic economy, and Congress has often increased category limits for special visas (H-1B) for that purpose. If current trends are not stanched and reversed, large numbers of specialized foreign technicians in critical positions in the U.S. economy could pose security risks.[63]

Along with the concern that the longer American students stay in school the poorer their performance, the report also notes the ripple effect of poor K–12 preparation and the declining desire among many American students to seek academic challenges. In addition, not only are other countries educating more students in advanced technical areas, but foreigners being educated in the United States are choosing to return home in record numbers:

- Fully 37 percent of doctorates in natural science, 50 percent of doctorates in mathematics and computer science, and 52 percent of doctorates in engineering at U.S. universities—the best in the world—are awarded to non-U.S. citizens [and], the percentage of science and engineering doctoral recipients with firm plans to stay in the United States is declining.

- In 1997, Asia alone accounted for 43 percent of all science and engineering degrees granted worldwide, Europe 34 percent, and North America 23 percent.
- [In 1997], China produced 148,800 engineers, the United States only 63,000.[64]

The authors of this report recommend requiring "higher levels of proficiency for all high school students," which will mean "changing enduring perceptions that taking four years of science and math in high school is only for the brainy elite." Clinging to that perception, according to the authors, would result in a disaster for this country—but this warning is not new. Writing in 1959, English philosopher C.S. Lewis noted that a movement against excellence

leads to a nation without great men, a nation mainly of subliterates, morally flaccid from lack of discipline in youth, full of the cocksureness which flattery breeds on ignorance, and soft from lifelong pampering. ... When such a nation meets in conflict with a nation where children have been made to work at school ... only one result is possible.[65]

Clearly, an educational system that is currently focused on the capricious tenets of coerced egalitarianism will, by its very nature, be unable to sustain the level of rigor necessary to ensure our freedoms in the future. As noted in Chapter 7, influences such as peer pressure, the deliberate actions of adults, and middle school policies and practices have all combined to thwart achievement among America's top students. As articulated above, the resulting coercive egalitarianism has serious national security implications.

MOVING TOWARD AN EDUCATIONAL RENEWAL

Words from *A Nation at Risk* ring as true today as they did two decades ago: "Our society and its educational institutions seem to have lost sight of the basic purposes of schooling, and of the high expectations and disciplined effort needed to attain them."[66] The question remains: How can we return to a culture of achievement?

Fostering a Culture of Achievement

American schools need to experience a rebirth of respect for achievement. For too long, high achievers have been treated with disrespect and ridicule. Some in the middle school movement appear to be belatedly awakening to this reality in that *Turning Points*, the manifesto that ignited the contemporary middle school movement, has been reissued with a more academic focus. However, this is little more than lip service to the issue, as middle school activists continue to insist on ascribing to non-academic issues a weight equal to (or greater than) academics as priorities for the middle school.[67]

As noted earlier, however, the standards movement may be helping schools move away from such an agenda and toward the fostering of respect for academic achievement. An important part of the standards movement is accountability for educational results, which are generally measured by student performance on standardized tests. With the exception of New York's Regents Exams, exit exams such as end-of-course testing is a relatively new requirement for high school graduation in the United States. However, other parts of the world have had such systems in place for many years. Do we see headlines reporting anti-testing protests and boycotts in other countries as we do here? No—and for good reason.

Professor John Bishop of Cornell University conducted an in-depth study that examined the impact of curriculum-based external examinations in Canada, where some provinces have such tests as a requirement to graduate from high school while others do not. The results he found should cause critics of standards and accountability to reconsider their views, as the presence of external exams is fostering a more serious attitude among students toward education, as well as a new respect toward high achievement:

The American adolescent culture rewards and respects sports ability, social skills, physical attractiveness and conformity to group norms. It denigrates the studious as "nerds." Nerds frequently become the object of harassment intended "to wear down [their] self esteem." The studious are outcasts because studying hard is counter to the interests of one's peers. . . . Peer pressure against learning is an almost inevitable consequence of the relativistic way American schools assess achievement and then signal it to colleges and employers. If academic achievement was defined relative to a fixed external standard and signaled that way as well, students would be less induced to pressure each other not to study.[68]

In other words, high standards, coupled with exit exams, can serve to refocus the culture of schools back to their original mission—providing a high-quality academic education. Yet anti-testing critics predict massive dropout rates among poor students who are being "forced" into higher and more rigorous curricula. Research indicates that this fear is just another myth.

Singapore, a country that regularly surpasses all others in international tests of student achievement, is a good example of the false nature of such claims. Secondary dropout rates in Singapore were 19 percent in 1980. But after the implementation of a series of reforms, including increasing the rigor of the curriculum, ratcheting up the difficulty of national exit exams, and implementing mandatory ability grouping, the dropout rate *plummeted* to 3 percent. According to Singaporean education official Poon Chew Leng, lower ability students gained confidence and had a more positive attitude toward school when they were allowed to work at their own pace, and higher ability students were not held back but were allowed to be challenged to the extent of their abilities[69]

A study of all California high schools examined the effect of an increase in the level of course difficulty and in the number of courses taken by economically disadvantaged students. The author states: "The results of this study do not support the hypothesis that higher levels of achievement or academic course enrollment are associated with higher dropout rates." He continues:

Although non-school socioeconomic and demographic factors are associated with dropout rates, they should not be offered as an excuse for defeatism. It is incorrect to draw the conclusion that educators can do little about poverty and therefore may live with the associated problem . . . the effects of poverty can be fought.[70]

This attitude is quite different from that of testing critic Alfie Kohn, who refers to testing as "educational ethnic cleansing."[71]

Another study examined nearly 77,000 students in 75 Florida high schools and found that requiring competency tests for high school graduation did not increase the dropout rate among minority students or students with poor academic records. The conclusion:

Numerous researchers have argued that competency tests are likely to have adverse effects on academically at-risk and minority students. The results of this study do not support these hypotheses.[72]

Although the results of these studies have not yet been replicated to see if they generalize to other situations, the fact remains that standards-based reform and accountability, such as that required by the federal *No Child Left Behind* legislation, are remaking the educational landscape. In the past, schools were not held responsible when students failed to learn, so the incentive to provide extra help for struggling students was lacking. However, the prevailing dynamic under the new federal law is that schools *must* be held accountable for student performance.

As can be seen in states that had already implemented such changes prior to 2002, two vocal groups have emerged: Those who are successfully rising to this challenge by strengthening the curriculum and using tests to measure student achievement in order to target remedial instruction and ensure that children of all abilities are demonstrating academic growth; and those who are expending their energies trying to destroy the return to an academic focus by attacking standards, tests, and accountability. As was described earlier, many middle school activists and social reformers continue to lead these attacks.

However, changing to a culture of achievement calls for more than changes in the K–12 arena alone. As noted in Chapter 8, professors in some American schools of education hold activist views that negatively influence the attitudes of teachers. The survey cited found that only around half of the education professors surveyed believe it is essential for teachers to have a solid understanding of the content they teach.[73]

This is not the only current source of criticism toward schools of education and the resistance of some of them toward a culture of achievement. As mentioned in Chapter 8, even the popular press has leveled charges against the education schools, stating that "many education professors undermine state standards" and that the reluctance to provide meaningful support for state academic standards means that some new teachers "are more inclined to scorn the standards than embrace them."[74] Indeed, it appears that there is a need to change the culture in a number of American colleges of education.

However, the negative attitudes emanating from some colleges of education may soon be on the brink of becoming less of an influence in American schools. A recent study indicates that growing numbers of teachers are now entering American classrooms through alternative routes to teacher certification, bypassing colleges of education altogether. According to Emily Feistritzer of the National Center for Education Information:

In each of the last three years, approximately 25,000 teachers were certified through alternative routes. Considering that an estimated 75,000 newly-minted teachers are now being hired per year, alternative routes could be contributing about one-third of new teachers hired [each year].[75]

This quiet revolution in teacher licensure may prove to have a profound effect on American education. As the schools of education begin to lose their influence, we may see an escalation in the growth of a culture of achievement as teachers enter the profession through other means, and as schools of education change to address such competition.

Intervention, *Not* Remediation

In too many cases, disadvantaged and minority children of all ability levels are not getting the K–12 educational opportunities necessary for academic success and required for access to higher education. Struggling students who have academic deficits need to be provided with educational interventions rather than wait for failure to occur. Unfortunately, the lack of interventions means that gifted/high ability students from disadvantaged families are often found in disproportionately low numbers in programs for the gifted. This is sometimes seen as an act of discrimination, and as such, a civil rights issue. But as Gallagher powerfully argues:

It is differential opportunities, practice, and motivation that appear to have been responsible for the differential proportions [of students from minority groups] found in programs for gifted students. . . . It is a problem of equity, certainly, since the disproportions indicate that there have been differential sets of opportunities for different groups of children.

The unfairness leading to the disproportions lies primarily in the imbalance of opportunities and environment, not in the selection process itself.[76]

To address this imbalance of opportunities, Gallagher calls for the creation of early enrichment programs targeted at all students, but with a special focus on disadvantaged students in order to reveal hidden talents among children whose opportunities have been limited.

It is alarming to note that, as evidence about the academic performance of disadvantaged students is evaluated, findings suggest that some of the most popular "progressive" educational policies and practices (such as those supported by middle school activists) are actually *harming* underprivileged children.[77] For example, researchers in England determined that children whose achievement was hurt the most by several decades of progressive policies were from the lowest socio-economic groups, because the progressive reforms were inconsistent with a belief in self-discipline and effort, therefore locking children into their existing social status with little hope of social mobility.[78]

This must change. According to Professor E.D. Hirsch of the University of Virginia:

Educational *progressivism* is a sure means for preserving the social status quo, whereas the best practices of educational *conservatism* are the only means whereby children from disadvantaged homes can secure the knowledge and skills that will enable them to improve their condition.[79] (emphasis added)

A COURSE OF ACTION

What can concerned citizens do? The tactics of many middle school activists reveal a disdain for average Americans who spend all day working, only to come home to use their family time to fight against forces—paid for (directly or indirectly) by their own tax dollars—which are intent upon implementing reforms with which they disagree. Concerned citizens are sacrificing their efforts and their personal time to organize grassroots groups in order to lobby their local school boards, local schools, and state legislatures for more responsive schools.

Former U.S. Secretary of Education William Bennett notes that we have come to a critical crossroads in education, and that it is crucial for citizens to become actively involved. He states:

What is critical is the task of regaining our institutions—and regaining our institutions not to then subject them to a narrow or rigid conservative ideology, but to let these institutions be governed by what works, by what makes sense, and by insisting that they remain true to their original purpose.[80]

Although Bennett speaks of admirable goals, the question remains: How can we achieve them? One answer may be found in the writings of C.S. Lewis:

If you are on the wrong road, progress means doing an about-turn and walking back to the right road; and in that case, the man who turns back soonest is the most progressive man. Going back is the quickest way on.[81]

"Going back is the quickest way on." Perhaps this best summarizes the strategies necessary for reversing the damage done to American public education by the policies of radical middle school activists. *Going back* to find scientifically based research which indicates the strengths or weaknesses of educational practices, *going back* to proven methodologies, and perhaps most importantly, *going back* to parents and empathetically listening to their concerns.

In a number of cities across the county, this is exactly what is happening. Conscientious educators are listening to parents and providing alternatives to the contemporary middle school concept. For example, schools in Milwaukee, Cleveland, and Cincinnati have "turned their backs on middle schools," changing instead to neighborhood K–8 schools with smaller enrollments.[82] Other school districts, such as those in Louisville and Paducah, Kentucky, are moving toward same-sex classes.[83] The goal for all of these traditional approaches is the same: to increase academic achievement and create an atmosphere that will encourage better student behavior.

When school districts are non-responsive to parents, officials often find that parents look for options other than the public middle schools. Home schooling is one option and private schools are another. Information from the National Education Data Resource Center indicates that very few private schools follow the middle school grade arrangement, opting instead for the K–8 model. In fact, it is reported that fewer than 1 percent of private schools use the 6/7/8 grade arrangement so common in public middle schools today.[84] However, it appears that it is not the grade level arrangement as much as it is the driving philosophy that causes parental concerns about middle schools.

Parents with children who have experienced a middle school that ascribes to the contemporary middle school concept may long for middle school alternatives, as described above. They may even agree with this policy expert:

I think we should abandon the whole middle school concept. Middle schools are a disaster. They slow down the intellectual progress that kids make in elementary school, and they effectively preclude readiness for college for many minority kids.[85]

CONCLUSION

James Gallagher has called a nation's investment in its gifted children "enlightened self interest."[86] He expresses the need for such investments as a national priority:

To be an effective advocate one has to sincerely believe in the cause. One belief that advocates of gifted education would share would be that investment in the educational stimulation of these children is one of the most constructive acts we could take on behalf of our society. . . . The athletic analogy is that all humanity is on the same team, and we have some formidable opponents: war, hunger, disease, ignorance. We will need the strongest performance of the best of our team members to prevail against such opposition. There is, in fact, no built-in guarantee that mankind will prevail against its enemies, and so we must make optimal the opportunities for our most talented team members . . . to do their best for us.[87]

How acute is the need to reject the precepts undergirding the radical middle school movement? According to the report of the U.S. Commission on National Security/21st Century: "If the United States does not stop and reverse negative educational trends . . . it will be unable to maintain its position of global leadership over the next quarter century."[88]

Returning our schools to their original function of providing a quality education is an imperative if we are to "secure the blessings of liberty for ourselves and our posterity." To do anything less will be a national tragedy. America's middle schools have been held captive by an activist agenda for far too long. While the standards and accountability movement appears to be steering middle schools away from the embrace of social engineers, middle school activists are desperately trying to reaffirm their control of America's middle schools.

We must not allow this to happen. Public schools must reassert their support for excellence and must actively move to become more responsive to the public. A number of middle schools have boldly and courageously rejected the radical middle school concept in favor of an academic focus, but this is just a start. The war against excellence must be ended if we are going to preserve our culture, our way of life, and the future of our nation.

NOTES

1. *A Nation at Risk: The Imperative for Educational Reform*, National Commission on Excellence in Education (April 1983), p. 1. Available on-line at http://www.ed.gov/pubs/NatAtRisk/.

2. "The Swedish model," *Wall Street Journal* (April 7, 1992).

3. P. Drucker, "The age of social transformation," *The Atlantic Monthly* (November 1994), p. 78.

4. S. Farkas & J. Johnson, *Given the Circumstances: Teachers Talk about Public Education Today* (New York: Public Agenda, 1996), p. 9.

5. "Information about Those Opposing Restructuring" (Denver, Colo.: Education Commission of the States, 1991).

6. National Middle School Association annual conference program (1994), p. 74.

7. National Middle School Association annual conference program (1995), p. 165.

8. National Middle School Association annual conference program (1996), p. 59.

9. National Middle School Association annual conference program (2000), p. 111.

10. J. Beane, Session 2322, National Middle School Association annual conference (November 2001).

11. V.E. Lee & J.B. Smith, "Effects of school restructuring on the achievement and engagement of middle-grade students," *Sociology of Education*, vol. 66 (July 1993), p. 178.

12. Ibid., p. 182.

13. Farkas & Johnson (1996), p. 37.

14. See D. Shearon, *On Meeting the Needs of High-Achieving Students*

and the Desires of Their Parents, presentation to the Metropolitan Nashville School Board (January 12, 1999); and P. Donsky, "Task force to study if schools are failing their best," *The Tennessean* (March 9, 1999).

15. D. Klausnitzer, "Middle schools would add three classes in plan," *The Tennessean* (September 16, 2001).

16. D. Shearon, e-mail correspondence (December 3, 2001). Material used with permission of the author.

17. For example, see J. Beane, "Middle schools under siege: Points of attack," *Middle School Journal,* vol. 30, no. 4 (March 1999a), pp. 3–9; J. Beane, *Curriculum Integration: Designing the Core of Democratic Education* (New York: Teachers College Press, 1997), p. 79; P.S. George, "Tracking and ability grouping," *Middle School Journal,* vol. 20, no. 1 (September 1988), pp. 21–28; P. George & W. Grebing, "Talent development and grouping in the middle grades: Challenging the brightest without sacrificing the rest," *Middle School Journal,* vol. 26, no. 4 (March 1995), p. 16, copyrighted material used with permission from the National Middle School Association (NMSA); NMSA annual conference program (1999), p. 103; A. Kohn, "Only for *my* kid: How privileged parents are undermining school reform," *Phi Delta Kappan,* vol. 79, no. 8 (April 1998), pp. 569–577; J. Oakes & A.S. Wells, "Detracking for high student achievement," *Educational Leadership,* vol. 55, no. 6 (March 1998), pp. 38–41; A.S. Wells & J. Oakes, "Potential Pitfalls of systemic reform: Early lessons from research on detracking," *Sociology of Education,* volume 69 (1996), p. 138; and A. Wheelock, "Winning over gifted parents," *School Administrator* (April 1995), p. 17.

18. L. Perlstein, "Suspicious minds," *Washington Post* (July 22, 2001), p. 5 (online edition).

19. N. Granstrom, "A parent criticizes middle school theory," *Basic Education* (May 1999), Council for Basic Education, Washington, D.C.

20. C.L. Mithers, "Gifted education: A broken ladder," *Los Angles Times* (August 5, 2001).

21. George & Grebing (1995), p. 17.

22. J.M. Rochester, "What's it all about, Alfie? A parent/educator's response to Alfie Kohn," *Phi Delta Kappan,* vol. 80, no. 2 (October 1998), p. 168. This was written in response to Kohn (1998).

23. T. Kariya & J.E. Rosenbaum, "Bright flight: Unintended consequences of detracking policy in Japan," *American Journal of Education,* vol. 107, no. 3 (May 1999), pp. 227, 228. Copyright © 1999 by the University of Chicago. Copyrighted material used with the permission of the University of Chicago.

24. National Middle School Association annual conference program (1979), p. 23.

25. Ibid. (2000), p. 52.

26. C. Yecke, *Policymakers' Views on Issues at the Middle School Level,* doctoral dissertation, University of Virginia (2001), p. 200. It should be

noted that the author is an anomaly. In 2003, she was appointed to serve as a state education commissioner.

27. Ibid., pp. 202, 215. (See comment in note 26.)

28. Ibid., p. 169. (See comment in note 26.)

29. Ibid., p. 89, Table 16.

30. Ibid., pp. 216–217. (See comment in note 26.)

31. C.A. Tomlinson, " 'All kids can learn:' Masking diversity in middle school," *The Clearing House*, vol. 68, no. 3 (1995), p. 165.

32. A. Bradley, "Muddle in the middle," *Education Week* (April 15, 1998), p. 38.

33. D. Brockett, " "School leaders, researchers re-examining middle reform," *School Board News* (1998), p. 5.

34. D. Ruenzel, "Coming of age," *Teacher Magazine*, vol. 9, no. 5 (1998), p. 32.

35. National Middle School Association annual conference program (1998), p. 123.

36. C.F. Toepfer, "What to know about young adolescents," *Social Education*, vol. 52, no. 2 (1988), p. 110.

37. National Middle School Association annual conference programs: 1998, session 2001; 1999, session 2321; 2000, session 2107; 2001, session 2642.

38. National Middle School Association annual conference program (2000), session 3205, pp. 140, 171.

39. Ibid., pp. 47, 115, 113.

40. Alfie Kohn, "Standardized testing and its victims: Inconvenient facts and inevitable consequences," *Education Week* (September 27, 2000), pp. 46, 47, 46.

41. National Middle School Association annual conference program (2001), pp. 97, 50, 67.

42. Ibid., p. 67.

43. J. Beane, National Middle School Association annual conference, Session 2322 (November 2001).

44. J.A. Beane, "Middle schools under siege: Responding to the attack," *Middle School Journal*, vol. 30, no. 5 (May 1999b), p. 6. Copyrighted material used with permission from the National Middle School Association (NMSA).

45. Beane (1999a), pp. 8, 6.

46. Beane (1999b), pp. 5–6.

47. P. George, "Threat and promise: Middle schools in Florida—Where are we now?" National Middle School Association annual conference, Session 2234 (November 2, 2001).

48. Ibid.

49. T. Dickinson, *Reinventing the Middle School*, book advertisement in the National Middle School Association Resource Catalog (2002), p. 23.

50. R.E. Slavin, "Mastery learning reconsidered," *Review of Educational Research*, vol. 57, no. 2 (1987), pp. 175–213.

51. S. Farkas & J. Johnson, *A Lot to Be Thankful For: What Parents Want Children to Learn about America* (New York: Public Agenda, 1998), p. 39.

52. Ibid., p. 35.

53. Farkas & Johnson (1996).

54. Yecke (2001), p. 182.

55. D.A. Rock & J.K. Hemphill, *Report of the Junior High School Principalship* (Washington, D.C.: National Association of Secondary School Principals, 1966), p. 34.

56. J. Valentine, D.C. Clark, N.C. Nickerson, & J.W. Keefe, *The Middle Level Principalship* (Reston, Va.: National Association of Secondary School Principals, 1981), p. 83.

57. J. Valentine, D.C. Clark, J.L. Irvin, J.W. Keefe, & G. Melton, *Leadership in Middle Level Education: A National Survey of Middle Level Leaders and Schools* (Reston, Va.: National Association of Secondary School Principals, 1993), p. 72.

58. H. Johnston, "Interview with John Lounsbury," *Middle School Journal* vol. 24, no. 2 (November 1992), p. 50.

59. *Losing America's Memory: Historical Illiteracy in the 21st Century* (Washington, D.C.: American Council of Trustees and Alumni, 2000).

60. J. Renzulli & S. Reis, "The reform movement and the quiet crisis in gifted education," *Gifted Child Quarterly*, vol. 35, no. 1 (Winter 1991), p. 30. Copyrighted material used with permission from the National Association for Gifted Children (NAGC).

61. A. Tannenbaum, "Pre-Sputnik to Post-Watergate concern about the gifted," in A.H. Passow (Ed.), *The Gifted: Their Talent and Development*, The 78th Yearbook of the National Society for the Study of Education (Chicago: University of Chicago Press, 1979), p. 12.

62. Ibid., p. 8.

63. *Road Map for National Security: Imperative for Change*, The Phase III Report of the U.S. Commission on National Security/21st Century (Washington, D.C., February 15, 2001), pp. iv, 39.

64. Ibid., pp. 39, 46.

65. C.S. Lewis, "Screwtape proposes a toast," in *The Screwtape Letters* (1942, 1959; reprint, San Francisco: HarperCollins, 2001), p. 206.

66. *A Nation at Risk* (1983), p. 1.

67. See Anthony W. Jackson and Gayle A. Davis, with Maud Abeel and Anne Bordonaro, *Turning Points 2000: Educating Adolescents in the 21st Century* (New York: Teachers College Press, 2000); J. Norton & A. Lewis, "Middle-grades reform," *Phi Delta Kappan*, vol. 81, no. 10 (June 2000); and K. Kennedy Manzo, "Middle school report urges academic rigor," *Education Week* (November 8, 2000).

68. J.H. Bishop, *Nerd Harassment, Incentives, School Priorities, and Learn-*

ing, Center for Advanced Human Resource Studies, paper 96–10 (Ithaca, N.Y.: Cornell University, 1996), p. 36.

69. *Overview of Singapore's Education System,* presentation by Poon Chew Leng, education official with the Singapore Ministry of Education, September 9, 2002.

70. M. Felter, "School dropout rates, academic performance, size and poverty: Correlates of educational reforms," *Educational Evaluation and Policy Analysis,* vol. 11, no. 2 (1989), pp. 109–116. Copyright 1989 by the American Educational Research Association. Reprinted with the permission of the publisher. See pages 114 and 115.

71. Kohn (2000), p. 47.

72. B.W. Griffin & M.H. Heidorn, "An examination of the relationship between minimum competency test performance and dropping out of high school," *Educational Evaluation and Policy Analysis,* vol. 18, no. 3 (1996), pp. 243–252.

73. S. Farkas, J. Johnson, & A. Duffett, *Different Drummers: How Teachers of Teachers View Public Education* (New York: Public Agenda, 1997), p. 7.

74. "Too many teacher colleges major in mediocrity," *USA Today* (March 18, 2002), available online at www.usatoday.com/news/comment/2002/03/18/nceditf.htm.

75. E. Feistritzer, "Alternative routes for certifying teachers escalate; Definition of alternative teacher certification emerges," press release (March 5, 2002), National Center for Education Information.

76. J. Gallagher, "Education of gifted students: A civil rights issue?" *Phi Delta Kappan,* vol. 6, no. 5 (January 1995), p. 410.

77. See B. Grossen, "Child-directed teaching methods: A discriminatory practice of Western education," *Effective School Practices,* vol. 12, no. 2 (1993), pp. 9–20; E.D. Hirsch, *The Schools We Need and Why We Don't Have Them* (New York: Doubleday, 1996).

78. R. Sharp, A. Green, & J. Lewis, *Education and Social Control: A Study in Progressive Primary Education* (London: Routledge & Kegan Paul, 1975).

79. Hirsch (1996), p. 7.

80. W. Bennett, "The war over culture in education," speech given at The Heritage Foundation (September 5, 1991).

81. C.S. Lewis, *Mere Christianity* (1943, 1952; reprint, San Francisco: HarperCollins, 2001), p. 28.

82. D. Harrington-Lueker, "Middle schools fail to make the grade," *USA Today* (March 15, 2001). Available online at www.usatoday.com/news/comment/2001-03-15-ncguest1.htm.

83. B. Schreiner, "Single-sex classes off to a good start," Associated Press report (August 22, 2002).

84. Ibid.

85. R. Mitchell, policy analyst with the Education Trust, as cited in

"Middle grades reform," *Phi Delta Kappan*, vol. 18, no. 10 (June 2000), p. 4 (online version).

86. See, for example, J. Gallagher, "Programs for gifted students: Enlightened self-interest," *Gifted Child Quarterly*, vol. 35, no. 4 (Fall 1991), p. 177.

87. J. Gallagher, "Equity vs excellence: An educational drama," *Roeper Review*, vol. 8, no. 4 (1986), pp. 234–235.

88. *Road Map*, p. 41.

Appendices

National Middle School Association Annual Conference Sessions on
Turning Points: Number of Sessions

Year	*Turning Points*	Year	*Turning Points*
1974	N/A	1988	0
1975	0	1989	1
1976	0	1990	1
1977	0	1991	3
1978	0	1992	1
1979	0	1993	2
1980	0	1994	16
1981	0	1995	10
1982	0	1996	4
1983	0	1997	2
1984	N/A	1998	3
1985	0	1999	0
1986	0	2000	2
1987	0	2001	6

Note: Programs for 1974 and 1984 were unavailable.
Source: NMSA annual conference programs.

Appendix B
National Middle School Association Annual Conference Sessions on Student Diversity: Number of Sessions

Year	Cultural Diversity	Gender Diversity	Academic Diversity
1974	N/A	N/A	N/A
1975	0	0	2
1976	0	0	0
1977	1	0	5
1978	6	3	12
1979	1	0	11
1980	1	0	13
1981	3	0	11
1982	1	0	9
1983	3	0	6
1984	N/A	N/A	N/A
1985	0	0	8
1986	1	0	14
1987	1	0	11
1988	19	0	35
1989	25	1	46
1990	37	2	51
1991	51	1	49
1992	54	2	33
1993	82	7	31
1994	48	12	28
1995	45	12	27
1996	39	10	27
1997	43	12	31
1998	28	13	26
1999	26	10	38
2000	19	9	34
2001	20	7	25

Note: Programs for 1974 and 1984 were unavailable.
Source: NMSA annual conference programs.

Appendix C
National Middle School Association Annual Conference Sessions on
Student Diversity: Percentage of Sessions on Student Diversity in
Each of Three Categories of Diversity

Year	Cultural Diversity	Gender Diversity	Academic Diversity
1974	N/A	N/A	N/A
1975	0	0	100%
1976	0	0	0
1977	14%	0	86%
1978	24%	12%	64%
1979	7%	0	93%
1980	6%	0	94%
1981	20%	0	80%
1982	7%	0	93%
1983	30%	0	70%
1984	N/A	N/A	N/A
1985	0	0	100%
1986	6%	0	94%
1987	8%	0	92%
1988	35%	0	65%
1989	35%	1%	64%
1990	39%	2%	59%
1991	48%	1%	51%
1992	54%	2%	44%
1993	66%	6%	28%
1994	55%	14%	31%
1995	47%	13%	40%
1996	48%	13%	39%
1997	47%	13%	40%
1998	42%	19%	39%
1999	35%	14%	51%
2000	31%	15%	55%
2001	39%	13%	48%

Note: Programs for 1974 and 1984 were unavailable.
Source: NMSA annual conference programs.

Appendix D
National Middle School Association Annual Conference Sessions on Academic Diversity: Number of Sessions

Year	Special Education	At-Risk	Gifted
1974	N/A	N/A	N/A
1975	2	0	0
1976	0	0	0
1977	4	0	1
1978	6	0	6
1979	5	1	5
1980	6	3	4
1981	7	2	2
1982	2	0	7
1983	1	1	4
1984	N/A	N/A	N/A
1985	3	2	3
1986	3	7	4
1987	2	6	3
1988	9	20	6
1989	12	18	6
1990	20	25	6
1991	20	21	8
1992	16	10	7
1993	17	10	4
1994	12	11	5
1995	17	8	2
1996	12	10	5
1997	15	8	8
1998	10	9	7
1999	14	8	5
2000	7	13	2
2001	3	12	3

Note: Programs for 1974 and 1984 were unavailable.
Source: NMSA annual conference programs.

Appendix E
National Middle School Association Annual Conference Sessions on Academic Diversity: Percentage of Sessions on Academic Diversity in Each of Three Categories

Year	Special Education	At-Risk	Gifted
1974	N/A	N/A	N/A
1975	100%	0	0
1976	0	0	0
1977	80%	0	20%
1978	50%	0	50%
1979	46%	9%	45%
1980	46%	23%	31%
1981	64%	18%	18%
1982	22%	0	78%
1983	17%	17%	66%
1984	N/A	N/A	N/A
1985	37.5%	25%	37.5%
1986	21%	50%	29%
1987	26%	57%	17%
1988	18%	55%	27%
1989	33%	50%	17%
1990	30%	49%	21%
1991	41%	43%	16%
1992	49%	30%	21%
1993	55%	32%	13%
1994	43%	39%	18%
1995	63%	30%	7%
1996	44%	37%	19%
1997	48%	26%	26%
1998	38%	35%	27%
1999	52%	30%	18%
2000	32%	59%	9%
2001	17%	67%	17%

Note: Programs for 1974 and 1984 were unavailable.
Source: NMSA annual conference programs.

Appendix F
National Middle School Association Annual Conference Sessions:
Sessions on Gifted and Talented Learners

Year	Total Number of Sessions	Total Sessions on Gifted and Talented Learners	Percentage of Sessions on Gifted and Talented Learners
1974	N/A	N/A	N/A
1975	50	0	0
1976	48	0	0
1977	134	1	.75
1978	228	6	2.63
1979	182	5	2.75
1980	195	4	2.05
1981	205	2	.98
1982	165	7	4.24
1983	198	4	2.02
1984	N/A	N/A	N/A
1985	231	3	1.30
1986	163	4	2.45
1987	421	3	.71
1988	441	6	1.36
1989	654	6	.92
1990	735	6	.82
1991	790	8	1.01
1992	717	7	.98
1993	761	4	.53
1994	739	5	.68
1995	775	2	.26
1996	806	5	.62
1997	679	8	1.18
1998	634	7	1.10
1999	593	5	.84
2000	586	2	.34
2001	550	3	.55

Note: Programs for 1974 and 1984 were unavailable.
Source: NMSA annual conference programs.

Appendix G
National Middle School Association Annual Conference Sessions:
Number of Sessions on How Students Learn

Year	Brain Periodization Theory	Learning Styles	Brain-Based
1974	N/A	N/A	N/A
1975	0	0	0
1976	0	0	0
1977	0	0	0
1978	0	0	0
1979	3	1	1
1980	1	3	0
1981	4	1	0
1982	2	3	0
1983	3	2	2
1984	N/A	N/A	N/A
1985	4	0	0
1986	0	1	1
1987	1	1	3
1988	1	5	0
1989	0	3	0
1990	0	4	1
1991	0	4	0
1992	0	10	3
1993	0	1	2
1994	0	6	0
1995	0	3	2
1996	1	3	2
1997	0	1	2
1998	0	2	3
1999	0	2	9
2000	0	1	9
2001	0	0	5

Note: Programs for 1974 and 1984 were unavailable.
Source: NMSA annual conference programs.

Appendix H
National Middle School Association Annual Conference Sessions:
Percentage of Sessions on How Students Learn

Year	Brain Periodization Theory	Learning Styles	Brain-Based
1974	N/A	N/A	N/A
1975	0	0	0
1976	0	0	0
1977	0	0	0
1978	0	0	0
1979	60%	20%	20%
1980	25%	75%	0
1981	80%	20%	0
1982	40%	60%	0
1983	42%	29%	29%
1984	N/A	N/A	N/A
1985	100%	0	0
1986	0	50%	50%
1987	20%	20%	60%
1988	17%	83%	0
1989	0	100%	0
1990	0	80%	20%
1991	0	100%	0
1992	0	77%	23%
1993	0	33%	67%
1994	0	100%	0
1995	0	60%	40%
1996	17%	50%	33%
1997	0	33%	67%
1998	0	40%	60%
1999	0	18%	82%
2000	0	10%	90%
2001	0	0	100%

Note: Programs for 1974 and 1984 were unavailable.
Source: NMSA annual conference programs.

Appendix I
Middle School Association Annual Conference Sessions: Number of Sessions on Grouping Options, Cooperative Learning, and Peer Tutoring

Year	Grouping Options	Cooperative Learning	Peer Tutoring
1974	N/A	N/A	N/A
1975	0	0	1
1976	0	0	0
1977	0	0	1
1978	1	0	1
1979	0	0	0
1980	3	0	0
1981	1	0	1
1982	0	1	1
1983	1	0	0
1984	N/A	N/A	N/A
1985	3	0	0
1986	0	5	1
1987	6	6	5
1988	6	16	3
1989	5	17	7
1990	26	34	6
1991	28	29	7
1992	49	25	5
1993	22	14	4
1994	44	35	4
1995	34	12	0
1996	18	17	2
1997	15	9	1
1998	17	7	0
1999	5	6	6
2000	10	0	0
2001	2	0	0

Note: Programs for 1974 and 1984 were unavailable.
Source: NMSA annual conference programs.

Appendix J
National Middle School Association Annual Conference Keynote
Speakers

Year	Keynote Speaker(s)	Year	Keynote Speaker(s)
1974	N/A	1989	Dudley Flood
1975	William Alexander	1990	Julia Thomason
1976	Gordon Vars		Paul George
	Donald Eichhorn	1991	George Walter
	Mel Heller		Crystal Kuykendall
1977	Nancy Doda	1992	William Purkey
	Marilyn Van Derbur		Henry Cisneros
	George Walter		Ann Lynch
1978	Ruth Love	1993	Jan Arnow
1979	Zacharie Clements		James Comer
	Harold Shane		Jacqueline Brown
	Wayne Dyer	1994	Patricia E. Russell-McCloud
1980	Art Garver		J. Howard Johnston
1981	Paul George	1995	Marian Wright Edelman
1982	Julia Thomason	1996	Neila A. Connors
1983	Conrad Toepfer	1997	Toni Morrison
	Mary Compton		Howard Gardner
1984	N/A	1998	Linda Darling-Hammond
1985	Robert Ricken		Alfie Kohn
	David Elkind		Mary Piper
1986	Betty Seigel	1999	Jesse Jackson
	Margaret P. Lathlan	2000	Harry Wong
1987	Zacharie Clements		Pat Schroeder
	Arthur Combs	2001	Lorraine Monroe
1988	J. Howard Johnston		Linda Ellerbee
	Conrad F. Toepfer		

Note: Programs for 1974 and 1984 were unavailable.
Source: NMSA annual conference programs.

Selected Bibliography

Allan, S. "Ability grouping research reviews: What do they say about grouping and the gifted?" *Educational Leadership*, vol. 48, no. 7 (April 1991), pp. 60–65.

Beane, J. "Middle schools under siege: Points of attack." *Middle School Journal*, vol. 30, no. 4 (March 1999), pp. 3–9.

Beane, J.A. "Middle schools under siege: Responding to the attack." *Middle School Journal*, vol. 30, no. 5 (May 1999), pp. 3–6.

Bestor, A. *Educational Wastelands: The Retreat from Learning in Our Public Schools*. 2nd ed. Urbana: University of Illinois Press, 1985.

Bishop, J.H. *Nerd Harassment, Incentives, School Priorities, and Learning*. Center for Advanced Human Resource Studies, paper 96–10. Ithaca, N.Y.: Cornell University, 1996.

Bloom, A.H. "What are you teaching my son?" *Educational Leadership*, vol. 53, no. 7 (April 1996), p. 83.

Bradley, A. "Muddle in the middle." *Education Week* (April 15, 1998). Available online at http://www.edweek.com/ew/ewstory.cfm?slug=31middle.h17&keywords=muddle.

Brewer, D.J., D. Rees, & L.M. Argys. "Detracking America's schools: The reform without cost?" *Phi Delta Kappan* (November 1995), pp. 210–215.

Brewer, D.J., D. Rees, & L.M. Argys. "The reform without cost? A reply to our critics." *Phi Delta Kappan* (February 1996), pp. 442–444.

Broaded, C.M. "The limits and possibilities of tracking: Some evidence from Taiwan." *Sociology of Education*, vol. 70, no. 1 (January 1997), pp. 36–53.

Callahan, C. *The Performance of High Ability Students in the United States on National and International Tests.* Washington, D.C.: National Association for Gifted Children, 1993.

Cassell, J. "Harms, benefits, wrongs and rights in fieldwork." In J.E. Sieber (Ed.), *The Ethics of Social Research: Fieldwork, Regulation and Publication.* New York: Springer-Verlag, 1982, pp. 7–31.

Clinkenbeard, P.R. "Unfair expectations: A pilot study of middle school students' comparisons of gifted and regular classes." *Journal for the Education of the Gifted,* vol. 15, no. 1 (1991), pp. 56–63.

Collier, C.S. "Collier comments on Mosteller." *Harvard Educational Review,* vol. 67, no. 3 (1997), pp. 603–605.

Feldhusen, J.F. "Susan Allan sets the record straight: Response to Allan." *Educational Leadership,* vol. 48, no. 6 (March 1991), p. 66.

Feldhusen, J.F. & S. Moon. "Grouping gifted students: Issues and concerns." *Gifted Child Quarterly,* vol. 35, no. 2 (Spring 1992), pp. 63–67.

Feldhusen, J.F., S.M. Moon, & P.J. Rifner. "Educating the gifted and talented: Strengths, weaknesses, prospects." *Educational Perspectives,* vol. 26, nos. 1 & 2 (1989), pp. 48–55.

Farkas, S. & J. Johnson. *Given the Circumstances: Teachers Talk about Public Education Today.* New York: Public Agenda, 1996.

Farkas, S. & J. Johnson. *A Lot to Be Thankful For: What Parents Want Children to Learn about America.* New York: Public Agenda, 1998.

Farkas, S. & J. Johnson. *Time to Move On: African-American and White Parents Set an Agenda for Public Schools.* New York: Public Agenda, 1998.

Farkas, S., J. Johnson, & A. Duffett. *Different Drummers: How Teachers of Teachers View Public Education.* New York: Public Agenda, 1997.

Figlio, D. & M. Page. *School Choice and the Distributional Effects of Ability Tracking: Does Separation Increase Equality?* Cambridge, Mass.: National Bureau of Economic Research, December 2000.

Gallagher, J.J. "Equity vs. excellence: An educational drama." *Roeper Review,* vol. 8, no. 4 (May 1986), pp. 233–235.

Gallagher, J.J. "Our love/hate affair with gifted children." *Gifted Child Quarterly* (January/February 1988), pp. 55–57.

Gallagher, J.J. "Education reform, values, and gifted students," *Gifted Child Quarterly,* vol. 35, no. 1 (1991), pp. 12–19.

Gallagher, J.J. "Programs for gifted students: Enlightened self-interest," *Gifted Child Quarterly,* vol. 35, no. 4 (Fall 1991), pp. 177–178.

Gallagher, J.J. "Academic effectiveness or social reform? A response to Robert Slavin and Jomills H. Braddock III." *The College Board Review,* no. 168 (Summer 1993), pp. 18–34.

Gallagher, J.J. "Comments on 'The reform without cost?' " *Phi Delta Kappan,* vol. 77, no. 3 (November 1995), pp. 216–217.

Gallagher, J.J., M.R. Coleman, & S. Nelson. "Perceptions of educational reform by educators representing middle schools, cooperative learning, and gifted education." *Gifted Child Quarterly*, vol. 39, no. 2 (Spring 1995), pp. 66–76.

Gallagher, J.J., C.C. Harradine, & M.R. Coleman. "Challenge or boredom? Gifted students' views on their schooling." *Roeper Review*, vol. 19, no. 3 (March 1997), pp. 132–136.

Goldberg, M.L. "Issues in the education of gifted and talented children." *Roeper Review*, vol. 8, no. 4 (1986), pp. 226–233.

Harrington-Lueker, D. "Middle schools fail to make the grade." *USA Today* (March 15, 2001). Available online at www.usatoday.com/news/comment/2001-03-15-ncguest1.htm.

Henry, W. *In Defense of Elitism*. New York: Doubleday, 1994.

Hofstadter, R. *Anti-Intellectualism in American Life*. New York: Random House, 1963.

Johnson, J. & S. Farkas. *Getting By: What American Teenagers Really Think about Their Schools*. New York: Public Agenda, 1997.

Johnson, J. & J. Immerwahr. *First Things First: What Americans Expect from the Public Schools*. New York: Public Agenda, 1994.

Kariya, T. & J.E. Rosenbaum. "Bright flight: Unintended consequences of detracking policy in Japan." *American Journal of Education*, vol. 107, no. 3 (May 1999), pp. 210–230.

Kulik, J. & C. Kulik. *Analysis of the Research on Ability Grouping: Historical and Contemporary Perspectives*. National Research Center on the Gifted and Talented Research-Based Decision Making Series, monograph no. 9204. Storrs: University of Connecticut, 1982.

Matthews, M. "Gifted students talk about cooperative learning." *Educational Leadership*, vol. 50, no. 1 (October 1992), pp. 48–50.

Matthews, M. "Gifted students respond to cooperative learning." Paper presented to the National Association for Gifted Children (November 1994).

Moon, T., C.A. Tomlinson, & C.M. Callahan. *Academic Diversity in the Middle School: Results of a National Survey of Middle School Administrators and Teachers*. Monograph number 95124. Charlottesville, Va.: National Research Center on the Gifted and Talented, 1995.

Nelson, S.M., J.J. Gallagher, & M.R. Coleman. "Cooperative learning for two different perspectives." *Roeper Review*, vol. 16, no. 2 (December 1993), pp. 117–121.

Renzulli, J.S. & S. Reis. "The reform movement and the quiet crisis in gifted education." *Gifted Child Quarterly*, vol. 35, no. 1 (1991), pp. 26–35.

Resh, N. "Track placement: How the 'sorting machine' works in Israel." *American Journal of Education*, vol. 106, no. 3 (May 1998), pp. 416–438.

Road Map for National Security: Imperative for Change. The Phase III Report of the U.S. Commission on National Security/21st Century (Washington, D.C., February 15, 2001).

Robinson, A. "Cooperation or exploitation? The argument against cooperative learning for talented students." *Journal of the Education of the Gifted,* vol. 14, no. 1 (1990), pp. 9–27.

Rogers, K. *The Relationship of Grouping Practices to the Education of the Gifted and Talented Learner.* The National Research Center on the Gifted and Talented Research-Based Decision Making Series, No. 1. Storrs: University of Connecticut, 1991.

Sapon-Shevin, M. & N. Schniedewind. "If cooperative learning's the answer, what are the questions?" *Boston University Journal of Education,* vol. 174, no. 2 (1992), pp. 11–38.

Schunk, D. "Peer models and children's behavioral change." *Review of Educational Research,* vol. 57, no. 2 (1987), pp. 149–174.

Shields, C.M. "A comparison study of student attitudes and perceptions in homogeneous and heterogeneous classrooms." *Roeper Review,* vol. 17, no. 4 (May/June 1995), pp. 234–238.

Sicola, P.K. "Where do gifted students fit? An examination of middle school philosophy as it relates to ability grouping and the gifted learner." *Journal for the Education of the Gifted,* vol. 14, no. 1 (1990), pp. 37–49.

Slavin, R.E. "Mastery learning reconsidered." *Review of Educational Research,* vol. 57, no. 2 (1987), pp. 175–213.

Tannenbaum, A. "Pre-Sputnik to Post-Watergate concern about the gifted." In A.H. Possow (Ed.), *The Gifted and the Talented: Their Education and Development.* The 78th Yearbook of the National Society for the Study of Education. Chicago: University of Chicago Press, 1979.

Tomlinson, C.A. "Gifted education and the middle school movement: Two voices on teaching the academically gifted." *Journal for the Education of the Gifted,* vol. 15, no. 3 (1992), pp. 206–238.

Tomlinson, C.A. "The easy lie and the role of gifted education in school excellence." *Roeper Review,* vol. 16, no. 4 (June 1994), pp. 258–259.

Index

About the Author

CHERI PIERSON YECKE is currently the Commissioner of Education for the State of Minnesota. Dr. Yecke was an award-winning public middle school and high school teacher before becoming a member of the Virginia State Board of Education, Deputy Secretary of Education, and Secretary of Education for the Commonwealth of Virginia. She also served as the Director of Teacher Quality and Public School Choice at the U.S. Department of Education.